The Virgin Birth of Christ

T0346533

The Virgin Birth of Christ

The Rich Meaning of a Biblical Truth

Richard A. Shenk

Paternoster:
thinking faith

First published 2016 by Paternoster
Paternoster is an imprint of Authentic Media Ltd
PO Box 6326, Bletchley, Milton Keynes MK1 9GG.
authenticmedia.co.uk

British Library Cataloguing in Publication Data

A catalogue record for this book is available from the British Library

ISBN: 978-1-84227-908-3
978-1-84227-914-4 (e-book)

Unless otherwise noted, the Scripture text used is the English Standard Version. Copyright ©
2001, 2007, 2011 by Crossway Bibles, a division of Good News Publishers.

Scripture marked NASB taken from the NEW AMERICAN STANDARD BIBLE®, Copyright ©
1960, 1962, 1963, 1968, 1971, 1972, 1973, 1975, 1977, 1995 by The Lockman
Foundation. Used by permission.

All quotations from the Greek New Testament are from Novum Testamentum Graece, Nestle-
Aland 27th Edition. Copyright © 1993 Deutsche Bibelgesellschaft, Stuttgart.

All quotations from the Septuagint are from Septuaginta (LXT) (Old Greek Jewish
Scriptures) edited by Alfred Rahlfs. Copyright © 1935 by the Württembergische Bibelanstalt
/ Deutsche Bibelgesellschaft (German Bible Society).

All quotations from the Hebrew Bible are from Biblia Hebraica Stuttgartensia (Hebrew
Bible, Masoretic Text or Hebrew Old Testament), edited by K. Elliger and W. Rudolph of the
Deutsche Bibelgesellschaft, Stuttgart, Fourth Corrected Edition. Copyright © 1966, 1977,
1983, 1990 by the Deutsche Bibelgesellschaft (German Bible Society), Stuttgart.

All of the above texts are cited from BibleWorks for Windows, version 9.x, Norfolk, VA:
BibleWorks, LLC, 2013.

Cover design by David Smart (smartsart.co.uk)
Printed and bound by CPI Group (UK) Ltd., Croydon, CR0 4YY

To Mark Carlton and Eric Wait,
my fellow pastors, my teachers, my friends,
who planted the seed thoughts for this project;
and to Rob Boyd
my friend and my lifelong mentor

Contents

Preface

This work began in discussions with my friend Mark Carlton. More than twenty-five years ago, Eric Wait, Mark, and I met each Thursday to preach our sermons to each other and learn from each other. At the time we lived and served in the wonderful high-desert town of Ogallala, NE. Eric, the most stable of us all, still lives in Ogallala, having served New Hope Church for more than thirty years. It was Mark who first motivated me to think more deeply about the *meaning* of the virgin birth when he preached his series 'The Great Christmas War'. He was the first to point out to me the 'challenge' which God made for himself when Jeremiah cursed Jehoiachin, cutting off the line of the Messiah. One possible *meaning* of the virgin birth arises from the (implied) adoption of Jesus by Joseph. Those were rich days together. God further developed this idea later in my discussions, as a theology professor, with my graduate theology students at Bethlehem College & Seminary. I am grateful for the opportunity to learn from men who are Christ-centred, biblically focused, brilliant, and also humble – a somewhat rare combination. Along with my reading over the years, they have challenged and extended these ideas first planted by Mark.

I am also grateful to many who helped me write (more) clearly, including my good friend and lifelong mentor, Rob Boyd; my mother, Ruth; and my wife and best friend, Lynne. I find godly wisdom in each of these people who are all students of the Word and lovers of Christ. They offered insightful comments on the ideas found here. And each of them is wonderfully intolerant of obscure phrasing and arcane words. And I am also grateful to my (long-suffering) teaching assistants Ryan Currie and Brian Verrett. They laboured to free my manuscript of its many typos and formatting errors (something I am congenitally incapable of doing!) and offered many suggestions for clarity of ideas and exegesis. Other friends worked their way through the whole manuscript, contributing both needed challenges and encouragements: Brian Tabb, my friend and dean; Jesse Scheumann and Mike Littel, former students and fellow labourers in God's work; Dr Greg Magee, my friend from doctoral seminars at Trinity Evangelical Divinity School; and Fr Stephen Edwards, my fellow student at the University of Wales, Lampeter, where God forged our friendship under our supervisor, Dr Simon Oliver. And I am grateful to Mike Parsons, now my former editor, who saw this manuscript through to submission before leaving Paternoster. He is discerning and brilliant! And now, in recent months it has been my pleasure to work with Reuben Sneller, Donna Harris, Becky Fawcett, and Suzanne Mitchell. Their expertise, excellence, and patience with me (an unknown academic whose contract they 'found in the drawer', left over from the 'former regime') was greatly appreciated. If God makes this minor manuscript useful, it is much to their credit. Indeed, God has made me rich by these friends who contribute far more to me than their help on this project.

How then shall this proposal be read? Certainly it includes errors and mistakes (which are mine despite the best efforts of friends and editors), and certainly some will disagree at points or at many points. Let me conclude this Preface with Augustine's words from his introduction to *The Trinity*:

> So, whoever reads this and says, 'This is not well said, because I do not understand it,' is criticizing my statement, not the faith; and perhaps it could have been said more clearly – though no one has ever expressed himself well enough to be understood by everybody on everything . . . On the other hand, if anyone reads this work and says, 'I understand what is being said, but it is not true,' he is at liberty to affirm his own conviction as much as he likes and refute mine if he can. If he succeeds in doing so charitably and truthfully . . . then that will be the choicest plum that could fall to me from these labors of mine . . . I do not doubt, of course, that some people who are rather slow in the uptake will think that in some passages . . . I mean what I did not mean . . . Nobody, I trust, will think it fair to blame me for the mistake of such people.[1]

Richard Shenk, Plymouth, MN, July 2015

Introduction

Nevertheless, the birth stories have become a test case in various controversies. If you believe in miracles, you believe in Jesus' miraculous birth; if you don't, you don't. Both sides turn the question into a shibboleth, not for its own sake but to find out who's in and who's out. (N.T. Wright)[1]

This position must be considered from a twofold point of view: first, with reference to the available New Testament testimonies on the subject; next, with reference to its dogmatic value . . . No one will wish to maintain that such acceptance of them introduces into our faith an element at variance with its true nature . . . [But] we are bound to grant that it is quite possible to believe in Christ as Redeemer without believing in his supernatural conception in this sense . . . [Moreover the Virgin Birth] betray[s] no dogmatic purpose. (Friedrich Schleiermacher)[2]

It was a code. In and of itself it had no meaning. A simple letter of the alphabet. The newly appointed reserve general had just won a great battle against Israel's enemies, the Ammonites. But now he had another problem: the hot-headed Ephraimites. In full battle dress they confronted general Jephthah, grumbling that they had not been invited to the front lines against the Ammonites. They liked a good fight, and they had missed it. But it was not Jephthah's fault; today they were just grumbling. Indeed their complaint was unfounded; the general had invited them and they ignored the call. Still, their blood was up and Jephthah had to fight them. But there was a problem: no unique uniforms. How would Jephthah's forces distinguish between friend and foe, since all were part of Israel, spoke the same language, and were brothers? Then he hit upon a difference: shibboleth. A letter of the Hebrew alphabet. It had no meaning in itself. It was a code. Yet the distinction of dialect ensured that the average sentry could distinguish friend from foe. You see – or rather 'you hear' – the Ephraimites had a bit of a lisp: 'sibboleth'. And by that code, that shibboleth, Jephthah could discern who was in and who was out. And in the battle he prevailed.[3]

The virgin birth has become just such a code. It is a means of distinguishing friend from foe. Those who believe in the virgin birth are in, and those who do not are out – at least from the perspective of Christian fundamentalists and their evangelical descendants. If some would charge that fundamentalists and evangelicals like a good fight a little too much, something akin to the reputation of the Ephraimites in Jephthah's day, that is perhaps credible. But the virgin birth is no trumped-up disagreement. Unlike the pointless grumblings of the Ephraimites, there is a real issue: naturalism versus supernaturalism. The battle over the possibility of miracles, and one foundational miracle – Christ's Virgin birth – cannot be ignored. It is helpful to divide the house over this issue. Jephthah was on to something! And as a shibboleth the virgin birth is a fair test with very few false positives or false negatives. Affirmation or denial separates us into camps: one camp affirms naturalism, a closed system, and the other affirms a personal God who rules over his creation as he pleases. Naturalism denies God this personal privilege in his world. Fundamentalists allow that God may sustain or intervene in ways that are distinct from his usual work. It is true that most theists, and all Christians, agree that it pleases God to act with continuity and in ways that are comprehensible to people in almost all situations. Yet naturalists, whether identifying themselves with Christians or not, must necessarily reject a personal deity who can and does do as he pleases, outside of natural law. So, it is helpful and right for the virgin birth to be a shibboleth. But how unlike the discerning letter of the Hebrew alphabet is the virgin birth; it has meaning in itself. So here I will pursue that meaning: What is the meaning of the virgin birth?

A bit of history will serve us before I address the meaning of the virgin birth. The virgin birth was affirmed and accepted by the church for millennia. The Apostles' Creed declares, 'conceived by the Holy Ghost and born of the Virgin Mary'. This creed needs no apostolic claim to be recognized or affirmed by the vast majority of Christians as 'The Creed'. The virgin birth was an issue that was so important that the authors not only made it explicit, but dedicated to its declaration *fully ten* of the seventy-six words of the original Latin.[4] Even so, this compound truth of fatherless conception and virginal birth was a foundation upon which the person and nature of Christ could rest. And yet, the virgin birth itself was not an issue for almost two thousand years.[5] In fact, it was not until the twentieth century that its denial came from within the church. This reality is perhaps surprising to those who have only known life within this dispute. Our tendency to assume continuity, something that serves us well in many contexts, can too easily project today's perspective on the past. Contrary to such assumptions, J. Gresham Machen reminds us that belief in the virgin birth has always been without dispute: 'According to the universal belief of the historic Christian Church, Jesus of Nazareth was born without human father, being conceived by the Holy Ghost and born of the virgin Mary . . . Whatever may be thought of the virgin birth itself, the belief of the Church in the virgin birth is a fact of history which no one denies.'[6] The change came in the nineteenth century with figures such as David Friedrich Strauss. In his seminal work, *The Life of Jesus*, he wrote: 'The statement of Matthew and of Luke concerning the mode of Jesus's conception, in every age, received the following interpretation by the church that Jesus was conceived in Mary not by a human father, but by the Holy Ghost.'[7] This division was not over the virgin birth but over a worldview; naturalism (modernism) was contending with supernaturalism (the freedom of God). The virgin birth represented this divide. Paul Badham, who wrote a centennial volume celebrating modernism, agrees that the virgin birth is central in this debate. He wrote, 'The importance of Christology to the classical Modernists was often obscured in the debates of the 1920s by their opponents, who believed that only Chalcedonian orthodoxy and total adherence to such beliefs as the Virgin Birth or the bodily resurrection of Jesus could safeguard Christ's divinity. But the modernists themselves had no doubt of their total commitment . . . They believed that the traditional doctrine had to be re-expressed in modern terms in order that it might continue to be believed.'[8] The camp was now divided between those who accepted the ancient creeds and submitted to the Bible as God's Word, and those who stood in judgement over the Bible's words and freed themselves from the creeds. And the virgin birth of Christ was a visible fault line.[9]

It is exactly because of this divide that the virgin birth became the shibboleth that distinguishes between camps, pulling in its train positions on biblical authority, theology of the Word of God, and Christology. In fact, when John Hick departed the ranks of the evangelicals in the middle of the twentieth century, his announcement was, 'I do not affirm the virgin birth.' He desired to stand with, as he imagined it, Mark, John, Paul, and Peter, the New Testament majority, who say nothing of the virgin birth.[10] This simple disaffirmation, opposing the virgin birth as a real event in history, was sufficient to predict the direction, if not the specific proposals, of his next fifty years of research. He lisped 'sibboleth', rather than speak the dialect of the fundamentalists, and marched with his new tribe. Such use of the virgin birth continued with the release of the Revised Standard Version (RSV) in 1952. According to Herbert May, writing in 1953, the publication was 'dramatized by the occasional Bible burnings which have taken place, and by the charges of liberalism, atheism, and communism levelled against the translators'.[11] Significantly at issue was the translation of Isaiah 7:14. Should *'almah* (the Hebrew word identifying the woman who would give birth) be translated as 'young woman' or as 'virgin'? The editors of the RSV selected 'young woman' and this decision provided a shibboleth.[12] This single choice was enough to determine the RSV's reception among many. I will consider the translation of *'almah* later; I do not mean to imply that the virgin birth of Christ is a trivial issue or not worth dividing over. Yet such limited use, as a shibboleth or badge of identification, hides its true beauty. It is this beauty that I seek.

For that reason, this is not a study of the validity of the church's historic teaching about the virgin birth of Christ, but a collection of ideas that explore and expose the theological value of the virgin birth. Many articles and many books have been written that defend the historicity and textual affirmation of the virgin birth or that seek to expose it as irrational or as myth. Indeed, there are so many that it is not possible to *survey* them here, nor is that the direction of this book.[13] My goal is to show the intent, beauty, and meaning of the virgin birth as intended by the biblical authors – what was on their minds as they wrote. Strangely, to the best of my knowledge, there exists no book-length treatment of the theology and meaning of the virgin birth for the church.[14] How can this be? If the virgin birth is a claim that God in his freedom chose to approach us in the flesh, how does this move of God reveal his glory to us, and how does this act of God make us free? Such a lack of significant reflection is not because it has become a shibboleth, for that is recent. Nor is it because the virgin birth has been deeply investigated by the church in the past and, therefore, has been thoroughly understood. In fact, discussions with students and church leaders incline me to think that this richness is often not discussed or taught by the church. Many continue to treat the virgin birth of Christ, first and foremost (and sometimes, finally), as a test case for acceptance within evangelical circles, or (in the case of others) a badge of distance from such circles. I am not arguing that we are unwise to use the virgin birth as a test case; shibboleths are helpful in their proper place. And we rightly define evangelicals as those who affirm biblical truthfulness and authority as grounding essentials to our epistemology and theology. But the virgin birth is more than a shibboleth. The purpose of this study is to present possibilities of rich, theological meaning that God intended for us in the virgin birth. I hope that many of the proposals in this book will strike the reader as obvious, once stated. I have no interest in novelty. My hope is that the aggregation of obvious ideas, ideas that are too little considered in this context, may help us see the richness of this truth and help us to live out this truth.

But is such an exploration valid? The quote at the start of this chapter from Schleiermacher would argue otherwise. Assessing the virgin birth textually and dogmatically, he rejected its dogmatic significance while admitting its textual affirmation. Quite a few would likely agree with him for their own reasons. Not least among these might be that some theological reasons given for the virgin birth early in the history of the church were not the best reasons. I will explore these arguments later. But Schleiermacher had his own reasons for failing to appreciate the dogmatic value of the virgin birth. In regard to dogmatics, and in regard to his project, centred as it was in the God-consciousness of Christ, the virgin birth did not contribute to this reality in any necessary way. In regard to the textual assertion and faith, he allowed for the belief in the virgin birth as something that was not at variance with the true nature of our faith – but also hardly necessary. And certainly it was not literally *true*. But warrant for exploring the theological value may yet exist. If you, the reader, find the virgin birth less securely grounded than I do, let us disagree. But I would urge you to continue this journey with me, exploring the *value* the virgin birth was *intended* to have for God's people. Indeed, Matthew and Luke, in their gospels, meant something by its inclusion, apart from our discussion of historicity. And I wonder, if we discover the virgin birth to be great and significant doctrinally, and rich in beauty, would that cause some to reassess its historicity, thus affirming it?

It is important to clarify terms right from the beginning. Christians often speak of the 'virgin birth', intending to suggest precisely what is meant by Matthew 1:18: 'before they came together she was found to be with child from the Holy Spirit', and by Luke 1:34: 'How will this be, since I am a virgin?' That is, Mary, never having engaged in intercourse, became pregnant by the Holy Spirit. This conception by the Virgin is the reason why many, rather than naming this event as the virgin birth, use the term 'virginal conception'. Matthew himself endorses this emphasis, citing Isaiah: 'the virgin shall conceive'. That Mary was a virgin at the time of the birth is also affirmed: '[Joseph] took his wife, but knew her not until she had given birth to a son' (Matt. 1:24,25). It becomes clear, despite our historical attachment to the term, that the idea of the virginal conception is emphasized and has temporal priority over the 'virgin birth'. Still, with a nod to historical usage by many in the church, I will use 'virgin birth' to mean both the virginal conception and virgin birth of Jesus Christ, taking the event as a whole.[15]

Let me help you understand the topography of this work. I will first review the history of the doctrine – lightly touched on already in this introduction. Then, I will consider traditional meanings given for the virgin birth. The first of these traditional meanings are misguided meanings: protection against the sin of concupiscence ('with lust') and the virgin birth as a way for God to 'bypass' original sin. I will also consider traditional meanings which are well grounded in Scripture: that the effect of the virgin birth was to reveal and preserve the divinity and the humanity of Christ and that the virgin birth stands against philosophical naturalism. Then I will investigate the virgin birth as a mystery revealed: how God bestowed the kingdom upon Christ by the virgin birth, and how God used the virgin birth as his means to keep information from the enemy. Then I will display an intriguing chiastic reversal (a particular structure discourse often used in the Bible). By this, I will show that the virgin birth reveals Mary to be wiser than Eve, and also consider that by it, God 'redeems' the reputation of women, which in Eve was ruined in the fall. Lastly, I will consider the virgin birth as a new birth for a new creation. This truth will display God's choice of adoption as his particular means and our adoption in Christ as a particular relationship to him. Then, we will also see the virgin birth as an analogy for the birth of faith in us. None of these are novel, nor are they meant to be. If they are correct theological reflections, they flow from the canon of Scripture and resonate with orthodoxy. Perhaps bringing them together will help us delight more deeply in the glory of God in the virgin birth. Perhaps God will use this approach to help us understand the deep value of the virgin birth as more than a shibboleth.

Lastly, this book is merely an initial investment, a first effort, which I hope to see exceeded by many others. It is not an end, but an exploration. Of course, the meanings displayed here do not exhaust the depths of what God offers us in this truth. It aspires to whet our appetites. There is more – much more! And perhaps some will disagree with one or two reasons that I have displayed. That is a wonderful part of the discussion and moves the conversation deeper. Further, I eagerly hope that you, as a reader of this book, will exceed my initial effort and go on to discover more of what God intends in the virgin birth, freed from its bondage as *just a code*. Discover with me the theological richness that pours out of this biblical teaching. It might take your breath away.

> Oh, the depth of the riches and wisdom and knowledge of God! How unsearchable are his judgments and how inscrutable his ways! 'For who has known the mind of the Lord, or who has been his counsellor?' 'Or who has given a gift to him that he might be repaid?' For from him and through him and to him are all things. To him be glory forever. Amen. (Rom. 11:33–36)

1

The Virgin Birth: A Short History from the Early Church Fathers to the Modernist Movement

By describing the Incarnation of the Word as the occurrence of a miracle the dogma of the Virgin Birth starts off with saying very clearly and impressively: within the continuum of actual human-creaturely history and without eliminating this or even so much as making a rent in it, the Incarnation of the Word is a divine beginning; grace, but grace of the free God; freedom, but freedom of the gracious God. Therefore there is indeed a unity of God and man; God Himself creates it; only God can create it; God creates it, because He wills to create it. (Karl Barth)[1]

The belief in the virgin birth was without dispute in the early church. Still, the lack of dispute, and even agreement, is no reason for holding or proclaiming this doctrine or any doctrine. If any doctrine might make us wonder 'Why? What does it mean?' the virgin birth would be in the top three for many, even most, people. Perhaps the virgin birth is a device invented to avoid some narrative difficulty within the newly inscribed gospel story? Certainly not. Rather the virgin birth created problems from the beginning for the church. Hans von Campenhausen affirms this reality: 'The history of the text also shows here that this obstacle is not merely modern, but that even in the earliest period, as soon as anything was known of the virgin birth, it brought difficulty and perplexity.'[2] Similarly, writing as a Jewish apologist and opposed to the very idea of a virgin birth, Gerald Sigal writes, 'God can create a human being from neither a man nor a woman, as in the case of Adam, or from a man without a woman, as in the case of Eve, which could also provide for a Davidic ancestry through the male's line. As such, what was the need for a virginal conception? Why was it alleged that God chose a method of conception so riddled with the myths of pagan idolatry?'[3] Sigal will offer possible answers to his question, but regardless of the answers, it is clear that both Sigal and von Campenhausen understand the challenge that the virgin birth makes for the church. So, while adopted early, perhaps even generally affirmed from the beginning, the virgin birth must have been important to the church, for it came with significant cost.

The 'cost' of this feature of the story is apparent with only a little reflection. The virgin birth certainly alerts the reader to a sharp distinction between this story and any other story that purports to be history. Moreover, it is a feature of the story of the incarnation that does not seem immediately necessary to many readers. It is a sticky point in the story that causes the reader to wonder: Why? To one way of thinking, the story does not need this sharp feature to accomplish its purpose. There is another cost as well. There is an antecedent tradition of pagan stories of sexual relations between gods and men, including virginal conception. Various suggestions have been made including the Roman god Mithras or even the Buddha. This question is not the focus of this study and I will leave the details to others. But I should acknowledge that, to some, the gospel nativity stories seem like copycat additions to God's story, a potentially costly embarrassment. Still, let me say a brief word in regard to these so-called pagan antecedents. Andrew T. Lincoln has recently written *Born of a Virgin?* This work of excellent scholarship challenges the virgin birth from the point of view of one who speaks from within the church. Indeed, he was disappointed and surprised that his position on the virgin birth disqualified him from serving in some schools – or even being granted an interview![4] Lincoln conceives that both Matthew and Luke are distinctly influenced by the Graeco-Roman world in their telling of the nativity. Of Matthew he writes, 'Once one accepts . . . some familiarity with accounts of the birth of major figures in the Graeco-Roman world, that a begetting by the divine Spirit could entail a virginal conception, then the other issues more or less fall into place.'[5] In regard to Luke his understanding is much the same.[6] He proposes this understanding as the means by which the gospel writers and the early church accredited Jesus as the Christ. Here I will bypass his full argument, which is both interesting and well made, and instead refer the reader to his work. He represents a significant position: Matthew and Luke were influenced by pagan sources in the telling of their nativity.[7] But in distinction to this position stands the work of J. Gresham Machen. His work is thorough and, if dated in places, is highly respected scholarship. He notes the great isolation of the Jewish world from the pagan world as a divide that could not and would not have been breached by the Evangelists. In regard to the possibility of later interpolation of pagan ideas he writes, 'it can be shown clearly that the verses attesting the virgin birth in Lk. i–ii are no later addition, but belong to the fundamental structure of the narrative.'[8] After reviewing pagan stories in detail and other writings contemporary with Matthew and Luke (or from the second century), Machen says, 'But what a gulf . . . between these pagan stories and the New Testament story of the virgin birth of our Lord!'[9] His work displays a point too often missed: though there may be surface similarities, the differences between the gospels and presumed pagan sources overpower the similarities.

On balance, the theory of infusion of pagan myth into Christianity simply does not work. N.T. Wright makes this point clear when he writes:

> This is how it would look: Christians came to believe that Jesus was in some sense divine. Someone who shared this faith broke thoroughly with Jewish precedents and invented the story of a pagan-style virginal conception. Some Christians failed to realize that this was historicized metaphor, and retold it as though it were historical. Matthew and Luke, assuming historicity, drew independently upon this astonishing fabrication, set it (though in quite different ways) within a thoroughly Jewish context, and wove it in quite different ways into their respective narratives. And all this happened

within, more or less, fifty years. Possible? Yes, of course. Most things
are possible in history. Likely? No.[10]

Again, I have presented neither extensive discussion nor the argumentation, merely conclusions. I leave it to the reader to explore in greater
detail. The point is this: there is sufficient reason to perceive distinction over the similarity in regard to the relationship between pagan
stories and this nativity from the Jewish culture. And there is reason
to doubt the likelihood of their adoption into Christian writings.

But before I move on, there is one more consideration. If there are
pagan virgin birth stories that are sufficiently like the Bible's story of a
virgin birth, which came first? Are the pagan stories fairly considered
antecedent to the gospel nativity narratives? Maybe not. Remember
that Satan is a liar who distorts reality, rather than one who creatively
invents a new one. When he lied in Genesis 3, he contradicted what
God had said – 'Did God actually say?' – rather than create a new
idea. Could it be that God told his story of a virgin first? Could it be
that God said, 'Adam, a time will come when a virgin will bear a child,
and that child will suffer and then die, but he will rise to life and then
return to conquer like a lion!'? There is no such record in Genesis. Yet,
if God did so, then all other stories of virgin birth would descend from
that one story. God's virgin story would antedate pagan stories. E.W.
Bullinger (1837–1913) considered just this possibility. He suggested
that when God gave the stars to people, he gave them as 'signs' (Gen.
1:14–19) to which he gave particular meanings. Specifically, Bullinger
suggests that God told Adam the whole story of salvation – with significant detail – through signs in the stars. Beginning with the story
of the Virgin with child and ending with Leo the conquering lion,
he says that God put the story of redemption before Adam and fixed
twelve specific signs in the stars to tell that story. He further speculates
that in Babylon, this story of God was distorted, becoming a wicked
tool for telling the future – something God never intended. Indeed,
God warned his people against mediums and fortune-tellers, and so
also horoscopes – the misuse of his stellar signs.[11] The glorious story
of the redemption offered by God to Adam may have become the

entertainment of Babylon. Again, Bullinger's book is long and I will not reproduce his whole argument here – an argument that, while intriguing, is not sufficient. Still, he gives us a possible way to read history which makes God's story of a virgin antecedent to the pagan myths. The value of observing Bullinger's proposal is not to incite speculation, but rather to show that there is sufficient reason to doubt the assertion that Christianity borrowed from the pagan culture. That is, if one possible reason can be offered which cannot be refuted as impossible, then the charge that borrowing is necessary, necessarily fails.

On balance, the pagan stories present an issue for the nativity stories of Matthew and Luke – for the virgin birth – which must be considered but then dismissed. Machen's arguments, and the arguments of those who came after him, are sufficient to answer this challenge. Now I return to the biblical text.

The virgin birth is affirmed in a limited number of texts in the New Testament, but is unambiguously declared where it is affirmed. The strong attestation found in Matthew and Luke is missing in the other gospels and the writings of Paul – quite conspicuously missing as many read the biblical text. Even in Matthew and Luke, the doctrine is constructed on only a handful of verses. This fact was not lost on the early church leaders, who were aware of the limited number of texts upon which the event rested. Yet the early theologians of the church prior to Nicea (325) affirmed the truth of the virgin birth against all challenges in this regard.[12]

Let's consider the texts that assert the virgin birth:

Matthew 1:18–23: Now the birth of Jesus Christ took place in this way. When his mother Mary had been betrothed to Joseph, before they came together she was found to be with child from the Holy Spirit. And her husband Joseph, being a just man and unwilling to put her to shame, resolved to divorce her quietly. But as he considered these things, behold, an angel of the Lord appeared to him in a dream, saying, 'Joseph, son of David, do not fear to take Mary as your wife, for that which is conceived in her is from the Holy Spirit. She will bear a son, and you shall call his name Jesus, for he will save his people from their sins'. All this took place to fulfill what the Lord had spoken by the prophet: 'Behold, the virgin shall conceive and bear a son, and they shall call his name Immanuel' (which means, God with us).

Luke 1:26–35: In the sixth month the angel Gabriel was sent from God to a city of Galilee named Nazareth, to a virgin betrothed to a man whose name was Joseph, of the house of David. And the virgin's name was Mary. And he came to her and said, 'Greetings, O favored one, the Lord is with you!' But she was greatly troubled at the saying, and tried to discern what sort of greeting this might be. And the angel said to her, 'Do not be afraid, Mary, for you have found favor with God. And behold, you will conceive in your womb and bear a son, and you shall call his name Jesus. He will be great and will be called the Son of the Most High. And the Lord God will give to him the throne of his father David, and he will reign over the house of Jacob forever, and of his kingdom there will be no end.' And Mary said to the angel, 'How will this be, since I am a virgin?' And the angel answered her, 'The Holy Spirit will come upon you, and the power of the Most High will overshadow you; therefore the child to be born will be called holy – the Son of God.'

There are at least two issues. First, as noted above, these are the only biblical texts that explicitly affirm the virgin birth. Second, Matthew seems to be dependent upon Isaiah for his affirmation of the virgin birth, but Isaiah may not be affirming what Matthew affirms either linguistically or historically.

Let's begin with Matthew. This gospel writer enlists Isaiah's support for his position: 'All this took place to fulfil what the Lord had spoken by the prophet: "Behold, the virgin shall conceive and bear a son, and they shall call his name Immanuel" (which means, God with us)' (Matt. 1:22–23). Matthew appears to depend on the Septuagint, a Greek translation of the Jewish Scripture (our Old Testament), which was current in his day (often designated with the initials LXX). This text seems to have been his source for the Isaiah quote. This trans-lation selected the Greek word *parthenos*, which in his day almost certainly meant 'virgin'.[13] However, the Hebrew text uses a word that is ambiguous: *'almah*.[14] The clear and primary meaning of the Hebrew term is 'young girl' or 'unmarried girl'. As such it has significant semantic overlap with 'virginity', yet this fact in no way indicates that it even sometimes means 'virgin'. John Walton put it this way: 'Someone could show me a thousand passages where "fiancée" was used to refer to a virgin, but that would not change the meaning [of fiancée].'[15] *'Almah*, as it stands in its context, cannot 'mean' virgin. His point is accepted by a majority of biblical scholars who note that Isaiah could have written *bethulah* – a virgin. Gerald Sigal puts this point even more strongly:

> Specifically, there is no reason to assume from the context that virginity is a critical factor in Isaiah 7:14. Nothing is known of the young woman's state of virginity at the time Isaiah spoke, nor is that knowledge critical for exegetical purposes. Moreover, no passage of Scripture may be properly interpreted outside its context. Whatever may have been the use of *'almah* in other biblical passages, whether to designate a married or an unmarried young woman, such use cannot be *a priori* presumed to establish what is the meaning of the word in Isaiah 7:14.[16]

From Isaiah alone, it is not possible, exegetically, to establish Matthew's point. This fact still leaves open the intent of the use of *parthenos* in the Septuagint. Sigal argues that Matthew took advantage of the Septuagint's use of *parthenos* for *'almah*. Rather than understanding the semantic domains of *'almah* and *parthenos* to overlap, he took advantage of this in order to read a new prophecy into the text, where such a prophecy did not previously exist.[17] Sigal goes on to say that *parthenos* evolved from the classical Greek of 'young woman' to the more technical and limited meaning 'virgin' only over time. Yet Matthew writes his gospel citing Isaiah 7:14 as his authority for his assertion of Mary's virginity. Sigal sees this choice as Matthew's error: to interpret *parthenos* in light of the technical meaning of his day, rather than the more general meaning it had at the time of translation, 150–200 years earlier.[18] Further, Genesis 24 speaks of Rebekah, using both *bethulah* and *'almah* of her, so using *parthenos* for *'almah* is fair if imprecise. Still, the LXX translation of Isaiah 7:14 with *parthenos* is an unusual use. What was on the mind(s) of the translators(s)? If we grant the enlarged and non-specific semantic domain for *parthenos*, we are still left wondering why it was selected only here without explicit warrant.

An example might serve. I grew up in Lebanon, Pennsylvania, near the town of Intercourse. Just telling someone the name of the town raises eyebrows. The word, which not so long ago had the general meaning of communication, now represents the most intimate of relationships, of communication, between the sexes. In fact, in technical writing the older meaning of 'intercourse' is still in use, but generally the narrower meaning is now the primary domain. It means sex. This example is a good reminder that semantic domains move and shift, shrink and morph. In the case of *parthenos* it is clear that caution should be used. Sigal is not alone in arguing well that, at the time of the translation of the Septuagint, the selection of *parthenos* for *'almah* does not require us to understand 'virgin' as the intent of the translator.[19]

However, this translation issue in no way diminishes the clear intent of Matthew's claim of virginity. Whatever decision is made in regard to Isaiah's intent or the intent of the translators of the Septuagint, still Matthew's claim of Mary's virginity is unambiguous. By his selection of the Greek word *parthenos* for the text of his gospel and in his day, he affirms a singular fact in regard to Mary: she is virgin, whether or not the prophetess of Isaiah was.[20] In the context of Matthew, *parthenos* unambiguously means 'virgin'. Clarity in regard to Matthew's use is also found in Mary's own response: 'How can this be since I am *parthenos*!?' But what then of Isaiah? Some could perceive that there is a dissonance between Matthew and Isaiah. Sigal and others perceive just this problem.[21] And if so, what then of our doctrines of the virgin birth and the Word of God, if this was not the intent of Isaiah? But such tension, if tension is perceived, is a false problem. Walton writes:

> If our formulation of doctrine demands something exegesis cannot deliver, rather than adjusting our exegesis we ought to think about

reformulating our doctrine. Is that not what biblical authority is all about? This is not to say that we abandon a theological tenet because of one ambiguous problem text. But, for instance in the issue at hand, if our perception of inerrancy is that it demands the interrelationship of meaning in passages where the NT uses the OT, yet we find numerous cases where sound exegesis does not provide such an interrelationship, how should we proceed? If we adjust our exegesis to conform to our perceived doctrinal need we are undercutting biblical authority on the exegetical, objective level to supposedly support biblical authority on the level of what we have formulated as the demands of inerrancy.[22]

If by this assertion Walton means that such tension is a false problem which only exposes our misunderstanding, then I agree. It is neither the virgin birth nor inerrancy that is challenged by this exegetical-lexical study. It may be, however, that our understanding of what is *included* in our affirmation of the virgin birth and inerrancy is challenged. We must work hard to affirm precisely what Matthew and Luke claimed when we affirm the virgin birth. In this move to affirm what the Evangelists intended and affirmed, I am instructed by Gerald Hawthorne, who wrote, 'Had Luke intended merely to convey to his audience that Mary was a young girl, and not more than that, there were any number of Greek words at his disposal for such a purpose – words such as *pais* (Luke 8:54), *paidiske* (Luke 12:45), or *korasion* (Mark 5:41). But he chose *parthenos* instead.'[23] Donald Macleod said this well: 'Of Matthew's use of Isaiah 7:14, whatever the merits of Matthew's exegesis, his assertion of the virgin birth is quite independent of it. Isaiah 7:14 may be difficult to interpret. Matthew 1:18,25 are not.'[24] So while warrant for Isaiah's use by Matthew may be unclear to us, this issue is distinct from Matthew's clear intent.[25] Luke's and Matthew's claims are in no way unclear: Jesus was born of the Virgin Mary, conceived by the Holy Spirit, without the help of any man. If the testimonies are few, nonetheless, both stand clear and unshaken.

There is one last observation to make in regard to the gospel texts and the differences. Only Matthew and Luke offer us nativity stories.

This point is rather obvious, but not always considered. While they alone declare the virgin birth, they alone offer nativity stories. So, of all biblical authors who relate the nativity story, all affirm the virgin birth. This observation proves nothing, but it is worth considering in discussion.

But what of the rest of Scripture? Is the virgin birth missing in the other gospels and in Paul's letters? The conclusion of John Hick and others, including Sigal, that the virgin birth can be dismissed for this reason is not warranted. Mark and John may be soft-spoken on the issue, but they are not silent. Mark refers to Jesus' apparent illegitimacy when he writes that people called him 'the son of Mary' (Mark 6:3). Similarly, John puts such words in the mouth of Jesus' adversaries: 'We were not born of sexual immorality!' (John 8:41, implying perhaps that Jesus was so born). Were these merely random slanders? Not likely. They were specific to Jesus and the rumours about him due to Mary's marital status at the time of his conception. They could count. John also speaks perceptively in his introduction. In John 1:12,13, addressing the spiritual birth of believers, John writes, 'who were born, not of blood nor of the will of the flesh nor of the will of man, but of God'. He writes these words just before his 'nativity': 'the Word became flesh and dwelt among us' (John 1:14).[26] John has given us a theological account of the nativity. Missing are the donkey, Joseph and Mary, the shepherds, and the stable. But very carefully, John sets the theological stage to show us that there is something quite different about the birth of Jesus. In fact, the very way he talks about birth 'not of blood nor of the will of the flesh nor of the will of man, but of God' (John 1:13) anticipates not only Christ's birth in the next verse – 'the Word became flesh and dwelt among us' – but also our own spiritual birth. For our spiritual birth is like Jesus' – without human will or a human father, and beyond anything of the flesh. This reality is precisely what Jesus explains to Nicodemus in John 3, something I will consider later. So while it is true that John and Mark are far from affirming the virgin birth explicitly, the virgin birth is a sufficient, if not necessary, solution to affirmations that are otherwise distracting. With the virgin birth as the key, the allusions fit the flow of the narrative.

What of Paul's massive writing, almost equal in length to the gospels and Acts? His declaration of the exalted Christ seems empty of any reference to the virgin birth – it certainly is empty of an explicit reference. But he could not have been ignorant of what Luke was thinking on this subject! James Orr writes, 'It would be going too far, however, to infer from this that Paul had no knowledge of the miracle of Christ's birth. Luke was Paul's companion, and doubtless shared with Paul all the knowledge which he himself had gathered on this and other subjects.'[27] Paul knew, and, knowing, it would be very strange if he did not object explicitly.[28] In fact, some (a distinct minority of those who oppose the doctrine of the virgin birth) yet cite Paul as the inventor. James Tabor, a New Testament scholar, wrote in a popular column that he observed that Paul, writing before the gospels, affirmed Jesus' divinity and his existence prior to his birth in many texts, including Galatians 4:4: 'But when the fullness of time had come, God sent forth his Son, born of woman.' Most would agree. But he went further: 'The implication of these texts is that Jesus' mother was merely the human receptacle for bringing Jesus into the world. It is not a far step from these ideas about Jesus' pre-existence, to the notion of Jesus as the first-begotten Son of God – eliminating any necessity for a human father.'[29] In context Taylor refutes the veracity of the virgin birth, yet he suggests that Paul, whose epistles seem to antedate Luke's gospel account (and others), anticipated the seed ideas that led Luke to propose the virgin birth. I cite him only as an example, a witness hostile to the concept of the virgin birth who nevertheless does not need to distance the idea of a virgin birth from Paul. Did Paul suggest it to Luke? This is not a necessary suggestion. Still the extensive companionship with Luke, over many years, suggests that these men discussed much more than is explicit in their writings. Certainly an idea as interesting as the virgin birth must have been discussed between them – either before or after Luke wrote his text. And it should also be noticed, and has been, that Paul's goal was not to write a gospel account, but to instruct the church in how to live in Christ. It is not surprising that the virgin birth was not an explicit concern, along with many other specifics of the gospel accounts that are missing from his letters.

But some have suggested that explicit affirmation of the virgin birth is also missing among too many, even the majority, of the Fathers of the church. Is this not a place where we might expect to find testimonies to the virgin birth in abundance, if it was generally accepted? Von Campenhausen, an authority on the early church, observes, 'The so-called "apostolic fathers" – with one important exception – do not seem to know of the virgin birth. At least in the *Letter of Barnabas* and *Shepherd of Hermas* this cannot possibly be due to chance, for both of them develop quite detailed speculations about the Lord's origin and earthly form.'[30] The *Shepherd of Hermas*, written early in the second century, is a writing much loved by the early church, a collection of five visions, twelve mandates, and ten parables. Much of this work is ethical in its focus, and so, perhaps, not interested in the narrative of Christ's beginnings. Indeed, Christ Jesus is never named in this text. Still, in regard to the Son the author does write, 'The Son of God is older than all His creation, so that He became the Father's adviser in His creation. Therefore also He is ancient.'[31] The author has a high Christology – Christ from above. And this ancient text affirms that the Son is the unique gate to the kingdom of God and that the Son sustains the world.[32] But there is no weight to von Campenhausen's expectation that the *Shepherd* should have affirmed the virgin birth. High Christology sets no necessary expectation for a reference to the virgin birth, nor does the lack of affirmation create a hole in the fabric of his argument.[33] So, rather than an argument from silence which counts against the virgin birth, it is possible that the silence implies the author's indifference to, or perhaps more likely the clear acceptance of, the virgin birth beyond need for comment. Indeed *Shepherd* says nothing explicitly of the cross, the Son's death or his resurrection, concerns he is not charged with dismissing or about which he would be said not to know.

Similarly the *Letter of Barnabas* offers a window into this early era. Quoted in the second century by Clement of Alexandria, it may have been written fifty or more years earlier. *Barnabas* has many references to Jesus, including an affirmation of his incarnation: 'Set your hope on Him who is about to be manifested to you in the flesh, even

Jesus.'[34] The author also affirms the unique power for salvation which flows to us from the crucified Lamb of God, our kingly substitute: 'Then there is the placing of the wool on the tree. This means that the Kingdom of Jesus is on the cross, and that they who set their hope on Him shall live for ever.'[35] This text focuses on theological matters, showing a concern that surpasses ethics. But even so, the absence of the affirmation of the virgin birth is hardly concerning, if it is still noteworthy. The author of *Barnabas* discoursed neither on Joseph nor Mary, nor explicitly on the birth of our Saviour. The silence, and the general silence of this generation of writers, is noteworthy, but does it weigh against affirming the church's early belief in the virgin birth? That does not seem to follow from these texts or others.

In fact, while the virgin birth is not of explicit interest to many, the evidence that we do find weighs in favour of an early affirmation of this doctrine. Ignatius, Bishop of Antioch, gives one of the earliest testimonies to the virgin birth. He was martyred in the early decades of the second century (perhaps as early as 107 CE), so this fact puts an early boundary on the date of his writing. In his day, there were those who believed that Jesus only appeared to be human – the Docetists, whose name came from the Greek word for 'appearance'. That is, for them, Jesus merely *seemed* to be human, but was actually only divine. There was no specific reference to 'Docetism' by name until Eusebius of Caesarea (c.260–c.339) wrote of the so-called *Gospel of Peter* (second century).[36] Even so, at the end of the first century or the beginning of the second, Ignatius argued against such beliefs. He affirmed that Jesus actually came *in the flesh* and, in so doing, affirmed the virgin birth. He wrote, 'And hidden from the prince of this world were the virginity of Mary and her child-bearing and likewise also the death of the Lord – three mysteries to be cried aloud – the which [*sic*] were wrought in the silence of God.'[37] Why include the virginity of Mary at Jesus' birth in his argument? Machen insightfully shows us that to refute the Docetists, Ignatius needed to prove only the real, physical birth of Christ; to assert the virgin birth was wholly unnecessary to his argument, even a distraction. This truth seems to testify to the general acceptance of the virgin birth in his day. As Machen puts it, 'The testimony of Ignatius, therefore, is unequivocal . . . [the virgin birth] was not a thing that had to be established by argument.'[38] Still the influence of docetic ideas continued. An example of such ancient ideas can be found in the pseudepigraphical[39] *Acts of John*:

> Another glory I will tell you, brethren. Sometimes when I meant to touch him, I met a material and solid body; and at other times again when I felt him, the substance was immaterial and bodiless and as if it were not existing at all . . . And there was set before each one of us a loaf of bread by our host, and he also received a loaf. And he would bless his own and divide it amongst us; and from that little piece each of us was filled, and our own loaves were saved intact, so that those who had invited him were amazed. And often when I was walking with him I wished to see whether the print of his foot appeared upon the earth – for I saw him raising himself from the earth – but I never saw it.[40]

Why was this teaching not refuted in a way that displayed the virgin birth? Or perhaps we should ask: Why was this generation relatively silent on the virgin birth? The answer is clear: the point was obvious among those of the church. The words of Ignatius reveal that the idea of the virgin birth was commonly held, and so there was no need to argue against such docetic teachings *within* the church. It is also not surprising that others (and certainly not docetic 'believers') would fail to take up this discussion on the point of virgin birth; the fundamental issue with Docetists was not the kind of physical birth, but a rejection of *any* physical birth. So, the fact that Ignatius did so at all is of great help, allowing us to perceive how commonly the virgin birth was held.

Justin Martyr (100–165) provides helpful insights also, as he deals with Trypho the Jew. He writes:

> Now it is evident to all, that in the race of Abraham according to the flesh no one has been born of a virgin, or is said to have been born [of

a virgin], save this our Christ. But since you and your teachers venture to affirm that in the prophecy of Isaiah it is not said, 'Behold, the virgin shall conceive,' but, 'Behold, the young woman shall conceive, and bear a son'; and [since] you explain the prophecy as if [it referred] to Hezekiah, who was your king, I shall endeavour to discuss shortly this point in opposition to you, and to show that reference is made to Him who is acknowledged by us as Christ.[41]

What does this passage mean? It means that both Justin and Trypho, writing in the middle of the second century CE, understood that the virgin birth was generally held by Christians and that it was an important difference between them.

We can say of the Apostolic Fathers and earliest creeds that, while testimony was minimal, all testimony to the virgin birth was positive. In the second century, even as early as Ignatius, the virgin birth had clear affirmation and was commonly held. By the third century, it was still not opposed from within the church (depending on one's understanding of the 'position' of the Docetists and Ebionites) and it was affirmed by creeds and leaders, including Eusebius, who did not see a need to affirm it in his own church's creed.

As the church matures, and opportunities to write theologically expand with time, we do find more affirmations. The catholic Christian rule of faith, our *regula fidei*, is becoming explicit. It developed from implicit agreement, through external challenge, to explicit affirmation. This development includes the affirmation of the virgin birth. At the end of the second century, Irenaeus writes, 'The Church, though dispersed throughout the whole world, even to the ends of the earth, has received from the apostles and their disciples this faith: [She believes] in one God, the Father Almighty, Maker of heaven, and earth, and the sea, and all things that are in them; and in one Christ Jesus, the Son of God, who became incarnate for our salvation; and in the Holy Spirit, who proclaimed through the prophets the dispensations of God, and the advents, and the birth from a virgin.'[42] Also in the later part of the second century, Tertullian (c.160–c.230) wrote, 'Him we believe to have been sent by the Father into the Virgin, and to have been born of her – being both Man and God, the Son of Man and the Son of God, and to have been called by the name of Jesus Christ.'[43] The church affirmed the virgin birth of Christ as part of its explicit *regula fidei* and creed.

It is worth observing that the virgin birth is represented in early creeds with simple bluntness: 'born of a virgin'. Historically, creedal affirmations or denials are often witnesses to a dispute. The effect is that the language reflects the details of those battles in the wording of the affirmation or denials. But for the virgin birth, those battles were yet to come. The affirmations of the virgin birth were guileless. Affirmation seemed to be generally accepted among the church; the words are simple. The earliest creed, as noted in the Introduction, may be the so-called Apostles' Creed. Machen dates its earliest form to no later than 150 CE, and likely much earlier.[44] It is a very early witness to the virgin birth and without nuance or polemic. Later, but still early, is the Creed of Caesarea, offered by Eusebius to the Nicene counsel in 325 CE. In regard to Jesus' birth, it reads: 'who was made flesh for our salvation', omitting any reference to the virgin birth, neither denial nor affirmation. The counsel revised his proposal under the influence of Arian conceptions: 'came down and was made flesh, and became man'. Still, they also felt no need to explicitly affirm the virgin birth. Later, revised again, and affirmed by Chalcedon in 451 (recorded by Cyril), the virgin birth became explicit: 'and was made flesh of the Holy Spirit and the Virgin Mary, and became man'.[45] The virgin birth seems to be assumed, then explicitly declared. Rather than receiving this reality as proof of a developing doctrine, it is instead an indication of an affirmation commonly held and not disputed. In the case of Eusebius the virgin birth was not unknown to him. Quite the opposite: he affirmed the virgin birth, yet saw no reason to insist on its inclusion in the creed.[46]

The Ebionites asserted that Jesus was born like all other men. They were early Jewish Christians whose name may have derived from the Hebrew for 'poor persons', though the actual etymology is obscure. In fact, like many movements, the Ebionites were not one group, but a collection of similar groups who existed during the second to sixth centuries after Christ. They followed Jewish customs, an important part of their identity, and they also accepted Jesus as a prophet. But for them, Jesus was not YHWH; he was not God. In fact, to call them Christians may represent a failure of categories. Irenaeus (130–202) provided the first reference to 'Ebionites'. He wrote:

> Those who are called Ebionites agree that the world was made by God; but their opinions with respect to the Lord are similar to those of Cerinthus and Carpocrates. They use the Gospel according to Matthew only, and repudiate the Apostle Paul, maintaining that he was an apostate from the law. As to the prophetical writings, they endeavour to expound them in a somewhat singular manner: they practise circumcision, persevere in the observance of those customs which are enjoined by the law, and are so Judaic in their style of life, that they even adore Jerusalem as if it were the house of God.[47]

It is not surprising that their gospel excluded Jesus' virgin birth. Specifically, Irenaeus charges, 'Vain also are the Ebionites, who do not receive by faith into their soul the union of God and man, but who remain in the old leaven of [the natural] birth, and who do not choose to understand that the Holy Ghost came upon Mary, and the power of the Most High did overshadow her.'[48] Denying Christ's divinity, they affirmed his adoption by God later in his life.[49] Although they began within the church, differing initially in customs rather than in theology, the distinction was in fact a different gospel. Their rejection of the virgin birth was therefore not from within the church, but from those who stood without, judging Jesus to be merely a man, not the God-man.[50]

In the fourth century, Athanasius (296–373) affirmed both the virgin birth and Isaiah's anticipation of that birth.[51] In the next century Augustine (354–430), Bishop of Hippo, perhaps because of his prior association with the Manicheans, was a bit more expansive: 'Thus we believe that our Lord Jesus Christ was born of a virgin who was called Mary . . . But nobody can say, "Perhaps Christ was born of a virgin" without prejudice to his Christian faith.'[52] From Augustine on, no one challenges this teaching as the position commonly held, and indeed there is reason to see it as the position of the church as far back as can be traced. Here is the key point: from the beginning a clear voice has sounded from the church affirming the virgin birth both implicitly and explicitly, and that voice has continued to sound its unwavering note for almost two thousand years.

The actual debate, or rather the divide, on the issue of the virgin birth waited for the advent of scholars such as David Friedrich Strauss. Writing in the time of Friedrich Schleiermacher, a mentor, Strauss wrote his seminal *The Life of Jesus* in 1836. His project accounted for the narrative claims of the Bible under the concept of myth. He exposed significant difficulties raised by the virgin birth, both philosophical and exegetical, resolving them by the Enlightenment mandate of naturalism. He proposes, 'Jesus was the offspring of an ordinary marriage, between Joseph and Mary; an explanation which, it has been justly remarked, maintains at once the dignity of Jesus and the respect due to his mother.'[53] Strauss would affirm that Joseph was the father of Jesus; that there was no virgin birth in history; and that the myth was overlaid on the historical events in order to fit the theological needs. But as noted above, this deviation from the historic assertion of the virgin birth was a wholly new idea *within* the church, as Strauss himself attested.[54] In fact, on both sides of the now visible divide, there was agreement: the virgin birth was newly contested.

In response to Strauss and others in the nineteenth century, *The Fundamentals: A Testimony to the Truth* was published at the turn of the twentieth century. Funded by Lyman Stewart in 1909, each section appeared as a pamphlet. Later, between the years of 1910 and 1915, it was published as a multi-volume set.[55] The first article, 'The Virgin Birth of Christ', was published in the first volume in primary position – an editorial decision that should not be lost on the reader.[56] In this article, James Orr relates the beginning of the modernist– fundamentalist controversy. He calls our attention to Pastor Schrempf, who in 1892 refused to use the Apostles' Creed in baptism over this article of faith. According to Orr, the affirmation of the virgin birth was uncontested: 'until recently no one dreamed of denying . . . this article.'[57] Of course, this was not strictly true. Citing Friedrich Schleiermacher (1768–1834),[58] or Strauss who followed him, could undermine Orr's overly specific claim. Yet Schleiermacher and Strauss were doing something rather new, a response to the Enlightenment and so to modernism, and so new within the church. And at least in the case of Schleiermacher, the intent was to restore and reinvigorate Christianity in the age of the Enlightenment. For that reason, and others, he rejected miracles. Or rather, he redefined them, writing, 'Miracle is simply the religious name for event. Every event, even the most natural and usual, becomes a miracle, as soon as the religious view of it can be the dominant [view]. To me all is miracle.'[59] Clearly his contribution to the conversation antedates, or perhaps sets the stage for, the modernist controversy. To Schleiermacher and Strauss we could add Unitarianism, Latter-day Saints, and many others. But Orr is still correct in asserting general agreement within the church for almost two millennia in regard to the virgin birth. Doubting the historicity of the virgin birth was a change.

Now, once raised as a new issue, the virgin birth became the central focus in the modernist–fundamentalist divide. 'The fundamentals', the focus of the publication, included five tenets, of which the virgin birth was only one: the inspiration and inerrancy of the Bible, the virgin birth of Christ, the atoning death of Christ, the physical resurrection of Christ, and the historical reality of Christ's miracles. As I pointed out above, this article by Orr on the virgin birth was placed first in this thousand-page collection of tracts because it was argued that the virgin birth had priority among the fundamentals, one that affected the whole of Christianity. Orr writes:

> Reading the Gospels, he [the ordinary Christian] feels no incongruity in passing from the narratives of the Virgin Birth to the wonderful story of Christ's life in the chapters that follow, then from these to the pictures of Christ's divine dignity given in John and Paul. The whole is of one piece: the virgin birth is as natural at the beginning of the life of such a One – the divine Son – as the resurrection is at the end.[60]

Of course, in opposition were the modernists. Paul Badham wrote in his centenary volume which celebrated the work of the modernists:

> The importance of Christology to the classical Modernists was often obscured in the debates of the 1920s by their opponents, who believed that only Chalcedonian orthodoxy and total adherence to such beliefs as the virgin birth or the bodily resurrection of Jesus could safeguard Christ's divinity. But the modernists themselves had no doubt of their total commitment . . . They believed that the traditional doctrine had to be re-expressed in modern terms in order that it might continue to be believed.[61]

The divide between the modernists and the fundamentalists was over the nature of truth. Modernists were interested in *preserving* the faith by updating it to fit modern, scientific, anti-supernaturalistic realities. Fundamentalists intentionally drew their source of truth from God's Word, not (always) rejecting scientific discoveries, but rejecting the position that science is the norm by which all is judged.[62] The divide often meant a mutual lack of respect, for while both sought to preserve it, they each thought the other was destroying the very thing they valued: Christianity.

Now the stage is set for the question of this study: What is the meaning of the virgin birth? I have outlined the divide over the virgin birth from the gospels to the modern era. I have tried to show that the virgin birth has been affirmed by orthodox Christians since the earliest days of the church. While this outline does not establish the doctrine, the fact of its acceptance by the church until recent times is not seriously contested. We have also observed the doctrine's importance, not merely as a shibboleth, but because the position that a person takes on the virgin birth is deeply connected to other fundamental positions, including the theology of the Word of God; God's right, ability, and willingness to intervene supernaturally; and the person of Christ. These are massive issues and the virgin birth is a shibboleth which represents these as well as the doctrine of the nature of

Christ's birth. This connection has been recognized at least since the fundamentalist–modernist controversy. But the question that drives me in this work is not these great issues. Instead, I ask: Believing that it is true, what does it mean? If Christ was born of a virgin, what does it mean to us who have inherited this great truth? This question is what I will now explore.

2

The Virgin Birth: Historic and Misguided Meanings

Our Lord Jesus Christ was born of a virgin only for the following reason: he was to bring to naught the begetting that proceeds from lawless appetite, and provide the ruler of this world with proof that God could form man even without human sexual intercourse. (Second-century fragment)[1]

For if it is established that God ought to become man, there is no doubt that he does not lack the wisdom and the power whereby this may be effected without sin. (Anselm)[2]

It was important to review the history of the understanding of the virgin birth in order for us to clear our heads and be free to think about why God might have brought Jesus into the world by a virgin birth. I considered the witness of Scripture and the writings of the early Fathers of the church, as well as the perspective of the church's near neighbours, such as the pagans, the Jews, and other streams of Christianity. Our look was brief, but we did see reason to believe that the virgin birth is affirmed by Scripture, that it has always been affirmed by the church, and also that it has been consistently rejected by the church's near neighbours. More recently it has come under attack even from within the church. As the Enlightenment matured in the nineteenth century, the virgin birth was not only disputed, but became a point of division, a fault line. Indeed, by the twentieth century, the division had a name: 'the fundamentalist–modernist controversy'. The virgin birth was the divide. It still is, as contemporary scholarship like that of Andrew T. Lincoln and Gerald Sigal indicates. But the ongoing disagreement over this shibboleth should not prevent us from moving forward to explore its meaning. Quite the opposite: this context is important because viewing it first and clearly can free us to think about what the virgin birth means. That is, acknowledging the historical topography frees our mind to focus on something deeper. As I suggested in the Introduction, everyone, even those who do not affirm the historicity of the virgin birth, would do well to join in an investigation of the rich theological meaning and value of the virgin birth. Indeed, the authors of the gospels, the Evangelists, meant something by it. What could that be?

It is here that I begin just that investigation. I will start by considering a few misguided meanings that have been suggested: the avoidance of the stain of concupiscence and the bypassing of original sin. I will attempt to show that these ideas fall short of being convincing; they are neither logically sufficient explanations nor historically or scripturally necessary. Anselm says it well in the quote above: God certainly can and did bring Christ into the world without sin, but it is not clear whether he did so by a virgin birth. I believe that these reasons for the virgin birth will be shown to be of little value to the life of the church, for understanding God, sin, or spiritual regeneration. Yet, whether in agreement or disagreement, these are reasons worth attending to because, as we will see, they are significant historically, and perhaps that history has something to teach us even yet.

To Avoid the Stain of Concupiscence

> He took our body, and not only so, but He took it directly from a spotless, stainless virgin, without the agency of human father – a pure body, untainted by intercourse with man. (Athanasius)[3]

It is quite impossible to write about the virgin birth without wading into the murky waters of sex and sexuality – waters made murky by our sinful state. This is the context for the concern about the 'stain of concupiscence'. As some early Fathers of the church understood concupiscence, it is the sin of engaging in sexual relationship out of desire, rather than in purity. Athanasius (296–373) provides us with an example of just this thinking (above). In this context, purity is the opposite of concupiscence; it is to engage in sex with one's spouse out of the simple desire to obey God's command to produce children – and nothing more. If concupiscence is a sin, and if human parents conceived the Messiah, then even the Messiah could be conceived in sin.

It is no different for many interpreters of these texts in our own day. Piotr Ashwin-Siejkowski observed that some hear the Creed's commitment to the virgin birth as if the Creed revealed that 'the early Christians were obsessed with the idea of "purity", "abstinence", "lifelong virginity" or sexual pollution'.[4] But is this what the Evangelists were thinking (was this in the mind of God?) when Matthew and Luke wrote of the virgin birth?

The textual fragment that is quoted at the beginning of this chapter is from an unknown author in the second century, although it is sometimes attributed to Justin. Without full context or certain authorship, it should not be given great weight; it does not necessarily reflect the thinking typical of its day. Yet it does show theological reflection on the virgin birth and it does raise the question: What does the virgin birth mean? The author is certainly clear in his own perspective: the virgin birth has one singular reason – to defeat concupiscence. He lacks no clarity.

But is there such a sin as the sin of concupiscence? Of course, and necessarily so, by definition. Colossians 3:5 speaks of the sanctifying work which is commanded of Christians: 'Put to death therefore what is earthly in you: sexual immorality, impurity, passion, evil desire, and covetousness, which is idolatry.' The Greek word for 'evil desire' is *epithumia,* which translates literally as 'desire', not 'evil desire'. The adjective 'evil' arises only from the specific context. It is this word which is translated into Latin as 'concupiscence' or *concupiscentiam malam* (again, the adjective *malus,* 'evil', is added due to context). The King James Version, reflecting the Latin and older English usage, translates this same text as 'evil concupiscence'. So concupiscence is the sin of following evil desires. But does this have specific application to marriage or to the virgin birth? It is hard to see that it does. Sex outside of marriage is either adultery (sexual relations when married to another) or fornication (sexual relations when unmarried). In both cases lust is involved, but neither case can apply to Mary and Joseph. Because Mary and Joseph were pledged to each other and would have married, any possible concern in regard to 'concupiscence' for the virgin birth can only be the possibility of lust within a faithful marriage, within the context of the sexual intimacy of a married couple. So we must ask whether God warns against concupiscence within marriage and if that in some way affects children born to a couple acting in concupiscence. And if so, could the virgin birth actually protect Mary, Joseph, or Jesus from the specific sin of concupiscence? The traditional answer to both questions is 'yes'. In the first case, the answer depends on showing that the reason for marriage is (only) to have children. But this is difficult to argue from Scripture. And in the second, it requires us to know something about the transmission of sin from parents to children. This too is a scriptural challenge.

Let us deal with the first. God intended marriage for much more than for having children. Indeed, God did command fruitfulness – children – but that is not all. In the Garden, 'God blessed them. And God said to them, "Be fruitful and multiply and fill the earth and subdue it, and have dominion over the fish of the sea and over the birds of the heavens and over every living thing that moves on the earth"' (Gen. 1:28). He repeated this command to Noah: 'And God blessed Noah and his sons and said to them, "Be fruitful and multiply and fill the earth"' (Gen. 9:1). Did this command to bear children exhaust the meaning of marriage? Clearly not. Something much greater was happening in regard to God's first people. Indeed, his first positive command was marriage. And Adam and Eve shared this with the fish and birds and beasts: the command to be fruitful. What they did not share with the animals was the union of many-in-one. This union, displayed in marriage, was shared by God's people uniquely with God alone. Here is how Genesis teaches this: Seeing that it was not good for Adam to be alone, God led him to name the animals. In doing so, Adam studied them, and, of course, they proved inadequate for this purpose; he was still alone. Then God made the woman and, like a father, he presented her to Adam, a wedding of sorts. They were married with God's blessing. Then comes the first sermon of the Torah: 'Therefore a man shall leave his father and mother and hold fast to his wife, and they shall become one flesh' (Gen. 2:24). This text, including the whole section from verses 18–25, is the conclusion to the second account of creation, and possibly to both the first and second accounts. It is clearly important because of its length – almost a third of the second account and more than a 'tithe' of both accounts. It also has a key position of importance, sitting in the concluding position. Whatever God intends by human marriage, it surpasses what he intends for the animals of his creation. People are not only to multiply, they are to be many and one: 'they shall become one flesh.' In this dual command to 'leave' and 'cleave' (if I may use the more pleasing rhyme of the KJV), God creates something new by his word: the two become one. In so doing, God reveals something in people that is very like himself. He did this in two stages. First, God created man in his own image: male and female. Then, by his word, he bound them both in the union of marriage. In so doing, the God who is many and one, three persons in one nature, caused the two to become one. And this new creation, marriage, reflected this very nature of God in his human creatures. That being so, the purposes of marriage are deeper than mere procreation. In the God-ordained miracle of two becoming one, human marriage reflects the very image of God, the Many-in-One – or, as he has revealed himself, the Three-in-One.

The meaning of marriage is not limited even to this glorious imaging. Beyond bearing and protecting children and beyond reflecting the image of God, God affirms his delightful intent for sex within marriage. This is not unimportant to understanding the meaning of the virgin birth – or unimportant to refuting confused meanings. From Genesis to Revelation, human marriage anticipates God's eschatological intention for his people: union with God in Christ. The first two chapters of his Book, Genesis 1 – 2, and the last two chapters of his Book, Revelation 21 – 22, both give pride of place to marriage: first that of Adam to Eve, which anticipates that of Christ to his church. As Paul writes, 'This mystery is profound' (Eph. 5:32). In the Song of Solomon we find a poem that celebrates God's love for his people. Still, the historical context is one husband's real delight in his wife, and it affirms God's real celebration of sexuality within marriage. The typological understanding, God's love for his people, is parallel to the human historical and poetic reality, neither overwhelming nor replacing it. Indeed, God created sexual relationships to be pleasurable and made marriage as the one context for the enjoyment of our sexuality. The Bible celebrates this. Proverbs advises each man to enjoy his wife and find satisfaction in sexual relationship with his own wife. And Paul, while advising singleness for the sake of the work of the kingdom, advises marriage specifically to avoid lust, because of the sanctified and sanctioned exercise of desire within marriage: 'it is better to marry than to burn with passion' (1 Cor. 7:9). Positively and negatively, marriage is declared as a proper place for enjoying the God-ordained beauty of sex in relationship with our spouse. Marriage is not merely for producing children. It is certainly that, but it also reflects the image of God in people, and it is God's intended haven for sexual delight.

What of the second concern? While marriage has a meaning beyond childbearing, and that meaning includes enjoying the sexual relationship within marriage, could lust lurk within marriage, and, if so, could a lustful conception transmit sin to a child? Having seen that a healthy marriage can be full of sexual desire without lust, the question may seem almost unnecessary. But of course, with the catastrophe of Genesis 3, the fall, everything in creation is distorted. Romans 8 tells us that all of creation has been subjected to frustration. That catastrophe certainly affected sex, which has come to be so tightly linked to the sin of lust since the advent of sin in the world. Does this mean that sex may be a 'Slough of Despond' at the heart of marriage? If so, concupiscence is, within the context of marriage, a 'bedbug' that bites even those with the best intentions. This seems to be the understanding of some in the church. If that is the case, the virgin birth might be a necessary response of God to save Mary and Joseph and Jesus – especially Jesus – from this stain.

For good reason, sex and lust was a serious concern in the early centuries of the church. It was early Gnostics who objected that sex in any context, including marriage, was sinful concupiscence, and Irenaeus (c.200) was one who confronted this distortion.[5] Tertullian (c.160–c.230) wrote in regard to Paul's admonition in 1 Thessalonians 4:3–4, 'that each one of you know how to control his own body in holiness', that marriage should, instead, be a sanctuary from concupiscence.[6] This affirms his understanding of the possibility of a marital sin of concupiscence, but also his optimistic view of the possibility of sanctification in this regard. This sample of two Fathers should help us see that it was not considered necessary that all sexual union within marriage fall into the sin of concupiscence. But sexuality is so powerful, and our world sufficiently distorted by human rebellion, that concupiscence seemed to many an unavoidable sin, even in the context of marriage. John Phillips, a modern theologian, observed that in the early church it was a common understanding that, if Adam and Eve engaged in sexual intimacy, they would have done so only for purposes intended by God: childbearing.[7]

What of Augustine, who wrote at the turn of the fifth century? When he was charged by Pelagius and Pelagians for condemning marriage, he responded with 'On Marriage and Concupiscence'. There he wrote, 'It is, however, one thing for married persons to have intercourse only for the wish to beget children, which is not sinful: it is another thing for them to desire carnal pleasure in cohabitation, but with the spouse only, which involves venial sin.'[8] This thinking represents the explicit possibility of the sin of concupiscence within marriage.[9] If correct, this represents a possible purpose and meaning for the virgin birth: to avoid such a sin.

This understanding continued, with standing, into the Reformation. Not a few have observed the depiction of Eve in Hans Baldung's 1511 woodcut *The Fall of Man* as an example that intentionally confuses reaching for the forbidden fruit with Adam's lustful reach for Eve's breast.[10] So at least some understood that concupiscence was a sin within marriage, though surrendering to this desire was a venial sin (minor), rather than a mortal sin (threatening our relationship with God).

What of the virgin birth? Logically, Mary and Joseph could have come together in marriage for the purpose of bearing children, without concupiscence, and so it would seem that there was no need for a virgin birth to prevent Christ from being the fruit of 'illicit desire'. But is concupiscence even a sin – an unavoidable sin – within marriage? Or, if it is a sin, are those born of such wrong desires ethically affected – tainted by sin? Augustine addresses both of these questions:

> Wherefore the devil holds infants guilty who are born, not of the good by which marriage is good, but of the evil of concupiscence, which, indeed, marriage uses aright, but at which even marriage has occasion to feel shame. Marriage is itself 'honourable in all' the goods which properly appertain to it; but even when it has its 'bed undefiled' (not only by fornication and adultery, which are damnable disgraces, but also by any of those excesses of cohabitation such as do not arise from any prevailing desire of children, but from an overbearing lust of pleasure, which are venial sins in man and wife), yet, whenever it comes to the actual process of generation, the very embrace which is lawful and honourable cannot be effected without the ardour of lust, so as to be able to accomplish that which appertains to the use of reason and not of lust. Now, this ardour, whether following or preceding the will, does somehow, by a power of its own, move the members which cannot be moved simply by the will, and in this manner it shows itself not to be the servant of a will which commands it, but rather to be the punishment of a will which disobeys it. It shows, moreover, that it must be excited, not by a free choice, but by a certain seductive stimulus, and that on this very account it produces shame. This is the carnal concupiscence, which, while it is no longer accounted sin in the regenerate, yet in no case happens to nature except from sin. It is the daughter of sin, as it were; and whenever it yields assent to the commission of shameful deeds, it becomes also the mother of many sins. Now from this concupiscence whatever comes into being

by natural birth is bound by original sin, unless, indeed, it be born again in Him whom the Virgin conceived without this concupiscence. Wherefore, when He vouchsafed to be born in the flesh, He alone was born without sin.[11]

Here Augustine explains why he understands concupiscence to be a sin, extrapolating from the concept of an 'undefiled bed'. He also implies that the virginity of Mary was the reason why Christ alone was born without sin passing to him from concupiscence. It would seem that, given his understanding of concupiscence, it would follow that no one could be of fully pure motives in regard to marital sex. So, by this way of thinking, virginity was a fence around such tainted desires. In his second book, refuting the same attacks, he writes even more succinctly: 'This has also, in fact, been said by Ambrose, of most blessed memory, bishop of the church in Milan, when he gives as the reason why Christ's birth in the flesh was free from all sinful fault, that His conception was not the result of a union of the two sexes; whereas there is not one among human beings conceived in such union who is without sin.'[12] So, by this thinking, the virgin birth provided a unique and necessary protection for Christ.[13]

However, as we considered above, this position has no biblical support; it is merely an argument from logic. If sexual concupiscence is a sin, it can have nothing to do with the virgin birth or with protecting Christ from the stain of sin.[14] Karl Barth writes, 'Here we cannot consider the quite un-biblical view that sexual life as such is to be regarded as an evil to be removed, so that the active sign is to be sought in the fact that this removal is here presumed to have taken place. The passage [often cited] is Psalm 51:5: "Behold I was shapen in iniquity and in sin did my mother conceive me," [which] by no means implies condemnation of the natural event as such.'[15] In this he is correct. Yet the informal idea that sex is not quite a Good in God's world and that it is not something God would want to be mixed up with persists for some. N.T. Wright observed, 'The birth stories have also functioned as a test case for views of sexuality. Some believers in the virginal conception align this with a low view of sexuality and a high view of perpetual virginity. They believe the story not because of what it says about Jesus, but because of what it says about sex – namely, that it's something God wouldn't want to get mixed up in.'[16] In a modified form, Wayne Grudem addresses this: 'All human beings have inherited legal guilt and a corrupt moral nature from their first father, Adam (this is sometimes called "inherited sin" or "original sin"). But the fact that Jesus did not have a human father means that the line of descent from Adam is partially interrupted.'[17] This leads us to a new idea: the transmission of original sin to our descendants. In this, concupiscence is not the problem. Instead, we wonder if sin may be inherited. This concern does not consider concupiscence a problem, nor does it view sexuality with suspicion. Rather, it raises the issue of the deeper concern of inherited original sin.

To Protect Christ from Original Sin

What is original sin? The word 'original' could make it seem to us that sin was original, as if the first humans created by God were made with a stain of sin. But this is not so; they were created good. Rather, the 'original sin' is the 'first sin'. This is the sin of Adam and Eve described in Genesis 3; original sin is the fall. Many theologians, ancient and modern, have understood that Adam's sin is transmitted to his descendants. If this is so, then we are guilty in Adam; he is our head. So we have inherited the original sin and stand condemned before God in Adam. To the shared sin of Adam – original sin – we each add our own sins and reinforce the condemnation. The question in our context is this: How does this original sin affect Jesus? Or more specifically, how did Jesus, fully God but also fully man, avoid the stain of original sin? Some propose the virgin birth to be the mechanism for this.

As noted above, original sin is a concern in regard to the virgin birth that is distinct from the concern of concupiscence. By concupiscence it is asserted (by some) that a child may inherit a stain of sexual sin from his or her immediate parents because they are his parents by sexual union. However, in regard to original sin, it is asserted that we inherit Adam's sin by transmission through the sexual union of our parents. So, in regard to original sin, the concern is to prevent Christ from the stain of the sin of Adam, rather than some (imagined) stain of the sexual desire of his parents.

Augustine again helps us understand how this issue was first conceived by the church. He believed that Adam was free to sin or not to sin. However, distinct from Pelagius, Augustine argued that, since Adam's fall, we are free only to sin.[18] This state of bondage to sin is the effect of original sin. But how is this original sin passed to us? Augustine understands that we receive original sin by inheritance. First, he affirms that the soul is not made uniquely for each individual, but is a product of the generation of life by sexual reproduction. He writes, 'For it is one of two things: if the soul is not derived by natural descent from the parent, it comes out of nothing. To pretend that it is derived from God in such wise as to be a portion of His nature, is simply sacrilegious blasphemy.'[19] That is, the soul comes by parental descent, not holy and pristine from God himself. I cite Augustine because he set the pace for the church. It should be noted that he held this loosely, subject to scriptural or rational refutation, if such refutation were possible without contradicting orthodoxy. He seemed to doubt this.[20] The effect of this view is that all who are born to man and woman, because they are born to man and woman, are understood to be born stained by sin.[21] The concern is that original sin is transmitted through parents. Like much of the argument for concupiscence, this is a logical problem. It is not very difficult to dismiss as a logical argument alone. But there is also a textual issue.

Luke 1:35 is the key text for this discussion: 'And the angel answered her, "The Holy Spirit will come upon you, and the power of the Most High will overshadow you; therefore the child to be born will be called holy – the Son of God."' The issue here is how the Christ's status as 'holy' is related to his conception. That is, is Jesus holy because he was conceived by the Holy Spirit, or is he called 'the Son of God' because he was conceived by the Holy Spirit?

Let's first consider John Calvin (1509–64). He writes:

> This is a confirmation of the preceding clause: for the angel shows that Christ must not be born by ordinary generation, that he may be holy, and that he may be the Son of God; that is, that in holiness and glory he may be high above all creatures, and may not hold an ordinary rank among men. Heretics, who imagine that he became the Son of God after his human generation, seize on the particle therefore as meaning that he would be called the Son of God, because he was conceived in a remarkable manner by the power of the Holy Spirit. But this is a false conclusion.[22]

Calvin seems to affirm that Christ's holiness is an effect of the Spirit's work in bringing about a virgin birth. Yet context matters here, as always. Calvin is arguing against those who would make Jesus Christ like any other man. He is not asking the specific question I am asking here. He is defending the truth that Christ's birth is not simply like every other man's – or any other's. Indeed, according to Luke, it is not. He is born of the Holy Spirit. For Calvin, Christ's birth maintains him in holiness, and he is who he is because he was born of God, the God-man.

Moving forward to the twentieth century and considering our key text in Luke, James Orr wrote, 'Miracle could alone effect such a wonder. Because His human nature had this miraculous origin Christ was the "holy" One from the commencement (Luke 1:35). Sinless He was, as His whole life demonstrated; but when, in all time, did natural generation give birth to a sinless personality?' Orr seems to understand that his miraculous nature, conceived by the Holy Spirit rather than conceived in some other way by God, made him holy. Grudem seems also to understand Christ's holiness as an effect of the virgin birth. He writes:

> The virgin birth also makes possible Christ's true humanity without inherited sin . . . All human beings have inherited legal guilt and a corrupt moral nature from their first father, Adam . . . But the fact

that Jesus did not have a human father means that the line of descent from Adam is partially interrupted. Jesus did not descend from Adam in exactly the same way in which every other human being has descended from Adam. And this helps us to understand why the legal guilt and moral corruption that belongs to all other human beings did not belong to Christ.[23]

But the question begins to press itself: *How* is a virgin birth sufficient to accomplish sinlessness at birth, avoiding original sin? Yes, it could be sufficient to say that the Holy Spirit made him sinless, but that is not exactly what is being claimed. What is claimed is that the mechanism of the virgin birth by the Spirit made him holy in distinction to a birth in some other way which was superintended by God's Spirit. This is a strong claim that a virgin birth was necessary to give holiness and protection from original sin. But what is it that we know of the biology of sexual reproduction that allows us to affirm that a virgin birth is some help against original sin? Alan Jacobs, in his book *Original Sin*, wrote on just this challenge. Referring to the 1854 Papal Bull of Pope Pius IX (1792–1878), in which he decreed that Mary 'was preserved free from original sin', Jacobs wrote, 'But it should be noted that although this language [and that of the early church Fathers before him] may capture rather well the condition of sinfulness, it doesn't do anything to help us understand how we all share in the sin of Adam. That is, it gets the "sin", but not the "original".'[24] Returning to Grudem's claim, I should add here that he did say in this context that nothing in the text asserts that sin is transferred to progeny by the unique contribution of the father. But if his assertion is based on Luke 1:35, it seems unlikely that Luke asserts that *virgin birth* provided the causal link to the holiness of the child. On reflection it is clear: we do not understand the mechanism of the transmission of this sin of Adam. Postulating a virgin birth to avoid original sin is a theory without foundation.

It is worth being careful – even technical – in regard to the text. At this point some may feel the need to skip to the next paragraph: I'd encourage you not to do so. A literal translation of the Greek text of Luke 1:35b could read, 'therefore also the one who is born holy will be called son of God'. The 'therefore also' tells us that this idea follows from what was established previously. This is what was established and it is two-fold: 'The Holy Spirit will come upon you' and 'the power of the Most High will overshadow you'. This is the ground for what comes next, and it echoes Genesis 1:2. Just as 'the Spirit of God was hovering over the face of the waters' anticipates the birth *of* creation, so the first part of verse 35, 'the Holy Spirit will come upon you', anticipates the advent of the Messiah *in* creation. It speaks of the creative work of God in Mary to produce a child, a virgin birth. Indeed, Mary clearly grasped this, as we saw from her previous question ('How will this be, since I am a virgin?', v. 34). This phrase in verse 35a is our ground and the answer to her question about bearing a child as a virgin. But what else, beyond the virgin birth, is to be attributed or implied by this creative work of the Holy Spirit in power? While the 'therefore' establishes a connecting link between the cause (the Holy Spirit's work) and the effect, what is that effect? This is the key question: Is it that the child will be born holy because of this work of the Holy Spirit, or that the holy child will be called 'the Son of God' because he is of the Holy Spirit – or both? The NASB translates in this way: 'and for that reason the holy Child shall be called the Son of God.' Their understanding is clear: it is because of the work of the Holy Spirit that the holy child is *called* 'the Son of God', not that he is holy because of the virgin birth.[25] At least in regard to this verse, the virgin birth is not the cause of his holiness, but the cause of his being called 'the Son of God'. It makes him clearly God and man, and affirms his persistent holiness as the God-man, but it stops short of declaring this a direct causal effect of the birth.

It is also worth considering Karl Barth in this regard. He also perceived a link between the virgin birth and Christ's freedom from original sin. He wrote:

> The decisive point of view, from which the *natus ex virgine* [virgin birth] was always regarded in early dogmatics, was rightly, therefore, the recollection of inherited sin, or original sin as it is better expressed

in the Latin *peccatum originale* [original sin], i.e., sin so far as man
does not live it out primarily and only in individual thoughts, words
and deeds, but lives it in the inevitability and totality of his existence
as one already fallen in Adam, because the *liberum arbitrium* [freedom
of the will] of obedience to God is missing, while the *servum arbitrium*
[slavery of the will] of disobedience is peculiarly his own. This human
nature is limited and contradicted by the *natus ex virgine*. It indicates
the existence of a Man who . . . because the *servum arbitrium* of disobedience is foreign to Him while the *liberum arbitrium* of obedience
is His own . . . The sign of that is *natus ex virgine*.[26]

Barth's affirmation of the virgin birth as the cause of Jesus' liberation
from original sin is significantly nuanced. While he begins by affirming that he stands with the early theologians of the church who decisively held that the virgin birth 'limited and contradicted' the fallen
human nature, still his understanding of this contradiction seems less
than causal. While referring to the virgin birth as a 'contradiction' to
the bondage of the will and an affirmation of the freedom of obedience, still he calls it a 'sign' rather than a protection against original
sin. In fact, in a later edition of *Church Dogmatics*, he adds:

It is well to remember again at this point that the *ex virgine* [from a
virgin] must always be understood as a pointer to this penetration and
a new beginning, but not as the conditioning of it. (Failure on my
part to make this distinction in the first draft of this book . . . meant
that the questions and answers involved were obscured). If there is a
necessary connexion between this sign and the thing signified, the
connexion is *not a causal one* (emphasis added).[27]

So what does he mean? Barth tells us that any connection between
the virgin birth and Christ's sinlessness must not be a causal link: the
virgin birth did not cause his sinlessness. Still, according to Barth, the
virgin birth is a firm link, a decisive link; a necessary (for us) pointer
to a deeper reality. What is that deeper and more important reality?
Barth is wise when he points to the veracity and importance of the

virgin birth: 'we must not under any circumstances expect elicitation of the *ex virgine*, to provide us, so to speak, with a technical proof of the conquest of original sin that took place in Jesus Christ . . . [Rather it points] to the conquest of original sin that took place in Jesus Christ.'[28] It is rightly a sign rather than an apologetic – an important distinction.

Anselm (1033–1109) wrote about virginal conception and its relationship to original sin; he understood the lack of causal necessity, as he describes with some clarity: 'It is true that the Son of God was born of a spotless Virgin. This was not out of necessity, as if a just offspring could not be generated by this method of propagation from a sinful parent, but because it was fitting that the conception of this man should be of a pure mother.'[29] God was not compelled to bring about Christ's birth from a virgin in order to achieve his goals; rather, this method was fitting.

But this quote raises another issue. I have so far avoided any discussion of Mary's own sinlessness (or perpetual virginity!). It is a topic both too great for this book and also not essential to this investigation. Yet I must touch on it here. The Roman Catholic Church pursued just this course – the sinlessness of Mary, her immaculate conception – in order to protect Christ from original sin. Of course the virgin birth was affirmed, but not to protect Christ from original sin. Indeed, it is insufficient for this goal. Removing only Joseph removed only one human parent. So, turning to Origen (182–254) and Augustine (354–430) for support, the Roman Church affirmed the sinlessness of Mary. On 8 December 1854 Pope Pius IX formalized this long-held commitment in *Ineffabilis Deus*. He wrote, '[Mary] was preserved free from all stain of original sin'; 'The most Blessed Virgin . . . ever increased her original gift, and not only never lent an ear to the serpent, but by divinely given power she utterly destroyed the force and dominion of the evil one.'[30] It is worth noting that, while affirmed by the Roman Catholic Church, it was not a consensus. Matthew Milliner noted, 'John Chrysostom, Bernard of Clairvaux, and Thomas Aquinas – hardly minor figures – each demurred from Mary's complete preservation from original sin.'[31] As is often the case, consensus followed the decree which came much later.

Anselm (1033–1109), writing in about the year 1100, wrestled with this same concern in his work *Why God Became Man*. Here he imagines a dialogue between himself and Boso (yes, 'Boso' does provide us with the antecedent for the name of our modern clown!):

Anselm: But that Virgin from whom the man about whom we are speaking was received was one of those who, before his birth, were cleansed of sins through him, and he was received from her in the state of cleanness which was hers.

Boso: He would appear to have [cleanness] from his mother, and not to be clean on his own account, but through her.

Anselm: *It is not so*. Rather, his mother's cleanness, whereby he is clean, would not have existed, if it had not come from him, and so he was clean on his own account and by his own agency.[32]

This makes the point made previously, that while Christ might seem to have avoided original sin by the virgin birth, it was also the holiness of Christ which purified Mary before his birth. Christ alone was sufficient to purify Mary, but not the reverse. So in arguing for the immaculate conception of Mary, the Roman Church is not dependent on the virgin birth to interrupt sinful inheritance; rather they have reached back to Mary's birth, protecting her from the curse of original sin, and, through her, Jesus. The virgin birth merely protects her status (concupiscence again) and so Christ's. While Jesus has the ability to bestow holiness on his mother in coming to her, the virgin birth does not have either biblical or logical ability to bestow sinlessness on the Messiah.[33]

The virgin birth does not provide the foundation for either evangelicals or Roman Catholics to keep the Messiah free from original sin. And while concupiscence is certainly avoided by the virgin birth, there is only logical purpose in this and no textual one. There is neither a biblically sufficient case that this is a sin married couples must avoid, nor (if it is a sin within marriage) that it affects their children. Both arguments lack the merit of sufficiency and necessity. Both are arguments from what we do not know. Moreover, in regard to original sin, we have no knowledge of *how* Adam's sin is passed to us, though indeed it is. The argument that it comes by sexual union is mere speculation. Just as we do not know how Christ's righteousness is imputed to us, neither do we know how Adam's federal headship corrupts us. It does not help to make Mary innocent, for the miracle worked in Mary, born naturally of sinful parents, could have been worked in Christ. So, though we may rightly avoid asserting the sin of concupiscence as passing on the original sin, we must also avoid asserting something we do not know in regard to how Adam's sin is actually transmitted.

It is good rather to say with Anselm, 'For if it is established that God ought to become man, there is no doubt that he does not lack the wisdom and the power whereby this may be effected without sin.'[34] In fact, we should instead affirm that the man-God Jesus was holy specifically because he is the man-God. As Athanasius put it, 'Not even His birth from a virgin, therefore, changed Him in any way, nor was He defiled by being in the body. Rather, He sanctified the body by being in it.'[35] As I said at the beginning of this chapter, these reasons for the virgin birth seem to be of little value to the life of the church and of little merit for understanding God, sin, or spiritual regeneration. Studying these historical missteps may help us identify better reasons, richer meanings. It is to this I now turn.

Doctrine: The Spirit's Call to Action

> My argument is that exegetes just find themselves believing in the author's mind (and intentional action) as a result of reading a text. (Vanhoozer)[36]

What do these non-meanings mean? What action does God's Spirit call us to, if we understand the virgin birth correctly – or refuse to misunderstand it? I should say a word here about 'meaning' and 'action' in relationship to the Word. Kevin Vanhoozer has rightly applied the insights of J.L. Austin and John Searle to the text of Scripture. God's words are God's acts. So, when we come to the words of authors of the gospels of Matthew and Luke, we rightly ask what they had in mind. I affirm the truth of Vanhoozer's quote above: 'My argument is that exegetes just find themselves believing in the author's mind (and intentional action) as a result of reading a text.'[37] The text is made of words penned by an author who had meaning and intent. Authors say something and intend to shape us for action – put it into action. To this end, we listen. Our listening includes the work of textual criticism (what words did the author actually write?) and exegesis (why these words, in this order, and in this place in the author's argument?). Then, believing that the author had a communicative intent beyond mere words, we anticipate that his words assert a meaning and intend to direct action, create new states, or express feelings. By doing the careful work of unpacking the intended meaning of the author in writing the words he wrote as he wrote them, we do the work of theology. Historical theology studies how others perceived the author. Biblical theology asks how this fits into the whole arc of the movement of God. Philosophical theology applies the rigour of clear thinking to the work of discernment. And systematic theology seeks to perceive a coherent mosaic of God's work of salvation which displays the glory of God in what the whole Bible says about each of his works. If we do this well, we are reading out the meaning from the mind of the author. If we do it poorly, we read our meaning into the words. But my belief is this: there is meaning in the text for the reader to discover – it is the mind of the author and the intent of the author. Even more strongly, the power of the Spirit of God is in the words to shape his people and move them to action. By discerning the meanings and discriminating against non-meanings, we hope to discern how the author, how God, would move us.

In regard to the virgin birth, this claim may be even more significant than it first appears. Though the virgin birth divides theological camps as a shibboleth, both camps accept that these are words written by an author (which author – human or divine, first-century follower or another – is not important to this observation) who intended something. So, even if someone does not believe the historicity of the account of the virgin birth, all should believe that the Evangelists wrote an account in Matthew and Luke, not merely for the account's sake, but with a meaning; that they said it as they said it, where they said it, in order to move their readers in some specific way. There is meaning in this text of the virgin birth; it is there for us to discern. And having discerned it, we discover the authors' intentions; we are to do something. These words are *creative* words.

Clearly, then, the truth of the words is important but not the only issue. And just as clearly, knowing the meaning is not the end of our work. Vanhoozer, following Austin and Searle, asserts that Scripture is a speech act of an author who moves us to action specifically because there is a mind behind the words. If there is meaning, it is that of the author, conveyed through a text, leading to an action, an effect, in us. I propose that this effect, this action, is our 'doctrine'. Those who object that 'doctrine' is a synonym for 'theology', a body of beliefs or teachings, have a fair point. Abundant examples could be given. And, strictly speaking, neither the word 'theology' nor the word 'doctrine' occurs in the Bible – but the concepts do. And in the biblical context, 'doctrine' is much more of a verbal idea than a noun. 'Theology' is a term based on the Greek word *theos* ('God') combined with 'ology' ('the study of'). As such, its focus is on meaning and truth: 'the study of God'. But 'doctrine', distinctly, is a word which is often chosen to translate the Greek word for 'teaching', and teaching always anticipates a change in how we live.[38] So, for example, in the Great Commission of Christ we are commanded to make disciples by 'teaching them to observe all that I have commanded you' (Matt. 28:19–20). The goal is obedience, not mere discernment of glorious truth. So I propose that this 'action-oriented' use of the word 'doctrine' has biblical precedent: the historical root of the word is 'teaching'. We might do well to reserve 'doctrine' for what the church *does*, rather than what the text *means*. This intensifies the question: How did the authors of the texts on the virgin birth intend us to live? What is the 'doctrinal' effect they intended by the words they asserted in the virgin birth?

To resolve this question I am attempting to distinguish in the mind of the authors the doctrine (action) from the theology (meaning) which arise from the words they wrote (text). What is the 'doctrine' of the virgin birth? We considered the historical understandings of the virgin birth as a means to prevent the passing on of the sin of concupiscence or original sin. I argued that this was not good theology. I argued that these were not the concerns of the authors as they wrote of the virgin birth. Where these meanings have been received as meanings of the virgin birth, they seem to have *flowed from* a poor theology of human sexuality, or perhaps *led to* a poor theology of human sexuality. The work I have done has made no attempt to distinguish between cause and effect – though I think this is worth pursuing. But as far as I have taken this, we can apply these rejected meanings of the virgin birth to our doctrine – what the church does. We can say that the authors of Matthew and Luke never had it in mind to cause us to live out such a distorted view of human sexuality, in which sin is intrinsic to sex. That is, were we to follow Augustine and others, we might think that was the case and so misfire in our doctrine of the virgin birth. Instead, on the basis of this investigation so far, we can affirm that the virgin birth cannot serve as a guide to help us understand what God thinks about sex or sexual sin. For this we must look elsewhere in the text.

So, how do we live in light of the virgin birth? As so far we have only considered and rejected meanings, our first doctrinal discovery is that we must not misapply the virgin birth in a way that causes us to derive an errant meaning of human sexuality. We now turn to more fruitful meanings, theology, and more hopeful doctrine.

3

The Virgin Birth: Historic and Biblically Grounded Meanings

Whatever the reasons, the fact itself is clear: the New Testament starts from above. (Donald Macleod)[1]

The church has thought much about the meaning of the virgin birth, but not always in productive ways. When the virgin birth is proposed as a means to protect Christ from the stain of concupiscence or from original sin, it may be misguided thinking. In regard to concupiscence we saw that the virgin birth is no 'help' because strong sexual desire is not necessarily a sin in the context of union within marriage, nor is there any reason to think that impurity would propagate to offspring. In regard to original sin, the virgin birth is no 'help' because it is not clear that Adam's sin is transmitted through the males only. Even if this were the case, it does not necessarily mean that God could not use the sexual union in order to produce a holy child. Anselm affirmed that it was fitting that God brought about Christ's birth by a virgin, but reasons could not be found to assert that the virgin birth avoided the stain of concupiscence or original sin, nor that it was intended to do so in the mind of either the gospel writers or God.

Now I will explore two other meanings of the virgin birth which are well grounded biblically and also more productive theologically. These meanings were likely on the minds of the gospel writers and have been the subject of significant reflection by the church. The first meaning is that the virgin birth reveals the full humanity and full divinity of the incarnate Christ in one person. Second, the virgin birth affirms the miraculous divine action of the incarnation against the simple (or closed-system) naturalism of a purely human birth. These meanings neither prove the virgin birth nor do they argue that the virgin birth is necessary. Still they may reveal the virgin birth to be justifiable – revealing God's sign which flows to us through their gospel context. Also, these meanings are fruitful, revealing something of God's character through his actions – helping us know and love him.

A word about my approach. Not a few theologians, among them Donald Macleod (1940), believe that the virgin birth is a critical starting point for our Christology, a Christology from above. In his Christology, *The Person of Christ*, Macleod intentionally distinguishes his view from that of others, including Wolfhart Pannenberg (1928–2014). Pannenberg begins with the man Jesus, rejecting the historicity and importance of the virgin birth but preserving the possibility of deity. His Christology is 'from below'. For Pannenberg and those in his camp, Christ's divinity, as we experience it, is emergent.[2] For Macleod and those with him, divinity is the initial assertion of the gospel writers, and this is deeply connected to the virgin birth. In fact, Macleod values the significance of the virgin birth so highly that he asserts and explains it in his first chapter, 'Virgin Birth: The New Testament Christology Starts from Above'. Both approaches have their merits. However, Macleod makes a good argument that the gospels, as written, intend a Christology from above. That is, there is no *progression* among the disciples from a 'low Christology' to a 'high Christology'. The nativity gospels, Matthew and Luke, present the virgin birth as an affirmation of Jesus' direct relationship to God, one shared by no other man. Even in those gospels that are silent in regard to the virgin birth, this is still the case. God speaks in Mark 1, declaring Jesus to be 'my beloved Son; with you I am well pleased' (v. 11). John has Nathanael exclaiming, 'Rabbi, you are the Son of God!' (John 1:49). While we should never ignore the tools of Christology from below as a helpful way to assess the text without presuppositions, 'Christology from below' is not a necessity thrust upon us by the text of the gospels.[3] Rather, I agree with Macleod that 'Christology from above' seems to be the authors' own perspective.

Given my own goal to hear from the Evangelists as they intended, I will follow 'Christology from above' as a method consistent with the style of the gospel writers whose claims I am hoping to understand.

To Reveal the Full Humanity and the Full Divinity of Christ

> The dogma of the Virgin Birth is thus the confession [which] eliminates the last surviving possibility of understanding the 'very God and very man' intellectually, as an idea or an arbitrary interpretation in the sense of docetic or ebionite Christology. (Karl Barth)[4]

The Ebionites and the Docetists are a picture frame around the person of Christ.[5] They are not in the picture. In contrast, the orthodox position holds that Jesus is one person with two natures. To put it another way: a 'person' is what Jesus is one of, and 'natures' are what he has two of – Oliver Crisp's axiom. The Ebionites and the Docetists are on the edges, framing orthodoxy, defining the boundary, but not in the picture. Both offer a distinct simplification that is attractive to some, but that distorts reality. Einstein is reported to have said of the nature of the world: everything should be made as simple as possible, but no simpler. The Ebionites and Docetists failed (and fail!) because they make a simple unity of Christ's nature, either human or divine, rather than preserving the necessary human–divine tension. Christian orthodoxy declared such simplifications 'Heresy!' They lie outside the picture that Nicea painted of Christ and which Chalcedon illuminated. Because the virgin birth is based on divine action in conjunction with human participation, affirming it is also active resistance to the error of over-simplification. Athanasius put it wonderfully: 'He formed His own body from the virgin; and that is no small proof of His Godhead, since He Who made that was the Maker of all else. And would not anyone infer from the fact of that body being begotten of a virgin only, without human father, that He Who appeared in it was also the Maker and Lord of all beside?'[6] The virgin birth displays Jesus' full deity and full humanity in one person.

This affirmation of the church is ancient and grounded in her history. Consider the Nicene Creed of 374 which says, 'We believe . . . in one Lord Jesus Christ, the only-begotten Son of God . . . of one substance with the Father . . . [who] was made flesh of the Holy Spirit and the Virgin Mary, and became man.'[7] This is a declaration of Christ's humanity and divinity in the one Lord Jesus Christ. Chalcedon was even clearer in this regard, as they searched for words to express what the church already affirmed:

> Our Lord Jesus Christ, at once complete in Godhead and complete in manhood, truly God and truly man, consisting also of a reasonable soul and body, and at the same time of one substance with us as regards his manhood; like us in all respects, apart from sin; as regards his Godhead, begotten of the Father for our salvation, of Mary the Virgin, the God-bearer [Greek *theotokos*]; one and the same Christ, Son, Lord, Only-begotten, recognized in two natures, without confusion, without change, without division, without separation; the distinction of natures being in no way annulled by the union, but rather the characteristics of each nature being preserved and coming together to form one person and substance [Greek *hupostasis*], not as parted or separated into two persons, but one and the same Son and Only-begotten God the Word, Lord Jesus Christ.[8]

The virgin birth unites the two natures in the person of Jesus: without discernible division and unconfused in the union.

Previously I mentioned the intentional connection Luke made between creation and virgin birth in regard to the Spirit's activity in both. It is worth looking at both texts. Genesis 1:2 reads:

> The earth was without form and void, and darkness was over the face of the deep. And the Spirit of God was hovering over the face of the waters.

And Luke 1:34–5a:

And Mary said to the angel, 'How will this be, since I am a virgin?'
And the angel answered her, 'The Holy Spirit will come upon you,
and the power of the Most High will overshadow you.'

Luke's Genesis allusions are clear when the texts are displayed together. We cannot ignore them, for Luke saw the parallels between
creation and the virgin birth. Initially, both the earth and Mary were
empty. Both were intended to be fruitful, but were, as yet, barren.
Then, in anticipation of a creative move which would relieve the un-
fruitful state, the Spirit of God hovered over each of them. In the first
case, Adam was the ultimate result on the sixth day, and in the second,
Jesus Christ. In both events, the Spirit is the creative agent, hovering
over the land and over Mary; and in response, both are generated.
But an asymmetry is also revealed that indicates more of the meaning
of this special birth. In the former case, Adam was created by God
from earth only, not born. Not so with Christ. The incarnation was
the result of God creating a man through a woman by birth. By the
virgin birth, two natures were joined in one person. As noted above,
this did not make the virgin birth necessary to God's work, but it was
sufficient to display this truth: a condescension of God, a sign to us,
that Jesus, who originated from the creative work of a divine-person
through a human-person, shares in both natures.

For Augustine, the virgin birth was such a sign, full of meaning. In
one of his letters he wrote to Lord Volusianus (in 412):

What if the Almighty had created the human nature of Christ not by
causing Him to be born of a mother, but by some other way, and had
presented Him suddenly to the eyes of mankind? What if the Lord had
not passed through the stages of progress from infancy to manhood, and
had taken neither food nor sleep? Would not this have confirmed the
erroneous impression above referred to, and have made it impossible to
believe at all that He had taken to Himself true human nature; and, while
leaving what was marvellous [*sic*], would eliminate the element of mercy
from His actions? But now He has so appeared as the Mediator between
God and men, that [*sic*: 'thus'?], uniting the two natures in one person.[9]

The occasion for this letter was questions, the first of which was this: 'Whether the Lord and Ruler of the world did indeed fill the womb of a virgin?'[10] Augustine's answer reflects not the proof requested, but rather the meaning of the virgin birth. This meaning is that the virgin birth confirmed 'to the eyes of mankind' that Jesus is the 'uniting of two natures in one person'. It was a sign of God's condescension to us.

Half a millennium later, Anselm reflected on this at length in his treatise 'Why God Became Man'. His conclusion was that the God-man *ought* to be born of a virgin woman. He argues that to redeem man, one from the race of man was required: 'Therefore, it is necessary that the man through whom the race of Adam is to be restored should be taken from Adam's progeny.'[11] Such a redeemer needed two conjoined natures: he needed to be the God-man, in one person. How might God accomplish this? Certainly there are many possibilities, and I suspect that most are not known to us. But there was a way which was sufficient to do just this. Anselm proposed: 'If, furthermore, these two natures, as wholes, are said to be somehow conjoined to a limited extent whereby man and God are distinct from one another and not one and the same, it is impossible that both should bring about what is necessary should happen . . . It is necessary for these two natures to combine, as wholes, in one person . . . for otherwise it cannot come about that one and the same person may be perfect God and perfect man.'[12] To this argument he adds an aesthetic one based on symmetry: Eve was born of virgin Adam without the help of a woman. This is the aesthetic and symmetric ground that makes it fitting that Christ should be born of a virgin, Mary, without the help of a man. His argument makes the case that the virgin birth provided Christ's qualifications as both God and man.

Isaiah says to us, 'The Lord himself will give you a sign. Behold, the virgin shall conceive and bear a son' (Isa. 7:14). God chose to give us a sign – this sign. Of course, there are other ways for God to have accomplished his plans. It is just here that Anselm's logic is not as tight as he thought it was. The virgin birth was not *necessary*.[13] Wayne Grudem explains that God could have created Christ in heaven, uniting his divinity and humanity, and then placing him on earth.

So also God could have formed Christ in the womb, the product of Mary and Joseph, uniting the deity to the humanity perfectly in the womb. So, rather than a logical necessity, the virgin birth is a marvellous condescension of God's grace; it reveals to us something of what God has accomplished. To this I hope Boso (of Anselm's creation) would typically exclaim, 'Nothing could be more solid!' This is no small point that Grudem emphasizes: '[in this way] his full humanity would be evident to us from the fact of his ordinary human birth from a human mother, and his full deity would be evident from the fact of his conception in Mary's womb by the powerful work of the Holy Spirit.'[14] While it does not arise as a necessity, this does seem a *sufficient* reason for God to have accomplished the incarnation by virgin birth. It grabs our attention and makes us ask: Why? When we do so, we discover that here is a sufficient reason for the virgin birth, a theological meaning that enriches and feeds our souls. Jesus is uniquely (as unique as is his birth) the God-man. He is, as we are led to see on reflection, one person with two inseparable and indivisible natures. The virgin birth was the means by which the Son of God condescended to us, becoming the God-man, and then died for us, and now lives for us.

Not everyone has agreed with this view. Schleiermacher had an interesting view, one perhaps idiosyncratic for a liberal scholar of his day (certainly for ours). He allowed for the legitimacy of belief in the virgin birth as being at least consistent with Christianity, though he affirmed a less specific, 'supernatural conception'. He wrote, 'but probably no one will wish to maintain that such acceptance of them [the gospel accounts] introduces into our faith an element at variance with its true nature . . . The general idea of a supernatural conception remains, therefore, essential and necessary, if the specific pre-eminence of the Redeemer is to remain undiminished.'[15] He is arguing that no one is required to reject the gospel accounts of the virgin birth for reasons of internal consistency in the gospels themselves or with the nature of Christianity. Yet by this he does not mean a literal belief in a virginal conception: 'anyone who cannot accept them [the gospel accounts] as literally and historically true is still quite free to hold to the doctrine proper of the supernatural conception.'[16] For Schleiermacher Christ's birth is miraculous in that it allowed Christ unrestricted participation and fullness in his God-consciousness, but it was not physically a virginal conception or birth. The virgin birth resulted from a normal conception between a man and a woman. Theologically, dogmatically, Schleiermacher rejected the plain meaning of the virginal conception, while retaining the testimony of a 'miraculous' birth and even conception.[17] What is he saying here? He understands the miracle of conception as the ground of the association of the natures – what he calls the 'state of union'. He notes that this association is not one which is on equal terms: 'the nature of the association, however, must at every moment be such that the activity proceeds from the being of God in Christ, and the human nature is only taken up into association with it.'[18] There is not a little truth in this. As we will explore later, this union is and must be asymmetric. Through the miracle he also wrestles with the meaning of the distinction and union of natures within Christ.[19] This too we must do, and as rich as is the virgin birth, its affirmation is only a beginning. Most significantly for this study, he affirms that this union of two natures is a personal one – implied by the 'virgin' birth, or rather the 'miraculous' birth. This should not be overlooked. Beyond this, I will not explore Schleiermacher's understanding – or his misunderstanding – of the relationship of Christ's natures within the one person, the hypostatic union. It is sufficient here to note that he affirms a connection (however limited) between the virgin birth and an asymmetric association of natures in the person of Christ.

It is into this conversation that Karl Barth (1886–1968) entered. He also understood the virgin birth to be a sign. This is perhaps reminiscent of Schleiermacher – a miraculous sign pointing to the deep things of God. Indeed, Barth affirmed that the primary object of the virgin birth was to signify rather than to accomplish; to demonstrate God's intention rather than be a means for God to effect an end. But Barth is actually in opposition to Schleiermacher and others, asserting not only the historical reality of the virgin birth, but also its didactic significance. For Barth, the virgin birth is God's dialectic 'Yes' and 'No' to his people. It is God's 'No' to any sufficient human participation in our own redemption and his 'Yes' to humanity as his self-determined and free act of revelation and reconciliation.[20] Yet neither the historical reality of the virgin birth, nor its significance, permits us to dissect this event as if we could fully understand God's means in this sign. Barth is clear: '"of the Virgin Mary" means born as no one else was born, in a way which can as little be made clear biologically as the resurrection of a dead man, i.e., born not because of male generation but solely because of female conception.'[21] By this, he does not mean that the dead will not be raised, nor that there was no virginal conception (the act prior to the actual virginal birth). Rather, he means that we cannot make biologically specific investigations and statements about the event on so little information, but we can make theological statements. Barth does:

> Now it is precisely the human father whom a human son has to thank for everything that marks his existence as belonging to him – his name above all, and with it his position, his right, his character as such and such an individual, his place in history. Thus His begetting by a human father could not be the sign of the existence of the man Jesus alone as the Son begotten of the father in eternity. This sign would rather describe Him as a man whose existence is different from the existence of God, and is proper to Himself.[22]

While the virgin birth was not necessary for God, in that God could have united the natures in another way, yet it is sufficient as a sign of the union of human and divine natures in the person of Christ.

In this joining of two natures in one person, we must notice an important asymmetry. I mentioned this above, but let me expand on this. Nothing about the virgin birth implies a joining of eternal equals. The second person of the Trinity, the Son of God, is co-eternal with the Father; the human Christ is created by God in history. God's condescension in coming to us as a human servant, as the God-man, was an event in the history of his universe. The virgin birth happened in time, at a place, and through a person, the virgin Mary. Oliver Crisp put it this way: 'The natures exist "in" Christ; they are possessed or instantiated by him. His divine nature is essential to him because he is a divine person. But his human nature is contingently related to him, as the nature he voluntarily assumes.'[23] The hypostatic union is the 'instantiation' of both natures in one person. And this union of two in one is the sign to which the virgin birth points, asymmetrically. Jesus Christ's divine nature has an existence apart from incarnation, but his human nature does not. This asymmetry is very important. Jesus is fully human, but because he is fully divine, he has a distinct relationship to that nature which no one ever had before or will have. This resists Docetism, which makes Christ only God. It equally resists the error of the Ebionites, which elevates the human nature. Rather the virgin birth affirms both, while the nature of the *hupostasis* resists a full parity of the natures. Because the virgin birth story permits a pre-existent divine nature and implies and affirms the creation of a human nature, it serves to sustain this critical nuance. I agree with Anselm: the birth of Christ by the virgin is fitting in every way.

The virgin birth is a sign of God's condescension to us in the incarnation, revealing himself as the unique God-man. Barth wrote, 'This thing is called the *nativitas Jesu Christi*. A miracle [which] points to the mystery of the true divinity and the true humanity.'[24] The sign of the virgin birth comes to us as a gift of God's freedom and grace. Even if God determined to give a sign, it would not be right to understand the virgin birth as required, as if God could not have accomplished his display of the union in another way. Yet it serves to affirm what is true of Christ, the God-man. Further, while we cannot pretend to understand how God accomplishes this great and mysterious work by the virgin birth, we can receive the sign with real joy. Immanuel!

To Stand Against the Bias of Naturalism

> It stands on the threshold of the New Testament, blatantly supernatural, defying our rationalism, informing us that all that follows belongs to the same order as itself and that if we find it offensive there is no point in proceeding further. (Donald Macleod)[25]

The virgin birth is a shibboleth for orthodoxy, but it is something more. It resists naturalistic explanation and so acts like fingernails on the chalkboard to a naturalistic culture. Naturalism, or materialism (there is only *matter* and energy), offers a worldview which is simple: a closed system in which the universe exists with no cause outside itself. Naturalism is a desire for a purely materialistic universe which explains itself within itself. In a naturalistic universe, all things can be explained from causes within our universe, outside of which there is nothing that could affect our universe. For example: Was it simply confusion or a longing for naturalism which gave birth to early theories of abiogenesis, life from non-life? Who was the first person to suggest that flies are created *de novo* (new and without antecedent) from dung? Is it really so different for Darwin to suggest the same idea over a much longer period of time? Perhaps, for he proposed a mechanism: chance mutation and natural selection.[26] In both cases the drive was to discover a cause for the universe from within the universe. But Darwin had done something new. Initially his work was rejected, but its real meaning soon became clear. He had built effective scaffolding from which others could now build a stout wall, enclosing the material universe from within. We did. And at each turn in the wall we posted signs: No Trespassing! God was no longer needed – or welcome. We are safe and alone inside! Laplace's famous rejection of the God hypothesis in the prior generation was now vindicated.[27] The world had its first effective apologetic for the materialist position. That his work was followed quite quickly by the modernist–fundamentalist controversy is really no surprise. *On the Origin of Species* was published in 1859. The modernist–fundamentalist controversy began at the end of the nineteenth century and was fully engaged with the publication of *The Fundamentals* in 1907. In fact, it was probably necessary that the virgin birth became a shibboleth between these two camps.

It is in just this context, this controversy, that the virgin birth stands as more than a shibboleth, and does so without shame. It declares God's intrusion into his world. Those who stand with the virgin birth stand against naturalism as an a priori belief and as a totalizing model. We stand with God's claims, even if, and perhaps especially if, they contradict the naturalistic philosophy of a world closed to God's action. The virgin birth insists on God's freedom to act as he pleases among us. We do this not *because* God's ways are opposed to the world or reason, and certainly not because God acts arbitrarily, but rather because we stand with God wherever he stands because of who he is. For this reason we affirm the virgin birth without shame, as a tenet that stands with God against naturalism, materialism, and the project of the Enlightenment (at least in so far as it is treated as a totalizing model of a closed cosmology). As Paul wrote of the gospel, 'Therefore do not be ashamed of the testimony about our Lord' (2 Tim. 1:8). The virgin birth is part of that call.

This position affirms the virgin birth against naturalism. Yet this is not a rejection of science or its methods. In fact, science's very foundation is the simplicity, consistency, continuity, and stability of the universe. This is something that Christians attribute to God himself. While affirming the virgin birth, many Christians understand physical creation in the framework of the Big Bang or some other theory of means, holding to a universe which is divinely created but billions of years old. And not a few Christians also understand life as evolving from non-life in our universe, holding to theistic evolution as their model of divine creation. Such positions can be held with an internal consistency that resists erosion. That is, Christians who affirm science as the investigation of the means of God can and do affirm a dauntless faith in God as Creator and Redeemer, and in his freedom to do as he pleases without necessarily revealing means. They can affirm the virgin birth as God's miracle. This is not like Schleiermacher's attempt. He intended to uphold the virginal conception as a miracle, but demoted it from the supernatural. To do this he added back the paternity of Joseph to the virgin birth. Such an attempt is misguided, and he failed.[28] Few, if any, modern liberals follow him in this.[29] Indeed, this position cannot be maintained. Christians hold the virgin birth over and against naturalism as a sufficient explanation for the universe. It needs no explanation within the universe.

Barth noticed that the virgin birth, like the empty tomb, resists any natural explanation. He wrote:

> Now it is no accident that for us the Virgin birth is paralleled by the miracle of which the Easter witness speaks, the miracle of the empty tomb. These two miracles belong together. They constitute as it were a single sign . . . The Virgin birth denotes particularly the mystery of revelation . . . The mystery at the beginning becomes active and knowable . . . The same objective content is signified in the one case by the miracle of the Virgin birth, in the other by the miracle of the empty tomb . . . The mystery at the beginning is the basis of the mystery at the end; and by the mystery of the end the mystery of the beginning becomes active and knowable.[30]

Barth is arguing that the virgin birth stands against naturalism because God stands at the start and end of Jesus' life, the mystery of revelation. We know this truth and witness God in this event only by God's readiness to be known to us in it – his free revelation to us. We are recipients. Dustin Resch argues, 'For Barth, the virgin birth should be regarded as an authentic element of the Christian faith; it is something to be retained and honoured precisely because it places a limit to our claim to mastery of that to which the sign attests.'[31] Barth says this in part in order to take his own stand against the sufficiency (or even the integrity) of natural revelation: 'Is it chance that in all of them recognition of the mystery of Christmas is menaced and weakened by being related to some form of natural theology?'[32] Here Barth comes close to accepting the virgin birth precisely because it is 'fingernails on the chalkboard' to anyone committed to understanding God through what he made. The virgin birth does and must stand against naturalism as a simple explanation of everything.

So should we affirm the virgin birth *because* it is a rejection of science – or rather, naturalism – to make a stand for supernaturalism? Of course not. To this point Barth wrote, 'The church has received this doctrine neither out of a capricious toying with logic nor out of an essentially profane pleasure in the supernatural nor out of a fanatical zeal to ascribe everything to God and nothing to man.'[33] We affirm it because it is revealed to us by God as truth. This stands not in opposition to science, but beside it. The methods of science are debated[34] but they include: physical testing rather than philosophical models; falsifiability rather than claims of authority; and distributed repeatability rather than unique anecdotal experience. Above all, the knowledge of science is something we work to achieve through these methods. Using these methods, and speaking the precise language of mathematics, theories can be constructed, predictions can be made and tested, and all can be communicated to others with the exacting precision allowed by the language. It works. Albert Einstein is an icon of such success. Building on the work of Ernst Mach (1838–1916) and others, he proposed a special theory of the relationship of space and time, and then the more general (and difficult) case of mass in that space-time universe when it is under acceleration. He first intended to call this 'Invariance Theory' – indeed, the speed of light is invariant in every reference frame. We know it as relativity. Success was first demonstrated when his elegant but not-so-simple equations were applied to the orbit of Mercury. The orbit of this 'rogue' planet was not sufficiently predictable by Newton's equations. Einstein restored order to Mercury's orbit and so to the universe. Such examples abound of the success of science. In light of this success, what future could exist for affirming any kind of supernaturalism, and especially the virgin birth? The virgin birth is not known by any means in our control. It is not testable or repeatable. It cannot be communicated by the language of mathematics. We affirm it, not because it lies outside the methods of science, and not because it is opposed to naturalism and a naturalistic philosophy of history, but because God affirms it. And so, without shame, we stand with God, the Author of the universe and of the methods of science.

Yet to many the virgin birth does stand *opposed* to science – or so it would seem. It is better understood as opposed only to naturalism. Alvin Plantinga is helpful here. In his recent book *Where the Conflict Really Lies*, he declares his thesis in the first paragraph: 'There is a superficial conflict but deep concord between science and theistic religion, but superficial concord and deep conflict between science and naturalism.'[35] In his careful manner, he works through this thesis throughout the rest of the book. He must do so carefully because this claim is a shock to many. It is for Christians who oppose science, for scientists who oppose religion, and for all the naturalists who believe that their project is more like science than religion. More than a shock, it is a challenge, and even a reversal of such worldviews. When religion, science, and naturalism meet, it is naturalism, not science, which is the odd man out. It is naturalism, not religion, that should be on the defensive in a scientific era. Our enemy is not science, but naturalism.

To make his case, Plantinga reflects on the New Atheists, among them Richard Dawkins and Daniel Dennett. Both claim that to reject evolution is to reject modern science and even reason. Citing Dennett, Plantinga writes, 'it is absolutely safe to say that if you meet someone who claims not to believe in evolution, that person is ignorant, stupid or insane (or wicked, but I'd rather not consider that).'[36] The claim here is not merely about positions, but about whether a person can reject the naturalist position with integrity. Those who hold this position assert that science, and not religion, is allied with reason and reality specifically because of the success of their method in an important domain – the physical world. But Plantinga would have us understand that this is a species of paternalism. Plantinga cites Feyerabend: 'Scientists are not content with running their own playpens in accordance with what they regard as the rules of scientific method; they want to universalize those rules, they want them to become part of society at large.'[37] Science (or scientists) assumed a methodological hegemony over every other domain, especially religion. But the claim perceived by Feyerabend is more modest. Dawkins and Dennett would go further, making questions about God out of bounds because God, or claims about a deity, lie outside scientific method. This is philosophical hegemony, based on method. It is worth observing that even if this charge against the overreach of science is true (as it is for the exemplars chosen), this objection against hegemony would not invalidate science within its own domain. In fact, it does not tell against science at all, but against naturalism. Plantinga explains that this argument between science and religion is one incited by naturalists – and it is a sham. He shows that any apparent concord between science and naturalism is superficial. He accuses the naturalists of wrapping themselves in the mantle of science 'like a politician in a flag'.[38] In reality, the naturalist is not in agreement with the scientist. The naturalist is feigning an alliance with science, and, in so doing, is dividing allies to advance a distinct agenda.

Are science and theism, especially Christianity, truly allies? It is, at least on the surface, confusing to some that science restricts its methods to those which find answers arising from within the universe and its laws. For the scientist, the assertion that 'God did it' is no answer. This hardly seems as if science and theism are allies. But they are. Such methodologically limited investigations are wonderful and important – and effective tools to understand God's world and *how* he did it. In fact, as per Plantinga, it is these very investigations that argue against naturalism. These investigations require us to do something anti-naturalistic: to ask 'how', when all that we should be able to do is to survive. Humans have a kind of 'excess mental capacity' which functions to take us beyond what might be expected for survival alone. It is beyond naturalism for humans to develop, by random mutation and natural selection alone, an ability to investigate the universe – simply in order to understand 'how'. Plantinga puts it this way: 'Theistic religion gives us reason to expect our cognitive capacities to match the world in such a way as to make modern science possible. Naturalism gives us no reason at all to expect this sort of match; from the point of view of naturalism, it would be an overwhelming piece of cosmic serendipity if there were such a match.'[39] Indeed, this would be an irrational evolutionary excess. In fact, Plantinga argues that naturalism, when understood through the lens of evolution, is self-defeating specifically because it uses the same kinds of arguments it disallows.[40] If this is the case, the combatants should not be science versus religion, for naturalism is an enemy of both.

The theist, on the other hand, has a reason for asking 'How?' Since we believe that God is personal and that God reveals his character in creation, it is a joy to discover him in his creation. Creation, as Calvin said, is the 'theatre of God'.[41] It may even be our responsibility to discover who God is by understanding his creation. Was it Solomon who said, 'It is the glory of God to conceal things, but the glory of kings is to search things out' (Prov. 25:2)? And are we not God's regents in his world? Could this not be construed as warrant for the question 'How'? So, the theist, the Christian theist especially, encourages the scientist to pursue such knowledge in God's theatre 'as if' there was no God, in order to discover God. Rather than providing a tension, Plantinga explains this as the distinction between methodological naturalism (how we investigate) and ontological naturalism (what actually is). It is a necessary method for any discipline to reject all answers which avoid the pursuit of an answer. 'God did it', as an end, would end such pursuits for a scientist. It is not an answer to the questions raised by science. The theist and the scientist are methodologically distinct but can share a common goal. John Polkinghorne, physicist and Anglican priest, puts it this way: 'We have a mind which is tuned to understand our universe because we were made in the image of the creator. We experience the universe's rational transparency to us and this wonderful intelligibility is indeed made comprehensible by the insights of natural theology. There is a supportive interaction between scientific and religious understanding.'[42] Still, it might be objected that methodological naturalism does not tell for or against ontological naturalism: Does God exist and who is he?[43] True. Yet it does show that we can discern that there is no essential conflict between science and theology, and that there is a place for methodological naturalism. The tension felt by scientists and theologians is not from the essence of their disciplines. Indeed, the essence of both disciplines is to model reality, but they have distinct methods and distinct domains. The methods of science seek for explanations *within* the universe, a domain that provides for repeatability and falsifiability. But this method can arise sufficiently from either of two assumptions: either God's personal works are understandable to us from within nature, or nature is the impersonal, uncaused cause. But the method and the discoveries do not discriminate between the two possible assumptions. We might say that science, as method, is agnostic. Naturalism, on the other hand, has an agenda to advance: a universe which causes itself and sustains itself. But naturalism cannot offer sufficient reason to draw science into its assumption of impersonal, materialist sufficiency. Christianity, however, proposes a transcendent personal God who invites people to discover his ways *within* what he created.

Such an alliance between science and religion, especially Christian religion, can be and is deeper still. Science can be a help to theology. Barth, as is well known, objected to deriving theological value from natural (general) revelation. Certainly it is true that general revelation is insufficient. Certainly there have been mistakes made in the exegesis of both natural revelation and special revelation. Polkinghorne observed this, but said, 'mistakes by natural theologians in the past do not preclude the possibility of success in the present. The science of 1750–1850 made plenty of mistakes.'[44] Neither stands alone as well as the two stand together. But many Christians reject science, eagerly affirming that all of their theology is derived from Scripture with no reference to 'natural theology' or, specifically, the conclusions of science. Plantinga objects, and so do I: 'My present point is that in some cases one can indeed acquire a defeater for a belief held on the basis of the Bible; I can come to see that what the Bible teaches isn't what I thought it was.'[45] Put another way, the proper exegesis of natural revelation can be a sheepdog for the exegesis of special revelation. That is not to say that conclusions from natural revelation, science, replace the theological exegetes or make any decisions for them, but that those conclusions may harass the exegetes onto a correct path – one otherwise not so easily discovered. So also, the exegetes of special revelation can serve as sheepdogs to the exegetes of natural revelation. Such statements will cause hair to be raised. Exegetes on both sides have examples of tyrannical abuse by the 'other side' matted, framed, gilded, and on their walls. Humility would serve both sides. The revelation, general and special, is the standard, not the exegetes. And when all exegesis is well done, though that is not to say completed, the exegesis will agree – because revelation testifies to its Creator and speaks truth about him.

Ultimately, naturalism should be considered in conflict with science. It certainly is the enemy of theism. As Plantinga argued, 'naturalism is a religion because it tells us what reality is ultimately like, where we fit into the universe, how we are related to other creatures, and how it happens that we came to be.'[46] And as was shown above, naturalism as a basis for evolution could have no particular interest in truth, but only in successful behaviours. He even notes that this was just the point that Darwin made: what an organism believes is not strongly coupled to successful behaviours; many beliefs can produce equivalently successful behaviours. Why, then, do humans care about truth and seek to discern it? Further, Augustine and others such as Michael Polanyi and Lesslie Newbigin have argued that real knowledge is also personal – something evolution cannot deliver.[47] However, it is not science but naturalism which struggles with either reality or personal knowledge. Ultimately, this is Plantinga's main point: 'Given that naturalism is at least a quasi-religion, there is indeed a science/religion conflict, all right, but it is not between science and theistic religion: it is between science and naturalism. This is where the conflict really lies.'[48]

If this line of argument is correct, then we are free, as theists, and certainly as Christians, to affirm the virgin birth – a miracle without naturalistic explanation – and to celebrate it as a sign of God's incarnation in Christ which is anti-naturalistic. Barth wrote:

In other words, if we are clear that with the Holy Spirit God Himself is declared to be the author of the sign of the Virgin birth, then we know that in acknowledging the reality of this sign we have *a priori* renounced all understanding of it as a natural possibility, even when we are tempted to do so by a consideration so inviting as that of natural parthenogenesis, for example. We are already committed, then, to an acknowledgment of a pure divine beginning, of a limiting of all natural possibilities, and this forbids us at the very outset to indulge in any reflection as to whether and how this reality can be anything else but a pure divine beginning.[49]

Barth declares the virginal conception ('parthenogenesis') as God's work to bring the Messiah into the world to be a declaration against naturalism. A commitment to this parthenogenesis is a stand against naturalism as a totalizing explanation of the universe. Indeed it is. Barth also forbids any reflection about how God did this great work, because the reality of this sign 'renounces all understanding of it as a natural possibility'. But, actually, one does not entail the other. Agreeing with Plantinga, rejection of an ontologically naturalistic explanation does not 'forbid' seeking also a scientific explanation. That is, it is logically possible that a person could discover how God did this great work, as we seek to do in creation. One could also doubt that God would permit such a mystery to be revealed. Barth did. Others do. Yet, because God uses means, the means of the virgin birth are not necessarily (and so by definition) undiscoverable as means and within nature. However, it is not coherent to have a virgin birth in a *merely* naturalistic world. In such a reductionistic world, God is not merely excluded from the investigation in order to discern his means (practical naturalism), but rejected even outside of the investigative system itself (ontological naturalism). Such presuppositions require that the virgin birth must be rejected. Indeed, it may be necessary to affirm the virgin birth boldly and specifically to object to ontological naturalism, endorsing supernaturalism as God does in this great sign which signifies his 'Yes' and 'No' to the world in Jesus. In the virgin birth God says 'No!' to man's sufficiency and to materialistic naturalism, and at the same time he declares 'Yes!' to his personal engagement with his world. This is a powerful and good meaning for the virgin birth.

In conclusion, I have looked at two ancient and well-considered and robust meanings. They have not only endured, but have gained strength in the eyes of the church. More than that, they seem to have been on the minds of the Evangelists. The virgin birth is a sign revealing the reality of the mystery of the union of Jesus' two natures in the person of Christ, and the virgin birth stands opposed to ontological naturalism. In the virgin birth Jesus is revealed as the ruler of his heaven and earth.

Doctrine: The Spirit's Call to Action

Again, we return to 'doctrine': What should the church do in response to the meaning of the text? The mind of the authors composed the words of the text, and these words have the meaning intended by the authors. When we discern this meaning, this is our theology. And the authors' meaning always intends action. This is our doctrine, the teaching that intends a change in us. So what are we to do once we discern that God reveals to us in the virgin birth the union of the two natures in the one person of the God-man, Jesus Christ? What are we to do once we discern the sign which God gives to us in the virgin birth – a sign that is 'Yes' to God and 'No' to materialistic naturalism?

Before answering those questions, I should acknowledge again the distinction between 'What are we to do?' and 'What did the authors intend to do in us?' The distinction is the shibboleth. If we believe the authors' veracity and historical accuracy about the events, the virginal conception and the virgin birth, then we ask, 'What are we to do?' But others balk at such a question. Believing either that the authors' integrity and veracity are suspect, or that the authors were deceived, they cannot submit to the authors' intended speech-act. Yet all can fairly ask, 'What did the authors intend to do in us?' I observe this in order to keep all my readers with me. However a person may respond to the shibboleth of the virgin birth, that response should not undermine this investigation. Meaning exists to be discovered. So, together, we all must ask, 'What did the authors intend by these meanings of the virgin birth?'

By the virginal incarnation, the authors revealed Christ as the God-man, and by his bold stroke, God displayed his glory in a way that is distinct from his usual work in normal birth. The authors are calling our attention to God's love for us, his glory, and his power. They intend that those who read these words will worship the God who meets us in our need and in a way that makes all this so clear – if we can accept it. Indeed, to the extent that the virgin birth reflects reality, it is God's condescension to us that we might understand the incomprehensible. And to the extent that God is displaying his power over, through, and in his creation by doing a new thing, the authors are calling us to worship him by strengthening our confidence in his bold and visible invasion into our desperate condition. The author reveals a mystery to incite doxology. This is seen in the citation of Isaiah: God is with us! It is displayed in the shocking obedience of Joseph to the angel. It bursts forth in Mary's song:

> My soul magnifies the Lord,
> and my spirit rejoices in God my Savior,
> for he has looked on the humble estate of his servant.
> For behold, from now on all generations will call me blessed;
> for he who is mighty has done great things for me,
> and holy is his name.
> And his mercy is for those who fear him
> from generation to generation.
> He has shown strength with his arm;
> he has scattered the proud in the thoughts of their hearts;
> he has brought down the mighty from their thrones
> and exalted those of humble estate;
> he has filled the hungry with good things,
> and the rich he has sent away empty.
> He has helped his servant Israel,
> in remembrance of his mercy,
> as he spoke to our fathers,
> to Abraham and to his offspring forever.
> (Luke 1:46–55)

4

The Virgin Birth: A Mystery Revealed

The whole messiahship of Jesus depends on his virgin birth. (Hans von Campenhausen)[1]

If we are perplexed by an apparent contradiction in Scripture, it is not allowable to say, The author of this book is mistaken; but either the manuscript is faulty, or the translation is wrong, or you have not understood. (Augustine)[2]

The two ancient reasons given for the virgin birth – avoiding the stain of concupiscence and freeing Jesus from original sin – do not stand up to consideration. They fail both scripturally and logically. We have considered two other historic reasons for the virgin birth that are well founded by the church: as a sign of the union of the two natures in the person of Christ and as a stand against ontological (rather than mere methodological) materialism. These two reasons are both scripturally strong and theologically fruitful. While sufficient, they do not make the virgin birth necessary. Still, God seems to have intended these as meanings of the virgin birth.

Now I consider the virgin birth as a mystery revealed. In Genesis, God promised a seed, the seed of the woman, who would defeat the serpent. Through progressive revelation, it becomes clear that he would be of the royal house of David, his direct descendant. Yet, at the time of the exile, God cursed this royal line. Specifically, Jeremiah condemned Jehoiachin (and his father, Jehoiakim), cutting off their descendants from ever ruling. What now? How would God fulfil his promise to David and to his people? The answer seems to be the virgin birth. It is through the virgin birth that God bestows the kingdom on Christ. In this we discover something of how God works, staying true to his promises but often by way of a mystery. The virgin birth is the mystery of God, a way of hiding and revealing, a strategic and surprising plan by which God defeats Satan.

To Bestow the Kingdom on Christ

But besides, if indeed He had been the son of Joseph, He could not, according to Jeremiah, be either king or heir. For Joseph is shown to be the son of Joachim and Jechoniah, as also Matthew sets forth in his pedigree. But Jechoniah, and all his posterity, were disinherited from the kingdom. (Irenaeus)[3]

Wherefore others said that Matthew gave the true genealogy of Christ: while Luke gave the supposititious genealogy; hence he began: 'Being (as it was supposed) the son of Joseph.' For among the Jews there were some who believed that, on account of the crimes of the kings of Juda [*sic*], Christ would be born of the family of David, not through the kings, but through some other line of private individuals. (Aquinas)[4]

The virgin birth permitted Jesus Christ to rule when royal descent alone could not have done so.[5] God used the virgin birth to bestow the kingdom on Christ. But it was not an obvious solution. Virgin birth alone did not confer the kingdom upon Christ. And human descent alone, even from the royal line of David, would not have bestowed the kingdom, but rather precluded Jesus' legitimate rule, as Aquinas observed was well known.[6] In the great work of God to bring forth the promised seed, the virgin birth is both a mystery and the solution to a mystery. The key to understanding this mystery of the hidden and revealed seed, the mystery of the virgin birth, is the prophecy of Jeremiah. I will begin by establishing the problem for royal descent from Jeremiah and then suggest why the virgin birth could be the solution. Then I will consider objections and alternatives to this view, showing the virgin birth to be a successful and sufficient solution, even if not a necessary one. We will watch as, through God's amazing history of covenant and curses, he bestows the kingdom on Christ in a most wonderful way: the virgin birth.

For almost four hundred years the line of David had ruled over all Israel, then the southern kingdom of Judah, and, in the last days, only Jerusalem. Yet, David's house stood. This long dynasty is no surprise to the reader of the Bible, nor to any Jew, for this is the house that God built by his unchangeable word. In 2 Samuel 7 (and 1 Chr. 17) God promised to establish the house of David, through Solomon, for ever. God declared, 'And your house and your kingdom shall be made sure forever before me. Your throne shall be established forever' (2 Sam. 7:16). Each of God's covenants – or each refining of the one covenant – made God's plan to fulfil Genesis 3:15 more specific: 'I will put enmity between you and the woman, and between your offspring and her offspring; he shall bruise your head, and you shall bruise his heel.' The woman, the first person to bring death, became 'Eve', the one whose seed would bring life. Then came Seth. And Noah, the new Adam, inherited that promise of life through the seed. Then Shem. And Abram, who became Abraham when he left Ur to follow YHWH to the Land. Then Isaac. And then Jacob. Of Jacob's sons, Judah, to whom Jacob gave the blessing of the ruling sceptre which would never leave him. Then, Perez. And then David, the first son of Adam, Noah, Abraham, Isaac, Jacob, and Judah who did hold that sceptre. Even as people multiplied on the earth, the light of God's promise fell with narrower and narrower focus. In Adam's darkness came the light of the promise of 'the seed'. As people multiplied, the focus was narrowed to Abraham, like a stage light. Then closer still, upon Judah, like a spotlight. Then closer still on David, like a laser. And for four hundred years it fell more narrowly with each generation, until . . . the light died.

In the year 598 BCE Jeremiah cursed the line of David by the word of the Lord. He declared for all to hear:

Is this man Coniah a despised, broken pot,
    a vessel no one cares for?
Why are he and his children hurled and cast
    into a land that they do not know?
O land, land, land,
    hear the word of the LORD!
Thus says the LORD:
'Write this man down as childless,
    a man who shall not succeed in his days,
for none of his offspring shall succeed
    in sitting on the throne of David
    and ruling again in Judah'.
(Jer. 22:28–30)

Coniah is one of the names of King Jehoiachin, King of Judah, the son of Jehoiakim. His father had reigned for eleven years, but his own reign was for a brief three months. He was taken into exile in 597 BCE by Nebuchadnezzar. Against Jehoiachin, God swears by his own name, YHWH, that Jehoiachin is to be written down in God's history 'as childless'. This has great and terrible implications for the coming of the Messiah. It has been too often overlooked by our standard canon of Bible stories, yet it stands as one of the key prophecies (curses) of the whole Old Testament. If Jehoiachin is 'childless', because he uniquely represents the royal line of David, how will God bring about the Messiah by the royal line of David?

This is indeed a terrible curse which troubled the people of Jeremiah's day for just that reason. Indeed, Jeremiah and his nemesis Hananiah struggled to the death over just this issue (Jer. 28). But as devastated as Judah may have felt at losing their king, God has made a problem for his own announced plans – for the integrity of his word. Or so it would seem. This curse threatens God's promised Messiah.

Returning to that promise mentioned above, consider the exact words of 1 Chronicles 17:10–14:

> I declare to you that the LORD will build you a house. When your days are fulfilled to walk with your fathers, I will raise up your offspring after you, one of your own sons, and I will establish his kingdom. He shall build a house for me, and I will establish his throne forever. I will be to him a father, and he shall be to me a son. I will not take my steadfast love from him, as I took it from him who was before you, but I will confirm him in my house and in my kingdom forever, and his throne shall be established forever.

This is God's eternal promise to David: an eternal kingdom from his house. Now Jeremiah has announced that David's only royal descendant is cut off. From where (from whom?) can the Messiah come?

But this was not the first time this very curse was lodged against the Davidic line. In Jeremiah 36:30–31 the prophet cursed Jehoiachin's father, Jehoiakim. This event, sequentially later in Jeremiah's non-chronological text, occurred earlier. It happened on the occasion of the burning of the scroll of Jeremiah by King Jehoiakim. In righteous anger, Jeremiah curses him:

> Therefore thus says the LORD concerning Jehoiakim king of Judah: He shall have none to sit on the throne of David, and his dead body shall be cast out to the heat by day and the frost by night. And I will punish him and his offspring and his servants for their iniquity. I will bring upon them and upon the inhabitants of Jerusalem and upon the people of Judah all the disaster that I have pronounced against them, but they would not hear.

So this devastating curse against the royal house of David is declared twice: first to the father and then to the son. The curse cuts off the line of David, leaving him with no valid heir – at least not through the line of Josiah–Jehoiakim–Jehoiachin.[7] Has God overthrown his own covenant with David?[8] To consider this idea, it may be helpful to

Family Tree of Jehoiachin

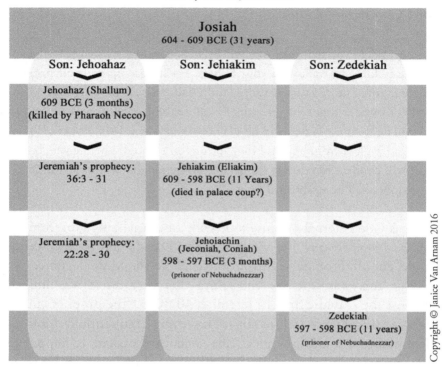

Josiah 604 - 609 BCE (31 years)		
Son: Jehoahaz	**Son: Jehiakim**	**Son: Zedekiah**
Jehoahaz (Shallum) 609 BCE (3 months) (killed by Pharaoh Necco)		
Jeremiah's prophecy: 36:3 - 31	Jehiakim (Eliakim) 609 - 598 BCE (11 Years) (died in palace coup?)	
Jeremiah's prophecy: 22:28 - 30	Jehoiachin (Jeconiah, Coniah) 598 - 597 BCE (3 months) (prisoner of Nebuchadnezzar)	
		Zedekiah 597 - 598 BCE (11 years) (prisoner of Nebuchadnezzar)

consider the table 'Family Tree of Jehoiachin' for clarity on the reign and relationship of these last kings. It is possible that this curse speaks only of a single generation: Jehoiachin's children will not reign. And, of course, Jehoiachin hardly reigned at all, sitting on the throne for only three months, before he surrendered to Nebuchadnezzar.

So the challenge is a seeming contradiction: How could any Messiah be the descendant of David and yet not the descendant of David? One obvious solution is to make an 'adjustment' to the royal line. When Nebuchadnezzar deposed and deported Jehoiachin, he appointed Zedekiah, Jehoiakim's brother, King of Judah (2 Chr. 36:10). Could the Messiah be descended from this king? While this move was unorthodox in the dynasty of David, it would satisfy the essentials of God's promise to David and the curse of Jehoiachin. But this move was not sufficient. Zedekiah, the last king to reign, also rebelled against God and the king of Babylon. Eleven years into his reign, he too was deposed and deported and *all of his sons were put to death before his eyes* (Jer. 52:3–11). He died in exile, childless. We might wonder if a son was saved, secretly, or produced later. That had happened before with Joash (2 Chr. 23). But Zedekiah never appears in *any* royal genealogy. His line ends. And with the death of Jehoiakim and Zedekiah, none of David's royal line was left alive except Jehoiachin (Jer. 52:31). And Jehoiachin was considered by God to be childless with no children who could reign in his place. No Messiah. If this was so, then this tree, the house of Jesse, David's father, had been chopped down to its roots. If this was the case, then the prophetic references to the coming Messiah as a 'branch' (Jer. 23), 'shoot' (Isa. 11), and 'root' (Rev. 5) take on a fuller meaning! Jesus is the source and the unexpected growth from the seemingly dead stump, cut down by God himself.

It is still worth considering what Jeremiah means by 'childless'. Jeremiah used this adjective only in Jeremiah 22. The word is seldom used in the Hebrew text – it appears only four times. Still, by its use, Jeremiah seems to draw close to an earlier threat to the covenant. In Genesis 15:2 Abram complains to God that he is 'childless' and will be survived only by his servant Eliezer, who is his heir. Despite this crisis, God promises Abram a 'great reward'. But this is of no value to Abram, who has no son with whom to share the reward! Now comes God's impossible promise to provide Abram, an old man with a barren wife, an heir. This is a reversal of his state of 'childlessness'. But the promise is not its fulfilment. Abram, now Abraham, sees his line threatened by this continuing state of aged childlessness. How can God keep his promise? From Abraham's perspective, the means and timing are not established. He has only God's promise. Yet Abraham believed God and waited in faith for the fulfilment (Gal. 3:1–15). The answer came about twenty-five years later with the birth of Isaac.[9] God overcame the curse of 'childlessness'. Now, almost 1,500 years later, the same challenge comes again: 'childless'. The messianic tree is cut down. How can the line of Jesse continue? This is the question that stood for the next five hundred years.

But how clearly was David's promise understood by Jeremiah's contemporaries? Did Jeremiah understand the challenge implied by his own words spoken for God? They understood it, and he understood it. Consider first the response of Hananiah to Jehoiachin's exile in Jeremiah 28. This event occurs four years after Jeremiah's curse and the exile of Jehoiachin (who is also called Jeconiah and Coniah). There is little doubt that Jeremiah's curse came as a painful wound to a people needing hope. Further, it seems quite possible that Hananiah's prophecy is a specific challenge to Jeremiah's curse.[10] So, in this context, Hananiah prophesied:

> In that same year, at the beginning of the reign of Zedekiah king of Judah, in the fifth month of the fourth year, Hananiah the son of Azzur, the prophet from Gibeon, spoke to me in the house of the LORD, in the presence of the priests and all the people, saying, 'Thus says the LORD of hosts, the God of Israel: I have broken the yoke of the king of Babylon. Within two years I will bring back to this place all the vessels of the LORD's house, which Nebuchadnezzar king of Babylon took away from this place and carried to Babylon. I will also bring back to this place Jeconiah the son of Jehoiakim, king of Judah, and all the exiles from Judah who went to Babylon, declares the LORD, for I will break the yoke of the king of Babylon.' (Jer. 28:1–4)

But as Jeremiah knew, and as God would soon reveal, Hananiah spoke out of his own desire, and not for God. To this prophecy, even Jeremiah replied, 'Amen! May the LORD do so.' I like Jeremiah's style! He continued, 'As for the prophet who prophesies peace, when the word of that prophet comes to pass, then it will be known that the LORD has truly sent the prophet.' But 'Jeremiah the prophet said to the prophet Hananiah, "Listen, Hananiah, the LORD has not sent you, and you have made this people trust in a lie . . . This year you shall die"' (Jer. 28:6,9,15,16). And in this battle of the prophets, Hananiah lost, dying in that same year, as predicted by Jeremiah. The yoke of Babylon was not broken. Jeconiah (Jehoiachin) was not released to return and to reign again. Neither were his sons. Ever.

Not as kings. Governor Zerubbabel, Jehoiachin's grandson, would appear as a leader in Israel (Hag. 1), and I will return to consider this confusing genealogical appearance later in this chapter. The point is this: the interaction between Hananiah and Jeremiah seems to indicate that bringing back Jehoiachin to reign was *a priority*. This interaction makes it seem that not only did Jeremiah understand the implication of his curse for the Davidic line, but so did the people. Whether they shared God's concern for the Davidic covenant or just wanted things 'back to normal', they could not have what they wanted through Jehoiachin.

Jeremiah shows us his own concern and understanding even more explicitly. Jeremiah emphasizes God's eternal covenant with David three times. If the curse was pronounced twice, Jeremiah stated the promise three times. In Jeremiah 23:5 we read, 'Behold, the days are coming, declares the LORD, when I will raise up for David a righteous Branch, and he shall reign as king and deal wisely, and shall execute justice and righteousness in the land.' We may be tempted to perceive these words to follow immediately upon the prophecy against Jehoiachin, and that may be the case. But Jeremiah is a book with a jumbled timeline that is hard to follow. While the patchwork nature of Jeremiah makes it impossible to be sure, it is at least the case that nothing in the text indicates otherwise. The message affirming God's eternal promise to David was at least intended to follow closely on the text of Jehoiachin's curse. The proximity seems to make Jeremiah[11] appear eager to comfort his readers with the real comfort that can be found: trust God, not men – not even the king. Though God has cursed the offspring of Jehoiakim and Jehoiachin, and in so doing he has now cut down the tree of Jesse, he will still raise up for David a righteous branch!

Hear this same word of promise in Jeremiah 30:8–11:

> And it shall come to pass in that day, declares the LORD of hosts, that I will break his yoke from off your neck, and I will burst your bonds, and foreigners shall no more make a servant of him. But they shall serve the LORD their God and David their king, whom I will raise up for them.

Then fear not, O Jacob my servant, declares the LORD,
    nor be dismayed, O Israel;
for behold, I will save you from far away,
    and your offspring from the land of their captivity.
Jacob shall return and have quiet and ease,
    and none shall make him afraid.
For I am with you to save you,
declares the LORD;
I will make a full end of all the nations
    among whom I scattered you,
        but of you I will not make a full end.
I will discipline you in just measure,
    and I will by no means leave you unpunished.

When did Jeremiah speak these words in relation to the curse? The last bit of temporal information that Jeremiah gave us was back in Jeremiah 29:2: 'This was after King Jeconiah and the queen mother, the eunuchs, the officials of Judah and Jerusalem, the craftsmen, and the metal workers had departed from Jerusalem.' This would seem to make it likely that this encouraging word of hope was given soon after the departure of Jehoiachin. If so, this reinforces Jeremiah's anger against Hananiah, but not because the yoke of Babylon would never be broken. Indeed it would! Instead Jeremiah was angry because Hananiah was declaring the hope to be still rooted in the divinely rejected Jehoiakim and Jehoiachin. Still Jeremiah knew God would keep his word in regard to David.

There is a third reaffirmation of God's promise to David in Jeremiah. This last one is his longest word of hope and is found in Jeremiah 33:15–26:

'In those days and at that time I will cause a righteous Branch to spring up for David, and he shall execute justice and righteousness in the land. In those days Judah will be saved, and Jerusalem will dwell securely. And this is the name by which it will be called: "The LORD is our righteousness."

'For thus says the LORD: David shall never lack a man to sit on the throne of the house of Israel, and the Levitical priests shall never lack a man in my presence to offer burnt offerings, to burn grain offerings, and to make sacrifices forever.'

The word of the LORD came to Jeremiah: 'Thus says the LORD: If you can break my covenant with the day and my covenant with the night, so that day and night will not come at their appointed time, then also my covenant with David my servant may be broken, so that he shall not have a son to reign on his throne, and my covenant with the Levitical priests my ministers. As the host of heaven cannot be numbered and the sands of the sea cannot be measured, so I will multiply the offspring of David my servant, and the Levitical priests who minister to me.'

The word of the LORD came to Jeremiah: 'Have you not observed that these people are saying, "The LORD has rejected the two clans that he chose"? Thus they have despised my people so that they are no longer a nation in their sight. Thus says the LORD: If I have not established my covenant with day and night and the fixed order of heaven and earth, then I will reject the offspring of Jacob and David my servant and will not choose one of his offspring to rule over the offspring of Abraham, Isaac, and Jacob. For I will restore their fortunes and will have mercy on them.'

This text is the strongest of Jeremiah's reaffirmations of the promise of hope. He connects God's covenant with David to God's faithfulness in his work of creation. God has not rejected his people, not fully. He has not abrogated his covenant with David. He will keep it as surely as the earth is on its foundations and is not moved. This word, too, seems to have come after the curses against Jehoiakim and Jehoiachin, for 33:1 tells us that this prophecy came while he was shut up in 'the court of the guard' under Zedekiah. It is a word of comfort to those who heard the curse and saw Jehoiachin taken into captivity with the only royal children after a brief three-month reign. As Nebuchadnezzar arrived, Jeremiah's curse was still hanging in the air of Jerusalem, echoing off the temple walls. Yet God had not forgotten his people or his covenant with David. God would restore. David's line would reign. The curse was given twice (in Jer. 22 to Jehoiachin and in Jer. 36 to his father, Jehoiakim); the promise three times (Jer. 23, 30, and 33). But how could God accomplish this?

Indeed, that is the key question: How could God accomplish this, for God had two words that seemed to be in opposition? This problem was noted by Aquinas, but his response merely sidestepped the issue and did not truly resolve it. In *Summa Theologica*, he raises just this objection. In regard to the question 'Whether Christ took flesh of the seed of David?' he answers, 'As Ambrose says on Luke 3:25, this prophetical passage does not deny that a posterity will be born of the seed of Jechonias. And so Christ is of his seed. Neither is the fact that Christ reigned contrary to prophecy, for He did not reign with worldly honor; since He declared: "My kingdom is not of this world."'[12] But this response ignores the problem that Jeremiah himself seemed so keenly aware of. Christ's rule seems imperilled by just this prophecy.

Chris Wright offers a synthesis of these perspectives: 'As far as Jehoiachin was concerned, none of his offspring would ever sit on the throne of David . . . until one of his descendants, "great David's great Son" would come to reign.'[13] This mediating position affirms the effect of the prophecy, uniting both perspectives of Jeremiah's words: a curse against a single generation and an eternal curse on the dynasty. Wright's confluence could find warrant in the gospel accounts, as I will show. If so, this must be what Jeremiah intended. Yet the challenge remains: How would God do this?

Leaving this challenge unresolved, I want to draw attention to the gospels and the genealogies of Christ found in Matthew and Luke. Let me begin with the ancient observations: these two accounts of Christ's ancestry are, on the surface, distinct in style and divergent in content. In Matthew readers encounter a highly structured genealogy which groups the generations into a series of three groups of fourteen (Matt. 1:17).[14] It is evident that Matthew's work is crafted (edited) to display a structure that serves his theological purposes. If we compare Matthew's line with Old Testament genealogies, differences become apparent. Much can be discerned from Matthew's explicit choices for his structure. He identifies the line of David through Solomon (1:6) down to Josiah (1:11), and then to his grandson, Jechoniah, who is also known as King Jehoiachin (or Coniah/Jeconiah). This king was the one cursed by Jeremiah: 'none of his offspring shall succeed in sitting on the throne of David.' Yet here he is in the ancestry of Jesus![15] How can this be? A further observation follows closely: while Matthew and Luke diverge, not only in different names but also in different lines, both lines terminate with Joseph. How can this be?

Let's first consider Matthew's genealogy and his unique features. Matthew identifies his genealogy as Joseph's (1:16), yet elsewhere Matthew insists that Joseph is not Jesus Christ's earthly father (1:18–25). N.T. Wright puts the question this way: 'Why does the genealogy finish with Joseph if Matthew is going to say that he wasn't Jesus' father after all? This cannot have been a problem for Matthew or he would hardly have followed the genealogy so closely with the story of the virginal conception.'[16] Wright is correct. Matthew is no fool. Still, however this issue is resolved, we still face the problem that Jeconiah is in this line. And Joseph is his son – his 'child'. This challenges Christ's right to rule as a descendant 'of Joseph'. But as Matthew and Wright noted, Joseph was not his father.

Now let me shift the focus to Luke's careful account and his genealogy – something that I suspect has come to the mind of many readers.[17] The divergence is quickly apparent. In chapter 3, Luke's genealogy begins with Joseph and works backwards. In contrast to Matthew's forward-moving structure, Luke's genealogy is inverted. More challenging is the fact that Joseph's lineage in Luke does not dovetail with Matthew's account of his lineage. While there is little difficulty matching the lines prior to David (though they begin at different points and emphasize different ancestors), they fully diverge in Luke 3:31, when Luke writes 'the son of Nathan, the son of David'. That is, Luke traces the ancestry of Christ, not through the royal line of Solomon (as does Matthew), but through David's son Nathan. So, not only are they divergent, but Luke does not track the royal lineage. This is critical because 2 Samuel 5:13–16 (and 1 Chr. 3:1–9) tells us of David's many sons. The list includes Nathan, who may have been named after David's friend the prophet. But Nathan never sat on the throne. While Nathan's line was truly Davidic, it diverged from that of his royal brother Solomon.

Yet these genealogies are not wholly divergent. Both Matthew and Luke include Zerubbabel, the son of Shealtiel; both son and father are direct descendants of Jeconiah (Jehoiachin): son and grandson. In this way, both genealogies are brought into alignment with the royal line of David. For this reason, it could be construed that both Matthew and Luke's genealogies are royal, since the dual-generation pairing of the key post-exilic leaders is unmistakable. But this is no real convergence. The challenge of the royal line seems more fundamental, a glaring and conspicuous divergence that does not disappear merely because of this overlap. To resolve this, some have suggested that Nathan may not be the son of David mentioned in 1 Chronicles 14:3–4. Instead, he could be a later and unknown descendant, many generations removed, but in the royal line of Solomon. Perhaps – but this does not relieve the problem of divergence in the genealogies; it deals only with the royalty problem. It would require that the genealogies re-converge as a result of intermarriage or levirate marriage.[18] In this way Joseph might possibly have two distinct but interwoven lines of descent, both of which trace back to David. This is a possibility, but one with no supporting evidence. Yet, even if divergent and re-converging lines are possible, Joseph would appear to have two distinct fathers. Perhaps both concerns must be ignored, as being without obvious reconciliation, and fairly so, given the paucity of evidence. Still, for those who affirm the truth of Scripture in all that it affirms, we desire to know what *these texts* affirm.

But what if the Bible is making a different claim? Instead of affirming two genealogies of Joseph, what if one genealogy is that of Mary? This is not a new idea. It is at least as ancient as Tertullian (c.160–c.230), who attributed Matthew's to Mary[19] and inferred that Luke's genealogy, distinct from Matthew's, is that of Joseph.[20] Considering the text of Matthew 1:16, 'Joseph the husband of Mary, of *whom* Jesus was born', Tertullian rightly notes that 'whom' is feminine and seeks a feminine antecedent, Mary. Yet that does not require that the genealogy is hers, but rather could speak only of the final move of God in Christ's birth through Mary. Later, others, observing that Matthew's gospel focuses on Joseph's story and Luke's on Mary's, suggested the reverse pairing of the genealogies.[21] On this reading of Luke, Joseph would be understood as the *son-in-law* of Heli. In Luke 3:23 we read, 'Jesus . . . the son (as was supposed) of Joseph, the son of Heli.' This proposal understands that 'Joseph, the *son* of Heli' might be taken as '*son-in-law* of Heli'.[22] If this were the case, then Luke's genealogy is that of Mary. But many contemporary scholars – including I. Howard Marshall and R.P. Nettelhorst and a host of others – reject any solution that associates either of the genealogies with Mary.[23] And for sound reasons. Gerald Sigal rightly notes that the 'lineal descent through the male biological bloodlines plays a decisive role in God's determination of who shall be chosen to do works on His behalf'.[24] Others, seeking a matrilineal example in the Old Testament, have referenced 1 Chronicles 2:34–41. The critical section of this reads: 'Now Sheshan had no sons, only daughters, but Sheshan had an Egyptian slave whose name was Jarha. So Sheshan gave his daughter in marriage to Jarha his slave, and she bore him Attai' (vv. 34–5). Those who point this out suggest that this is a genealogy which not only mentions the mothers (as does Matthew), but is a matrilineal exposition in which a woman stands for her generation. This too Sigal rejects, denying that this can be used as such an example since 1 Chronicles 2 is hardly a female line, but rather a male line with a female mentioned because of the lack of a male heir in her particular generation. Fairly argued. Even more significantly, he argues that Mary's line, if it existed, would be of no help to overcome the curse of Jeremiah in the case of Christ.[25] He concludes, 'Luke's lineage through the non-royal family of Nathan is irrelevant whether it is that of Joseph or Mary respectively.'[26] The point is that Luke's genealogy establishes Davidic ancestry, but not royal ancestry. He is correct.[27]

Are we then left with confusion, however unsatisfying it may be? I should be precise on this point: as evangelicals we may (must!) confess our confusion at many points *of biblical interpretation*, but that is not to affirm confusion *in the text*. J. Gresham Machen acknowledges this apparent confusion and moves toward his own solution. First, he rejects a sometimes suggested grammatical solution to the Gospel of Luke. This alters the construction (the punctuation) to make Jesus the son of Heli: Jesus 'being the son (of Joseph it was supposed) of Heli'. This grammatical sleight-of-hand removes Joseph from the lineage, implying Mary instead. Machen rightly called this reading 'unnatural'.[28] However, he does accept as more 'natural' that Joseph (the supposed father) could be the son-in-law of Heli in Luke's account. This requires no grammatical gymnastics, but simply that we understand 'son' as 'son-in-law'. In this case, Mary is Heli's descendant, for he has no male heirs. By marriage, Joseph becomes his 'son' and heir. Machen argues correctly that this falls within the semantic domain of 'son' in the text and that Mary, unnamed here, could be the legitimate heir of her family, if she had no brothers (Num. 27:1–11). This means, 'Every link in the genealogy would be joined naturally to that which precedes; Jesus would be represented as the "son" of Joseph, Joseph as the "son" of Heli, Heli as the "son" of Matthat.'[29] Some have suggested that something like this must be understood in order to find Shealtiel and Zerubbabel in both lines: Matthew's (from David through Solomon) and Luke's (traced through Nathan, David's non-royal son). For Shealtiel to appear among the names of descendants, a valid means of merger is needed, such as inheritance of daughters or levirate marriage.[30] If such a solution is necessary to join the lines, it implicitly offers validation to the Heli thesis for Luke in particular. But Machen sets this proposal aside. He suggests that it is more likely that Luke gives us the actual line of Joseph, and Matthew the legal and royal line. But if this is so, it seems that we are left with confusion *in* the text. As noted by Sigal, that is problematic for two reasons: the foremost being that Joseph would not stand in line to rule through Nathan (whether he was David's son or a later descendant, he was not royal). Machen is aware of this problem. His solution is to assume a broken royal line between Zerubbabel and Joseph. This would mean that Joseph's true father was Heli, and only by a complex of unknowable and undocumented moves (a sort of shell game or thim-blerig) could the line be traced by God alone and through marriage (though not blood or genealogies).[31] While possible, this seems most unsatisfying because so much is demanded from outside the text, and is, as I hope to show, unnecessary.

To counter objections to assigning either genealogy to Mary, further support might be found in Mary's familial relationship to Elizabeth, who is of the line of Aaron. If Mary is also of the Levites and priests, she cannot be of any line of David (Solomon or Nathan, Matthew or Luke). We know that Elizabeth was of the priestly line, a Levite descended through Aaron ('a wife from the daughters of Aaron', Luke 1:5). In Luke 1:36 the author puts Mary and Elizabeth together: 'And behold, your relative Elizabeth in her old age has also conceived a son, and this is the sixth month with her who was called barren.'[32] If the relationship between the two women is by blood, then Mary is a descendant of Levi, not of the clan of Judah. That would make her no relative of David, excluding her from either Matthew or Luke's genealogy. Clearly one possibility is that Mary is a Levite descended from Aaron. This would not preclude her from marrying into the tribe of Judah. This was proposed by no less a figure than Aquinas, who cites Gregory of Nazianzus.[33] This would have the salutary effect of making Jesus also a priest, quite fitting for his role. However, this faces a challenge. The Aaronic line of Christ is never explicitly mentioned elsewhere, although Hebrews refers to his non-Aaronic priesthood by analogy with Melchizedek.[34] In the rest of the text, Old and New, it is only the Messiah's descent from David which is mentioned. This is a compelling reason to think that Elizabeth is related only by marriage, but it is not a necessary one. She could be a Levite.

What, then, is the case? Despite Machen's proposal that the two genealogical lines draw together into one in Joseph, his suggestion must be set aside for the reasons given, as also must Sigal's. What then? I think we too quickly pass over the fact that the Evangelists have two distinct emphases in their birth narratives. Matthew focuses on Joseph's thoughts and feelings, and so, if he has provided us with Joseph's genealogy, this would be consistent with telling Joseph's story.

Similarly, Luke focuses on Mary's story from her perspective, and if he provides us with her genealogy, we are only challenged by his attribution to Joseph and not to her. Machen's 'natural' solution seems fitting. If this were the case, then both Mary and Joseph are descendants of David, but only Joseph stands in line to rule while Mary does not. This allows the distinct possibility that these are respectively the Davidic lines of Joseph (Matt.) and Mary (Luke). If this is the case, it would accord with Jeremiah's prophecy, putting Jesus in the line of David, but not physically in the royal line. However, it is not necessary to distribute the genealogies, one to Mary and one to Joseph. We need only observe that, if both genealogies are of Joseph and can be synchronized in some way we cannot prove, then Joseph has the right to rule. If Jesus is conceived by a virgin who is married to Joseph, then Jesus does not stand in the line of Jehoiachin, and so stands outside God's curse on the line of David. He is Joseph's son by marriage, not blood. For this reason, adoption into the line is made possible by the virgin birth, a solution to the problem posed by Jeremiah's prophecy.

Of course, I have not yet examined the issue of adoption. While I will address this later, let me offer a brief glimpse that shows why adoption, or something very like it, is required for anyone who affirms the virgin birth, however the confusion noted above is resolved. Whether or not Mary's genealogy is given in Luke,[35] it cannot be the case that Mary's genealogy is given in Matthew, because of Jeremiah's prophecy. So consider, for argument's sake, that both genealogies apply to Joseph and grant that the divergence is solved by some solution not yet discerned, as Machen would have it. That may be the case. If so, it remains that all who are committed to the virgin birth must affirm that Jesus is not biologically related to Joseph, but only to Mary (and God). This is the decisive feature of the virgin birth (virginal conception), not only for those who accept it, but also for all who reject it.[36] So Jesus is related to Mary only, who is without genealogy and without explicit connection to David. In fact, her only 'genealogy' seems to point to Aaron. Without Joseph as the natural father, on either account of the genealogies, there is no biblical testimony to Jesus' Davidic and royal line. It becomes necessary that adoption, or something with identical function, must take place to accomplish what is accomplished in the story. Without it, Jesus cannot be of the royal dynasty. Worse, in light of Jeremiah's prophecy, it seems distinctly problematic to have Joseph in the royal line. Again, adoption, or something functionally equivalent, is required.[37] More on this later, when we consider this again in Chapter 6.

However, the Bible is very conscious of Jeremiah's prophecy condemning David's line in Jehoiakim and Jehoiachin. The language of the Messiah reflects this. Of this dead stump in the line of David, God says, It will sprout![38] Somehow, from this stump of a family tree will arise the legitimate Davidic kingdom. How can that be? The virgin birth provides a distinct solution. The Christ is born to Mary, who is not of the royal lineage (implicit if her royal genealogy is not stated, or explicit if hers is preserved by Luke). Then Christ may be adopted by Joseph, who is of David's line (explicitly by either Matthew alone or by a harmonization of the genealogies from Matthew and Luke). In this way, Jesus inherits all the rights, but avoids the prophetic sanctions of Jeremiah – as long as Mary is not a royal descendant of David, and Joseph is. That is, both genealogies could be Joseph's by the mechanism noted above or some other, and so Joseph is in the royal line. As a result, Joseph could not himself rule, nor could his children, for the prophecy precludes this. But he *could adopt* Jesus, who was not of the royal line by birth, into the royal line. In adoption, God re-establishes the Davidic covenant and the royal line. But the key is the virgin birth, rather than direct descent through the royal line. In this way Christ Jesus is the son of Mary but not of Joseph. Joseph is free to adopt, and both the prophecy and the covenant are fulfilled. The virgin birth bestowed the kingdom on Christ, a shocking reversal of Jeremiah's prophecy.

To Hide Information from the Enemy

Now the virginity of Mary was hidden from the prince of this world, as was also her offspring, and the death of the Lord; three mysteries of renown, which were wrought in silence, but have been revealed to us. (Ignatius)[39]

But why would God choose such a circuitous route as to have Jeremiah curse God's appointed king so that there were no more heirs? If we believe that every leader is appointed by God (Rom. 13:1–2) and that God directs the heart of the king (Prov. 21:1), surely God was not 'forced' to select either Jehoiakim or Jehoiachin. My understanding of God is that he not only has foreknowledge of all things, but also that he foreordains all things. But surely, even if one were to take the position that God merely foreknows, that would be of no help to explain this predicament in which God puts himself regarding his eternal covenant with David. Supposing that God did not like what they would do (in his complete foreknowledge, bereft of the ability to foreordain), he could have selected them because 'on balance' they satisfied his purposes. If this is granted, we are still left with God's free and deliberate choice to curse David's line, seeming to end the messianic dynasty. This action and its consequences were fully intended by God unless this declaration was made in a fit of pique, later regretted – an option that lies outside of orthodox consideration. If this reasoning stands, we are left with the question: Why? I propose that one of the possible answers may be that God, at times, hides his plans from the enemy, Satan. This is not an idea that can be proven, but perhaps it may be profitably explored. It is interesting to pursue this as a theme within Scripture and wonder what it might mean if that were the case in regard to the virgin birth.

This is the proposal: by God's action of cursing these two kings – and also affirming his commitment to David by the same prophet – God may have been effectively hiding the Messiah from the enemy. It was like turning out the lights so that darkness seemed to enclose God's plans. This was not a darkness that meant the death of light, but a strategic move to keep information from the enemy. Then, in the fullness of time, light came into the world and he made his tabernacle with us. If God did this through Jeremiah's curse, these were not new tactics for God in Jehoiakim's day. An investigation of such a strategy would begin in the Garden. In Genesis God revealed his will: his image-bearers would obey him and delight in him. Greg Beale and John Sailhamer make the case that Adam was God's priest and the Garden was God's temple.[40] Beale argues that Adam failed in his role to 'serve and guard' as a priest:

> Genesis 2:15 says God placed Adam in the Garden 'to cultivate it and to keep it'. The two Hebrew words for 'cultivate and keep' (respectively, *cäbad* and *shämar*) can easily be, and usually are, translated 'serve and guard'. When these two words occur together later in the Old Testament, without exception they have this meaning and refer either to Israelites 'serving and guarding/obeying' God's word (about ten times) or, more often, to priests who 'serve' God in the temple and 'guard' the temple from unclean things entering it (Num 3:7–8; 8:25–26; 18:5–6; 1 Chr 23:32; Ezek 44:14) . . . Therefore, Adam was to be the first priest to serve in and guard God's temple.[41]

How Satan must have celebrated the destruction of God's only priest and the desecration of his hand-made temple! It may have seemed to him that he had completely thwarted God's plans. But, immediately and without hesitation, God announced his plans to conquer in Genesis 3:15: 'I will put enmity between you and the woman, and between your offspring and her offspring; he shall bruise your head, and you shall bruise his heel.' Adam, fully taking God's point, and acting now as prophet and king, changes Eve's name. In verse 20 Adam renames her 'Eve', because she is 'the mother of all living'. Stephen Wellum said, 'It is evident that Adam is reclaiming dominion in faith through naming his wife the mother, which cannot help but allude to the more specific role she will have as the one who will provide a seed who will strike the serpent.'[42] So we have the destruction of God's previously announced plan, followed by God's promise to restore. But God's exact means are now less clear. Our information is severely limited: Eve and her seed.

One might assume that her firstborn child would be that seed. Indeed, this may have been what Eve herself thought: 'Now Adam knew Eve his wife, and she conceived and bore Cain, saying, "I have gotten a man with the help of the LORD'" (Gen. 4:1). Perhaps Satan followed that misdirection, as seemingly confirmed by Eve: it was Satan who 'inspired' Cain to kill his brother Abel. Indeed, Satan was a murderer from the beginning. But was murder his only desire? Is it not possible, even likely, that his intention was to 'desecrate' the seed, and so thwart God's plan? For in murdering Abel, it was Cain who was really taken out, apparently foiling God's plan. Should not information be kept from such an enemy? Perhaps it was. It may be that God's plain-in-sight plan was not as plain as Satan thought.

Then Moses records that God gave Seth to Adam and Eve. He continues this story of painful redemption through the genealogy in Genesis 5, which begins with Adam through Seth and ends with Noah. Each generation echoes the punishment of death: 'and he died'. Picking up the story in Genesis 6, Moses speaks of the sons of God. Could these sons of God be the descendants of Seth traced through the previous chapter – or are they angels, as some suppose?[43] Lest we be distracted by the mapping of 'sons of God' to its antecedent, trying to prove the unprovable, I only raise the question.[44] But if these verses in Genesis 6 make reference, not to angelic beings, but to the line of Seth as the 'sons of God', such a proposal would serve a biblical theology of the war between the two seeds. On this proposal, Genesis 6 reveals Satan's attack on the seed of promise: intermarriage between the 'sons of God', descended from Seth, with those of Cain. When God declares his wrath against humanity, the flood, did Satan perceive a victory? Yet the flood claimed the lives of almost all – but not all. God saved eight from the line of Seth. But another apparent victory came when this father, saved through the flood, got drunk. Mocked by his own son and grandson, he cursed them. Yet, in Shem, Seth's line was still intact. Descending through Shem, the line was enlarged, and in this way, God blurred the focus. As people spread out over the earth, the many sons of Seth became too many. The Seed, the seed of the woman, who would be Messiah was hidden deep amid the corruption and death. Was God hiding information from the enemy?

The pattern of the seed hidden, revealed, Satan's attack, and then hidden again, continued. In retrospect, hundreds and thousands of years later, Moses recorded the genealogy of Genesis 11. Years of the seed hidden. But then God called Abram from Ur of the Chaldeans. And in Genesis 12:1–3 God revealed his plan again: 'Now the LORD said to Abram, "Go from your country and your kindred and your father's house to the land that I will show you. And I will make of you a great nation, and I will bless you and make your name great, so that you will be a blessing. I will bless those who bless you, and him who dishonors you I will curse, and in you all the families of the earth shall be blessed."' Now the enemy had a focus. After the strange lamp-lit night of covenanting (Gen. 15), Satan inspired Abraham to give away his wife for his own self-protection (Gen. 20). In this act, the promise, which included Sarah as deeply as it included Abraham (Gen. 18), seemed to be thwarted by the enemy. Satan may well have felt on the cusp of winning everything when Sarah entered Pharaoh's palace. But God interceded, and Pharaoh let God's people go; he returned Sarah to Abraham. A near miss. And then, after the child was born, did the enemy cry with delight as Abraham raised the dagger over his son bound on the altar – even as Abraham obeyed God?[45] But again, in God's plan, God's plan was not undermined – no matter how it may have looked to the enemy or philosophers.

Following Abraham, most strangely for generations, God consistently rejected the socially mandated firstborn in favour of the second – or even the fourth, confusing hundreds of millions of people even today.[46] Did this rejection of primogeniture, the law of the firstborn, hide information from the enemy and confuse him? Did it move the enemy's attacks in the wrong direction as God rejected Ishmael, Esau, Reuben, Simeon, and Levi, taking Isaac, Jacob, and Judah? But of course, Jacob's blessing tipped God's hand: 'The scepter shall not depart from Judah, nor the ruler's staff from between his feet, until tribute comes to him; and to him shall be the obedience of the peoples' (Gen. 49:10). But even so, the ruling seed was hidden in Egypt, a socially unacceptable shepherd. No ruler, Jacob, but a rather undistinguished son of a Hebrew about to become a slave, multiplying into tens and hundreds of thousands. Hidden like sand in a desert.

So hope was hidden in abundance, for Israel grew in the womb of slavery. Later, freed by God through Moses, Satan moved again. He inspired rebellion as he had in the Garden. For here, at the threshold of returning to the Garden of God, they were offered the same promise: serve and guard, or be thrown out, again. Satan won. They refused to enter the Land and all died in the desert – but not all. The children of promise survived and God took them into his promised land. And now the secret plan of God, so clearly announced, was hidden in multitudes and hidden deeper in their sin. Could God bring a seed out of this rotting tree?

But, from them, God called out one. His name was David, a man after God's own heart – so God had knit him in his mother's womb. Now the enemy had a target, again. Indeed the enemy often tempted this proto-seed. He tempted him with pride, and as a young man he rejected sin and followed God in humility. The years of humility as a shepherd resulted in the conquest of giants – something God's people failed in only five hundred years earlier. He tempted him with power, and he rejected this, serving the living king or running from him, rather than taking what was his as promised to him by God. But David surrendered to lust. And then murder. Did Satan cry with delight now? Did he think he had cut down the tree and thwarted God's plans? We can only imagine; I do so imagine. But God's mercy is new every morning; and one who had killed the lion and bear put his own pride to death and confessed. This turn of story could not have been imagined. Not by me; perhaps not by God's enemy. And God forgave. And David lived to give birth to – this is amazing – the royal heir through the woman secured by murder. This grace is too much for God's enemy to comprehend. God has hidden his plans from him under the cover of grace; he kept information from the enemy. Yet still God announced his plans in 1 Chronicles 17. He would build the messianic house through David – uniquely through David's royal line.

From the days of David onwards, every time a king turned to idols and rejected God, Satan must have hoped he had won. Sometimes the prophets seemed to reinforce Satan's victories! Though we are ignoring the failed kings of Israel, looking only at Judah, David's line was still fully corrupt. God did not accept even Josiah's revival as sufficient. During Josiah's reign, Jeremiah entered as God's man. Then came Jehoiakim. And his son followed: Jehoiachin. Then came the curse: the line of David is cut off! The promised family tree is a stump! So what is God's plan now? Is this a victory for Satan – or for God? But rather than a threat, perhaps the curse is used by God to hide his plans: they are hidden again. Clearly announced, clearly restated with passion by Jeremiah himself; but how would God bring them about? He has hidden them from the enemy. Where should Satan deploy his venom?

My retelling of the unfolding story of God's redemption is slanted to lead us to this conclusion: God is hiding information from the enemy, while clearly announcing his plans. Yet there is another telling of this story in Revelation 12:1–6:

> And a great sign appeared in heaven: a woman clothed with the sun, with the moon under her feet, and on her head a crown of twelve stars. She was pregnant and was crying out in birth pains and the agony of giving birth. And another sign appeared in heaven: behold, a great red dragon, with seven heads and ten horns, and on his heads seven diadems. His tail swept down a third of the stars of heaven and cast them to the earth. And the dragon stood before the woman who was about to give birth, so that when she bore her child he might devour it. She gave birth to a male child, one who is to rule all the nations with a rod of iron, but her child was caught up to God and to his throne, and the woman fled into the wilderness, where she has a place prepared by God, in which she is to be nourished for 1,260 days.

Doesn't this telling of the story as a war – however unequal – support the idea that God is constantly hiding information from the enemy in plain sight?

For then, when it was time for the birth, the angel came to Mary, one perhaps hidden away from the royal line of David. Ignatius was correct: 'Now the virginity of Mary was hidden from the prince of this world, as was also her offspring, and the death of the Lord; three mysteries of renown, which were wrought in silence, but have been revealed to us.'[47] Who could have anticipated this? Then came the revelation to God's people. The angel announced and the Spirit came upon her and she conceived; Jesus was born of a virgin. Then that baby was adopted by Joseph, a man who stood to inherit the royal throne, but could not because of Jeremiah's curse. What was hidden was now revealed! But God, as he always does, had his way. Christ was adopted; a royal adoption. All this God accomplished by the virgin birth.

Doctrine: The Spirit's Call to Action

What, then, is our doctrine? How do we respond? Again we must ask about the response that the authors intended by these meanings. Words do not have meanings, but rather convey the meaning of the authors. And authors intend not only meanings, but a response in their readers. We have considered two powerful and related meanings in this chapter under the heading 'a mystery revealed'. The first meaning is that the Messiah's coming was seemingly cut off by God, through Jeremiah, so that it might have seemed impossible for God to preserve his covenant. Yet Jeremiah himself declared that God's covenant with David was as solid as his covenant with the day and the night. Indeed, by adoption, God accomplished his purposes. And because of the nature of the adoption, the coming of the Messiah was strategically hidden from the enemy. This enemy, according to Revelation 12, sought to swallow the Messiah at birth. But when? And where? This was impossible to discern because the line was cut off. He was hidden. After Jehoiachin there was only a root, a stump, a dead branch. But through Joseph, who had the right to the throne, God revealed Jesus as rightful heir through the virgin birth. God did his great work and, in so doing, he revealed the great mystery. If this is a valid meaning of the authors, what response did they intend in us? I believe that from Jeremiah to Matthew and Luke, their intent was to raise our confidence in God. Our God always keeps his word, even if to us it seems impossible. Despite the fact that the family tree was cut down to the stump, yet our God was gloriously moving to keep his word and provide for his children. This was as sure as his covenant with the day and the night. God's covenants stand. God's enemies are powerless. God's people can have confidence.

Another response which might be in keeping with Christ's adoption, and our adoption in Christ, may be our own adoption of unwanted or orphaned children into Christian families. Within Western culture, adoption, while not without misuse and stories of tragedy, has a rich history. But this is not the case in all cultures. Only recently, a Christian family in the Middle East was arrested when their adopted daughter died of an illness, one which had plagued her prior to adoption. The charges made against Matthew and Grace Huang included child-trafficking and intent to sell the organs of their deceased daughter. The evidence did not include facts that would substantiate such charges. Instead, it included the 'obvious' fact that the children they adopted (for they had adopted three children from Africa) were not of their culture. This Islamic country, which honours much of the Mosaic law, has no concept of adoption. I might speculate that the adoption of Christ by Joseph has deeply affected cultures penetrated by the gospel – even among those who do not affirm Christ themselves. Without a deep cultural affirmation of Jesus' adoption by Joseph, we might have no basis for valuing and understanding adoption in our own families. Is Joseph's adoption of Christ, and God's adoption of us, a call to adopt children into our families? Perhaps.

5

The Virgin Birth: A Chiastic Reversal

God can create a human being by four methods. To be specific: he can do this either from a man and a woman together, as the usual practice demonstrates, or from neither a man nor a woman, as in the case of Adam's creation, or from a man without a woman, as in the creation of Eve, or from a woman without a man – which he has not yet done . . . It has been kept in reserve for the very undertaking which we have in mind. (Anselm)[1]

So far I have rejected two common meanings of the virgin birth: protection of Christ from hereditary concupiscence and protection from original sin. I've also proposed as basic to the virgin birth that it is a sign from God which reveals the full divinity and full humanity of Christ and also acts as a move in opposition to ontological naturalism. Somewhat more speculatively, though with historical and biblical support, I have shown that the virgin birth is a mystery which hid information from the enemy as God's means of establishing the kingdom. Now I will examine the virgin birth as a means God used to reverse the damage done by Eve when she was deceived. This damage was primarily toward God, but she also inflicted damage on the reputation of women. In the virgin birth, God reverses the role of the woman, contrasting Eve in her 'conception' of sin with Mary's conception of the Christ.

I find Augustine insightful: 'It was suitable that man's liberation should be made manifest in both sexes. Consequently . . . it was becoming that the liberation of the female sex should be manifested in that man being born of a woman.'[2] This is just the territory I want to explore: the 'liberation' of the female sex manifested in the way in which Christ was born – of a woman alone. This particular and unique act of God was a grace of God to women. Anselm's observation displayed above is a most helpful place to begin to examine this. Let me lay it out as a chart:

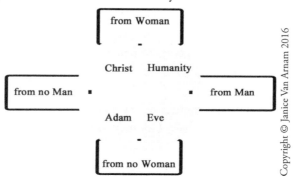

What Anselm offers is an observation of symmetry – a truth table of sorts. God has used every logical combination of man and woman for the generation of humans. By looking at the diagonals in the table, we can see an interesting pairing of Adam with Humanity and Eve with Christ:

Adam: from neither a man nor a woman
    (is like)
        All (other) Humanity: from a man and a woman
            (for either both or neither are involved)
BUT:
Woman: from a man without a woman
    (is like)
        Christ: from a woman without a man
            (for only one or the other is involved)

I want to help us observe a wonderful chiastic reversal here for women. A definition may be in order. A chiasmus is a 'term of art' for theologians which indicates an argument that displays progressive and parallel ideas in order to make a point to the reader. A chiasmus is a creation of the author intended to highlight his point. By this structure, the point is often displayed by working into the middle, where the key idea is highlighted, and then backing out with symmetry. Of course, it is only usual and not necessarily the case that the central idea is the focus. Let me give an example:

> God alone is all good;
>> We were made good, but became evil;
>>> God overcame our evil on the cross;
>> In Christ we are made good eternally;
> Now we can enjoy God's goodness.

This chiastic structure provides a way to display a cross-centred reversal, which spans the text from Genesis to the gospels. With it written in prose, we might not notice it. But with it set out as it is above, we can see how the first and last, and second and fourth, statements are parallel, and that the middle statement is the focus of the message. In this case, it is also the basis of the reversal – a chiastic reversal. So it is for women in the virgin birth. While we will explore this at length, let me display the ideas of creation and the incarnation here as a chiasmus, a suggestion for how to understand these events:

> Eve came into the world through a man without a woman (God's special creation);
>> By Eve, who was deceived by Satan, evil undermined all of God's creation;
>>> God promised that, through the woman's seed, the enemy would be destroyed;
>> By Mary, who obeyed God, the Saviour was born into God's creation;
> The Saviour came into the world through a woman without a man (God's virgin birth).

In this chiasmus, Woman, represented by Eve, who came into the world from a man (but by no woman), failed in her duty. So, Woman, represented by Mary, through whom came the virgin birth of Christ by a woman (but by no man), succeeded in her duty. This was the anticipated hope of redemption for which all men and women waited for millennia. The key to this telling of the story is God's promised redemption (Gen. 3:15), but the means is the joyful chiastic reversal of the role of woman from deceived to obedient. This reversal is accomplished by the birth of the Saviour by a woman with no man: the virgin birth. Of course, the reader must decide if this chiastic reversal is actually in God's mind as author of the creation and the incarnation, and in the mind of the Evangelists (and Paul in 1 Tim. 2, as we will see later in this chapter) as the immediate authors of the text, and whether the central idea is truly the focus of all the authors, divine and human.

What impact does this have on our understanding of the meaning of the virgin birth? I propose that this symmetry helps us see in the virgin birth a sign which reveals Mary to be wiser than Eve, and also highlights the 'redemption' of women.[3] We will see this by comparing the annunciation with the fall narratives, as well as by an investigation of 1 Timothy 2:12–15.

To Reveal Mary to Be Wiser than Eve

And behold an angel was before (her) saying: 'Do not fear, Mary; for you have found grace before the Lord of all things. You shall conceive from his Word.' (*Protevangelium of James*)[4]

But each person is tempted when he is lured and enticed by his own desire. Then desire when it has conceived gives birth to sin, and sin when it is fully grown brings forth death. (James 1:14,15)

There is a particular beauty in the virgin birth which we do not always pause to witness. We are familiar with the glory of the angel, the beauty of Mary's submission, the heroic integrity of Joseph, and the breath-taking miracle of the virginal conception. But our familiarity, and even our delight, with these glories may make it difficult to perceive another glory. This glory arises out of the symmetries: Eve's beginning and Mary's conceptions are opposites. Eve's failure in the Garden is gloriously reversed in Mary's submission to God in Nazareth. Mary's seed defeats Eve's deception. And also, comparing their 'conceptions', Mary is revealed as wiser than Eve. This too is a chiastic reversal for women.

Why was Jesus *born* to Mary, as a virgin, instead of being created from the dust, as was Adam? Even before Anselm (1033–1109), Irenaeus (130–202) gave a clear answer:

> If, then, the first Adam had a man for his father, and was born of human seed, it [was] reasonable to say that the second Adam was begotten of Joseph. But if the former was taken from the dust, and God was his Maker, it was incumbent that the latter also, making a recapitulation in Himself, should be formed as man by God, to have an analogy with the former as respects His origin. Why, then, did not God again take dust, but wrought so that the formation should be made of Mary? It was that there might not be another formation called into being, nor any other which should [require to] be saved, but that the very same formation should be summed up [in Christ as had existed in Adam], the analogy having been preserved.[5]

Irenaeus is saying that for Jesus to be like Adam he could not have a man for his father, for Adam did not have a man for his father. And indeed, in the previous section, Irenaeus has already ruled out the possibility of Christ ruling if he was related to Adam, due to the curse of Jeremiah. So Joseph must be rejected as an option. Quite possibly, we might imagine that, like Adam, Jesus could be made from the dust. But this would make him too distinct from all other humanity, 'another formation', and so a second distinct line in need of salvation. This connection between Adam and Christ is made very clear in Scripture, specifically in Romans 5 and 1 Corinthians 15, where Paul speaks of Christ as the new Adam. This is no casual pairing for Paul, but rather one that undergirds his deep understanding of the workings of our salvation. But Irenaeus has ruled out two ways to be connected to Adam. Instead, Irenaeus is pointing us to the need for Christ to be born through Mary, through whom Christ possesses continuity with Adam, as Anselm agreed.

Irenaeus is also among those who extrapolate from the connection between Adam and Christ to see connections between Eve and Mary. These are neither trivial, nor few. Both Eve and Mary were young when they 'conceived'. Eve, following immediately after her creation, 'conceived' sin, and Mary, a young girl just engaged, conceived the Messiah. At each conception, both listened to angelic beings who spoke to them. And both were betrothed to their husbands by God himself. To Adam, God acted as a father bringing his daughter: he 'brought her to the man' (Gen. 2:22b). So too, in the case Joseph, already betrothed but planning to divorce because of the pregnancy, God came bringing him a wife. He said through an angel, 'Do not fear to take Mary as your wife' (Matt. 1:20). So both women were committed to a man and under his protection. Also, both Eve and Mary continued as virgins beyond the betrothal and into the marriage, at least until their respective 'births'. In Mary's case, betrothed but still a virgin, she became pregnant by the Holy Spirit (Matt. 1:18). Though Joseph then married her (v. 24), they did not consummate the marriage until she had given birth (he 'knew her not until she had given birth to a son', Matt. 1:25). So also Eve, married to Adam in Genesis 2:22–25, did not immediately fulfil the blessing and the command, 'Be fruitful and multiply' (Gen. 1:28). Seemingly in no rush to consummate the marriage, that waited until after the 'birth' of sin. Only then does the text tell us, 'Now Adam knew Eve his wife' (Gen. 4:1). So in both relationships, Adam and Eve and Mary and Joseph, the consummation seems to have been delayed; the women are virgins at the time of their first 'conception'. There are also obvious contrasts. Eve was disobedient, and Mary obedient. One participated in bringing death, and the other participated in bringing life. Irenaeus writes, 'The knot of Eve's disobedience was loosed by the obedience of Mary. For what the virgin Eve had bound fast through unbelief, this did the virgin Mary set free through faith.'[6] These are the similarities and differences that can be observed; were they on the mind of the authors? We must ask: What did Matthew and Luke have in mind? Does the extensive allusion of the Evangelists to the Genesis story make it likely that these parallels were intentional? It may do. Further, this rather expansive chiasmus testifies to God's plenary and superintending intention as well. I suggest with Irenaeus that both God and the gospel writers were directing our attention to a reversal in which Mary is shown to be wiser than Eve.

Another interesting source that helps us see this connection, one which is even richer and fuller, comes from the *Protevangelium of James.*[7]

The author of this second-century writing is unknown to us. Relative to the canonical New Testament, it is a late and apocryphal writing. It is pseudepigraphic, that is, not written by James, the brother of the Lord, as it claims.[8] This book is part of the tradition of the infancy narratives of Christ, and is, like other such extra-canonical works, distinctly *unhelpful* if our desire is to know about the life of Christ. Yet the author may be helpful to us as an early commentator on the theological significance of Jesus' birth when he observes some interesting connections between the stories of Mary and Eve.[9] These connections are not new to Roman Catholics, and I believe them to be intentional and helpful in seeing the meaning of the Evangelists Matthew and Luke.

The story told by the author of the *Protevangelium* begins with Mary's birth. Joachim and Anna were barren. After they sought God, he granted a girl-child, Mary, with an angelic prophecy that her name would be known throughout the earth. Like Samuel, Mary was presented in the temple and dedicated to temple service in her third year. In her twelfth year, at God's direction, she was betrothed to Joseph, after a sign of God appeared out of his staff. While betrothed, she was chosen to spin the gold, linen and silk in order to make a new curtain for the Most Holy Place. While carrying out this occupation in the temple of Jerusalem, Mary heard the voice of the angel making the announcement of her virginal conception. The additions to and discrepancies with the gospel account are obvious – even glaring. Not least among these is the location in Jerusalem rather than Nazareth. This is the story of the *Protevangelium* right up to the announcement.

The differences notwithstanding, the unknown author may help us reflect on some of the real connections between the announcement of the nativity and the fall. First, neither Adam nor Joseph was present at either 'conception'. Let's take the most obvious first: Joseph. Luke's account excludes him from the announcement to Mary, and this is reinforced by Matthew. In Matthew's account the angel came to Joseph separately and after Mary had conceived, in order to testify to the truth of the virginal conception and to command Joseph to marry her. What of Adam? Prior to the coming of the angel, the *Protevangelium* (13.1) depicts Joseph comparing himself to Adam, who is absent from Eve at the decisive hour, and so, according to this account, Joseph, like Adam, was not there to protect his wife. But that does not seem to be the case according to Genesis. The text of Genesis says, 'she also gave some to her husband who was with her, and he ate' (Gen. 3:6). A simple reading seems to imply that they must have been together, side by side at the tree of the knowledge of good and evil. Adam was there in the Garden, but he was standing by as a silent partner. Yet there are two other possibilities. The text could mean something like, 'who was with her *in the Garden*'. In this case, turning from the tree with the half-eaten fruit, she moved (some indefinite distance in the Garden) to Adam's side and offered him the fruit. Is this the intent of the author or stretching a point? Another possibility is to repoint the text so that it reads, 'and she gave it to Adam, her people'.[10] If this is the author's intent, then Adam's proximity is not at issue, but his lack of protection may be. What should be seen is this: whether Adam was somewhere nearby in the Garden or at her side, he had effectively removed himself from the story, from leadership, and from any proactive participation. In this sense at least, he was not for her; he did not serve her; he was not with her. For if Adam was there, he did not speak or intervene to protect her from the deceit of the serpent. Quite the opposite; he listened to the voice of his wife instead of God. Effectively, and perhaps physically, Adam and Joseph were both absent from their wives when they conceived.

Second, both Eve and Mary conceive by hearing (by ear). Gary Anderson notes how significant this is in church history.[11] In the Garden Eve *hears* the serpent *speak*: 'You will not surely die. For God knows that when you eat of it, your eyes will be opened, and you will be like God, knowing good and evil' (Gen. 3:4–5). And through this conversation, Eve conceived sin, 'by ear'. And she confirmed this with her mouth: 'she took of its fruit and ate' (Gen. 3:6). Hearing resulted in the flaming of the desire which gave birth to sin – all by hearing. Then, with her mouth, she confirmed the conception. Mary followed the same path to the conception that brought salvation through the Messiah. Mary heard the angel, and conceived by her hearing. And by her mouth she declared and confirmed this great conception: 'Behold,

I am the servant of the Lord; let it be to me according to your word' (Luke 1:38). While these allusions between Luke 1 and Genesis 3 are not clearly semantic, they do constitute a constellation of conceptual allusions. Both include an angelic being,[12] a discussion with that being, conception by ear, and a confirmation by mouth. And indeed, from that hearing and confession by mouth, Christ was conceived in Mary by the Holy Spirit. And so the act of Eve and the act of Mary mediated opposite and decisive changes in the world.

This idea of 'aural conception' (conception by ear) also clarifies and distances itself from strange interpretations and even sexual misconceptions in regard to the creedal words 'conceived by the Holy Spirit'. Barth noticed this: 'God Himself takes the stage as the Creator and not as a partner to this Virgin. Christian art in earlier times attempted to reproduce this fact, that here there is no question of a sexual event. And it has been well said that this procreation was realized rather by way of the ear of Mary, which heard the Word of God.'[13] In both accounts, those of Eve and of Mary, and so in both acts, only eisegesis, reading in our concerns rather than those of the authors, could discern a 'sexual event'. The conceptions are 'aural', and by Mary's obedient reception the Saviour will be born.

Third, Eve and Mary responded to the angel differently, but perhaps not as we might expect. Again, Gary Anderson helps here by noting that the responses show that Eve was gullible, but Mary was not. Eve responds to the fallen angel only with statements, but Mary responds to the angel with scepticism. To the serpent's first challenge: 'Did God say you must not eat from *any* tree of the Garden?', Eve responded with a confused and seemingly 'helpful' correction. Yet this undermined God's word to Adam by at least three misstatements.[14] To the serpent's flat rejection 'No, you won't die!', she listened. She offered no challenge. No questions. Then she conceived sin in her heart, with no argument. In short, she was gullible. When we come to the gospels, we meet another young woman, Mary. She too is confronted with an angelic visitor who tells a strange story. Both will conceive by ear, but there is a contrast. Mary is almost impertinent with the angel. She exclaims, 'How can this be?' What is the meaning of this? Perhaps it is an expression of wonder. Perhaps she is challenging the angel's story, as if the angel is impugning her character. It certainly is not an expression of disbelief, in contrast with Zechariah.[15] In contrast to Eve's 'politeness' to the lying serpent, Mary before the angel is not naive. This question comes from a young woman who is deeply frightened, in contrast to Eve, who, in her comfort, did not keep her head. In the end, the calm and polite Eve sinned. But the anxious young woman Mary kept her head in this situation and obeyed. Mary responded as the covenant partner of God that she was: 'Behold, I am the servant of the Lord!' And Jesus was conceived.

Mary is revealed to be wiser than Eve. James wrote in his letter, 'But each person is tempted when he is lured and enticed by his own desire. Then desire when it has conceived gives birth to sin, and sin when it is fully grown brings forth death' (Jas 1:14–15). Is James reflecting on Eve's failure in the Garden of Eden? For in the Garden she conceived sin, and, in her, sin was given birth. How different was Mary, who also followed her desires – her desire to submit to God and obey him – and then conceived Jesus, giving birth to the Saviour! Mary is shown to be wiser than Eve. The similarities between the stories show the connection of type and anti-type. The differences show the success of Mary over Eve. And in this, God grants a marvellous victory to women, solely through the person of Mary. This is not the salvation of the race, nor was Eve blamed for the death of the race. But woman was blamed for her being deceived, as she herself confessed in Genesis 3:13. But now this is reversed in Mary! If, through the disobedient conception of Eve, Adam was led into trespass, and this led to the condemnation of all people, so also through the obedient conception of Mary, the virgin birth of Jesus took place, and by his obedience came the justification of all men! In this we have a reversal of Mary over Eve, a chiastic reversal of the roles, a mercy of God to all women and a joy for all men.

To 'Redeem' Women

As Eve's disobedience introduced death into the world, so Mary's obedience led to life. (Gary Anderson)[16]

The woman's seed, the product of her childbearing, will some day bruise the serpent's head. As the woman was deceived by the serpent, so she shall avenge herself through the seed which she bears. (Roberts)[17]

We have seen Mary revealed as wiser than Eve by comparing the Garden deception to the Nazareth Magnificat. Both are virginal conceptions, with one virgin rejecting God and the other receiving God. One is the great grief of the world and the other brings joy to the world. Seeing this contrast and comparison is a step toward perceiving God's gracious work of 'redeeming women' by means of the virgin birth. In this virgin birth, men make no contribution, but, instead, God works uniquely through a woman to repair the damage a woman initiated. Just as Adam failed to participate in the first conception, so Joseph contributes nothing to the second. The conception of sin is between a woman and the father of lies, and that of Jesus between a woman and the Holy Spirit who comes upon her. In the virginal conception and birth, women are redeemed in that they are uniquely co-labouring with God to deliver the One who will redeem.

The key text for this second part of the investigation is 1 Timothy 2:13–15 (displayed below) – a troublesome text indeed. This text is often 'used' (in every negative sense of the term) to 'prove' (in every imagined sense of the term) either the egalitarian or the complementarian position regarding the roles of men and women. It has also been exegeted fairly to argue both positions. This is an important discussion but one that is not my interest here. I am interested in Paul's connection with Genesis 1 – 3 and especially with 3:15, a connection which may link Christian women with Eve. I also want to anticipate Eve's connection with Mary, seeing in them a type and anti-type relationship. Yet, in so doing, I will not argue for either the truth of pseudepigraphic works (works with false claims of authorship) that recognized this connection, nor for the full scope of the doctrines of Mariology. Rather, I hope to show that the virgin birth helps us understand the redemption that came through a woman – the 'redemption' of women. It is a reversal – a chiastic reflection of Eve and Mary in Christian women – and a point of joy that women have a unique and critical role in the story of redemption, not only in that of the fall.

In order to set expectations, I want to reveal my approach for this fairly technical section. The text of 1 Timothy 2:13–15 must be considered exegetically, though the full scope of exegesis is beyond what I intend for this book. I will state textual concerns, the most significant scholarship, and my reasoning and conclusions, but further clarification of argumentation and language issues will be restricted to the footnotes, most often as pointers to the works of others.[18]

1 Timothy 2:13–15 reads this way:

> [13]For Adam was formed first, then Eve; [14]and Adam was not deceived, but the woman was deceived and became a transgressor. [15]Yet she will be saved through childbearing – if they continue in faith and love and holiness, with self-control.

I will show why this text should be read as a commentary on the Genesis account, relating Eve's creation, fall, and redemption as the ground for Paul's teaching to the issues facing the Ephesian women.[19] This will help us see Paul's 'redemption' of women – their place in redemption with Mary which overturns their place in the fall with Eve. Paul does this by tracing women's role in creation, the fall, and redemption.

First Timothy 2:13 is grounded in the creation of Eve in Genesis 2. The dependence of this verse on the account of the creation of Eve is clear enough; there is little debate or confusion. Yet it is worth noticing that Paul draws from Genesis 2 in contrast to Genesis 1. In Genesis 1 Adam and Eve were created with no temporal distinction ('male and female he created them'). But in Genesis 2, we encounter the jarring and shocking words 'not good' (v. 18), the first such occurrence in the Bible. This judgement is completely at odds with the expectation established in Genesis 1 by the oft-repeated coda, 'God saw that it was good'. Here in this second and more detailed telling of human creation, God makes a woman for Adam from his rib, second-born as it were, and presents her to him in marriage.[20] In 1 Timothy 2 Paul makes his point in verse 13; it is an argument from the order of creation.

Verse 14 follows verse 13 as the fall follows creation in Genesis 2 – 3. What is Paul's point? In some cases, students of this text have misconstrued the meaning as if Paul is placing blame on Eve while exonerating Adam. However, this is not the case. Andrew Spurgeon is helpful and clear:

Paul's statement – 'Adam was not deceived; Eve, being deceived, came into transgression' – was his summary of the fall of humanity. Elsewhere Paul placed the blame of humanity's sinfulness on Adam: 'Through one man sin entered into the world' (Rom 5:12); 'In the transgression of one man, many died' (Rom 5:15). The apparent discrepancy of holding either Eve or Adam accountable for transgression is resolved when proper stress is placed on *deception*: whereas Adam was not *deceived*, Eve was *deceived* (1 Tim 2:14). Adam's disobedience was willful, a violation of the direct command that he received from God. Eve's transgression was deception, that is, the serpent's false statements deceived her. She said so to the LORD when he asked her why she ate from the tree: 'It was the serpent. He deceived me, and I ate' (Gen. 3:13). So following the 'creation' account (1 Tim 2:13), Paul summarized the 'fall' account in this verse but with the added emphasis on deception (1 Tim 2:14).[21]

I judge that, so far, my readers are with me. So far, the link of 1 Timothy 2:13–14 to Genesis 2 – 3 is clear. Paul's point or the validity of his point is debated, but the link with Genesis is not – at least in these verses. The challenge comes when we consider 1 Timothy 2:15. Not a few have suggested that Paul is responding to erroneous teaching and the danger of the Ephesian women succumbing to these errors. David Kimberley suggested specifically that '1 Timothy 2:15 is expressed in response to erroneous Gnostic teaching in Ephesus to the effect that childbearing was an occasion for condemnation for Christian women'.[22] These views are interesting, but not my primary concern here. I want to understand Paul's choice to follow the career of Eve through her creation, fall, and also her redemption in Christ through Mary. To be clear, I will argue that Eve is the subject of the verbal noun 'childbirth', the one who 'will be saved'. Yet Paul is directing our attention also to Mary, who is never the subject or antecedent of any of his pronouns, yet who stands in the place of ultimate fulfilment, the mother in the one childbirth that leads to salvation for all. I will work through the exegetical issues, one at a time, building translation as we go.

The first concern in this text, verse 15, is the question: Who is 'she'? Spurgeon traces the subject of this pronoun back to the closest match in gender, number, and case: 'woman' in verse 14, and, driving back further, 'Eve' in verse 13. The options, however, are varied and include Christian women, Ephesian women, or even Mary. Along with Spurgeon, I judge that the continuity of argument distinguishes between these options decisively: the 'she' of this text references 'Eve'.[23] In speaking of Eve, Paul is admonishing and encouraging the Ephesian women and all women to a certain kind of life. I'll return to this detail later.

What, then, does it mean for Eve to be 'saved'? The options are many and include physical preservation in childbirth, preservation from deception by Satan, 'salvation' from the ban on teaching, and reconciliation in general. I will not here present specific arguments against these; others have done so. Rather, the context and Paul himself seem to allow room for only one meaning: salvation from sin. This is not only Paul's most frequent use, but it is also the context for Paul's argument in chapter 2: 'Christ Jesus came into the world to save sinners' (1 Tim. 1:15). Stanley Porter, along with many others, argues for this common use of Paul when he writes:

> Most plausible, it seems to me, is to take 1 Tim. 2.15 as a concluding statement of the entire section (1 Tim. 2.8–15) . . . In the light of the above cumulative evidence and in particular in the context of 1 Tim. 2.15, σωθήσεται is virtually guaranteed a salvific sense (the passive voice is probably a divine or theological passive, that is, God is the agent of salvation).[24]

Paul is consistent in using 'save' (*sozo*, σώζω) in just this way – soteriologically, that is, in regard to God's work to redeem us in Christ. For Paul, 'save' is always Christological. This, if it is sustained, refutes any understanding of Paul's use of '*sozo*' as 'salvation by works'. We could say this quite strongly: Paul limits his use of this word 'save' to our salvation from sin through Christ.[25] So this verse reverses the problem raised in the previous verse: Eve's failure; she 'became a transgressor'. This overwhelming problem is now reversed by a new idea: 'she will be saved.'

Now we turn to the next exegetical challenge: What is the function of 'through'? In Greek, this preposition (*dia*, διά) can have several meanings. These include temporal, so 'will be saved through the time of childbirth'; or means (instrumental), so 'saved by childbirth'; or attendant circumstances, so 'even though she must bear children'.[26] Let me consider these from last to first, that is, starting with the one most difficult to understand. The use of '*dia*' for 'attendant circumstances' is a use of the prepositional phrase to explain something that is also true but not entailed by the context. That is the meaning of 'even though' above. Doug Moo argues for understanding '*dia*' in just this way: 'she is saved, *even though* she must bear children'; '*dia*' is not a means of her salvation nor does it specify the time of her salvation. We might understand this as we do Paul's charge to us all in Philippians 2:12: 'work out your own salvation with fear and trembling.' In this case, 'fear and trembling' do not save us, but 'attend' our salvation experience.[27] However, Paul is quite consistent in his instrumental use of '*dia*' with 'save', and if a consistent translation can be made instrumentally, that must be favoured. That translation is at hand: 'saved by means of'. This wording might give us pause if it sounds as if we are setting up Paul to affirm a means of salvation which is distinct from the work of Christ. But this is not the case. We must listen to the end of Paul's argument here before we judge. Having come this far, I propose we read: 'Eve will be saved by means of . . .'

What, then, does the 'childrearing' denote? The initial question is this: Does Paul, by his use of the definite article ('the') with the noun ('childbirth'), intend to make a generic noun a specific one, or is the articular noun still generic? For example, someone from the USA could say, 'I went to the hospital', and that person could intend by this either a (generic) hospital, or the specific hospital known to both persons in the conversation. The former possibility is a generic use of the definite article. However, a British person could say, 'I went to hospital', and intend by that a specific hospital, avoiding the article by convention. Both are equivalent, and discernment is required by the listener. What of Paul? Philip Payne has done an extensive study of Paul's use of the article in 1 Timothy. He argues that Paul's use of the article always intends to make a noun specific (non-generic) or to distinguish one class from another. Paul's use of the article with a noun is never generic in 1 Timothy.[28] Payne's analysis is not conclusive; it does not carry the weight of necessity and so decisively determine our understanding of Paul's usage here. Yet he certainly has put the burden of proof on those who would argue necessity in this (or any) generic use of the articular noun in Timothy. This implies strongly that Paul's use of the article with 'childbirth' points to a particular and specific birth. To which birth should we look? The context for Paul here, based on verses 13 and 14, which point to Genesis 1 – 3, is Genesis 3:15, the protoevangelium. This is the text I have considered above at some length: 'I will put enmity between you and the woman, and between your offspring and her offspring; he shall bruise your head, and you shall bruise his heel.'[29] In this context, Paul could intend no birth other than the birth of Christ, the one who crushed the head of Satan on the cross.[30] With this in mind, our text so far would read like this: 'Eve will be saved by means of the childbirth [of the Messiah].' The strength of this proposal begins to emerge when 'saved' (used soteriologically) is brought together with 'the childbirth' (pointing to Christ). However, we also begin to see a possible double meaning. Mary, by participating in the salvation of all by this childbirth, is revealed in contrast to Eve. Eve earned the self-given reputation for being 'deceived' – she exclaimed it herself to God (Gen. 3:13)! But Mary, for the sake of all women, acts to 'save' (redeem) the reputation of all women. By her willing and obedient reception of the holy offer, the childbirth that provided for the salvation of the people of God, Mary has redeemed the reputation of women!

So we face the last exegetical question in the final clause: 'if they continue in faith and love and holiness, with self-control.' What is the antecedent of 'they'? The options here are similar to those in the issue of the subject 'she' in the previous clause (v. 15). Yet now the pronoun seeks a plural antecedent. Options include Christian women, the

Ephesian women, Adam and Eve, or Eve's descendants. Consistent with the choice of Eve as the subject, Eve's descendants seems a good fit, though this could be identical with 'Adam and Eve' taken to stand for themselves and all their progeny, the larger group of their descendants. Payne represents this well when he writes, 'Paul uses the plural because he includes Eve's descendants in Eve, so named "because she would be the mother of all the living" (Gen. 3:20), just as he includes "the many" in Adam in Rom 5:19. The grammatical shift from singular to plural is a direct reflection of the Genesis narrative's reference to the woman giving birth to children (plural τέκνα = בָּנִים) in 3:16.'[31] I agree.

With this understanding of 'they' we now address the meaning of the conditional clause: 'if Adam and Eve, along with their descendants, continue in faith and love and holiness, with self-control.' Why must they continue so? Again, Paul exclusively uses the Greek word for salvation as an expression of his Christology, and so here in verse 15 Paul does not intend 'salvation by works', certainly not by the *work* of childbirth. The explanation, the ground for this affirmation, is found in Genesis 3:16, which follows the protoevangelium of 3:15. Moses writes, 'Your desire shall be for your husband, and he shall rule over you.' Jesse Scheumann observes that, whether this is understood as a pronouncement of marital tension or harmony (a much-debated point in its own right), Paul's condition here aligns with this same text:

> In order to preserve the line of promise until the coming of Christ, Adam and Eve need to remain together (understood as either over-coming the judgment of Gen 3:16b or according to its promise) in certain virtues. According to Paul, the virtues are πίστις, 'faith/faith-fulness' (toward God and his promises), ἀγάπη, 'love' (for God and one another), and ἁγιασμός, 'holiness' (no longer defiled by the de-ception of Satan). All of these virtues are covered μετά σωφροσύνης, 'with a sound mind' (no longer deceived by Satan's lies). If Eve is to be saved through the childbirth of Christ, it makes sense that Adam and Eve (along with their progeny) must remain in faith, love, and holi-ness, with a sound mind, extending the line of promise until Christ.

This act of Adam and Eve provides the necessary cause or ground for Eve to be saved through the childbirth of Christ.[32]

I take Scheumann's point to be an overstatement of the attendant circumstances of faith, love, and holiness. They are a condition, but a condition ultimately met by God himself by the childbirth. Certainly, God called his covenant people, Israel, to holiness as the womb of Christ and called the church to the same holiness. But this condition is subordinate to the promise of the protoevangelium, *the* childbirth in Paul's text, not the other way round. This is a good thing, for sadly, as we have already seen, neither they nor their descendants have done this well. To Jeremiah's curse could be added all the words of the many prophets. Yet it is the case that this was God's command to his people and it was for the purpose that God would, through the line of Adam and Eve, overthrow Satan by the coming seed, the Messiah. This line is restricted, following Seth, Noah, Abraham, David and Solomon, but not following many other lines of Adam and Eve. The privilege of participating in the coming of the Messiah is restricted, not open. All who are related to Adam are not in the line of the seed. Paul rightly represents this line as those who live by faith, love, and self-control, reminding us of the example of many of the patriarchs who *by faith* pleased God – such is the final judgement of Hebrews 11. The condition is demanded, but met antecedently in *the childbirth*.

If we put this together, the following translation seems likely:

> For Adam was formed first, then Eve; and Adam was not deceived, but the woman was deceived and became a transgressor. So, she [Eve, with her progeny] will be saved by means of the childbirth [of the Messiah], if Adam and Eve [and their descendants as well] continue in faith and love and holiness, with self-control.

How does this serve us in regard to the meaning of the virgin birth? As stated above, this is the 'redemption of women' – the restoration of the honour of women. The virgin birth is a gracious condescension of God to bring about the birth of the Messiah through Mary alone, the descendant of Eve. Barth writes of this conception by Mary alone:

> Once again and now from the human standpoint the male is excluded here. The male has nothing to do with this birth . . . Man is not simply excluded, for the Virgin is there. But the male, as the specific agent of human action and history, with his responsibility for directing the human species, must now retire into the background, as the powerless figure of Joseph . . . The woman stands absolutely in the foreground . . . That Mary does so and that thereby the creature says 'Yes' to God, is part of the great acceptance which comes to man from God.[33]

It is Mary alone, with Joseph powerless in the background, who has the redeeming privilege to say 'Yes!' She says 'Yes' to God for all women, for all men, and for all of God's wilful creatures. It is a 'Yes!' which echoes eternally, overcoming Eve's, 'No', through Christ. Robert Wall states it this way: 'Eve does not mention Adam's role in her child-bearing; that is, this above all else is an experience that distinguishes women from men and thus defines the prospect of a woman's experience of partnership with the Creator.'[34] In fact, as Payne noted, Paul specifically selected the phrase 'the childbirth' rather than 'Christ' in order to 'highlight the positive role of women' in this great work of undoing the deception of Eve.[35] In this move, God has restored the honour of women; God has 'redeemed women'.

Paul, like all good authors, does not use throwaway lines. So in Galatians 4:4, when he wrote, 'But when the fullness of time had come, God sent forth his Son, born of woman, born under the law', he did not write 'born of woman' merely to identify God's Son, as distinct from another son they might have confused him with. Rather 'born of woman' is precisely that bit of this Son which is important for his point. This Son was not born of man. Redemption came through the Son born of woman. By this means, we gained redemption from sin. But in one respect, women, too, are 'redeemed'. By the glory of the virgin birth women are freed from the injury to their reputation and restored to their place of honour before God and all creation.

Doctrine: The Spirit's Call to Action

What is our doctrine? How do we now live? What do Matthew and Luke intend by these meanings, if we have rightly discerned their intent? I must confess that this 'doctrinal' section is rather more difficult for me. An egalitarian, if I can presume to speak for him (I say 'him' with intention here), might argue that in light of this reversal we behold in the virginal conception and birth, we should certainly treat women differently; indeed, I suspect an argument would be made that we should eliminate traditional roles that are 'imposed' by culture. Thus far, I would agree, though not on the basis of this text. I believe the Bible repeatedly destroys cultural traditions, including the mistreatment of women — but that is not a discussion for this book. The authors' intention, apart from issues that are named as 'egalitarianism' or 'complementarianism', was to celebrate God's kindness to women, reversing their role in the fall just as he had promised. Our response is to rejoice in this God who rescues the weak, delivers his enemy, and lifts up the sinner. Women no longer bear the scar of the garden deception. They are offered not only salvation in Christ, as are men, but something else as well. Indeed, God has redeemed women in a glorious chiastic reversal. Eve fell historically, tearing down her husband. God singled her out in his charge against Adam: 'because you listened to the voice of your wife!' But now, since the childbirth and the work of Christ that followed from that birth, Eve, and all women, stands in Mary, glorifying God and magnifying the Lord who keeps his promises even to wretched sinners! And the Lord is revealed through her to us all as the One who lifts up the estate of the humble so that they are called blessed. We are to rejoice in this God, and honour his daughters, our sisters, as blessed by God, deceived no more.

6

The Virgin Birth: A New Birth for a New Creation

> The incapacity of human beings to bring about the incarnation, described in the virgin birth, even indicates the incapacity of human nature as such to be adopted by the Son of God. (Dustin Resch)[1]

> The birth of Christ, in which the initiative and power are all of God, is an apt picture of God's saving grace in general of which it is a part. It teaches us that salvation is by God's act, not our human effort. The birth of Jesus is like our new birth, which is also by the Holy Spirit; it is a new creation. (Justin Taylor)[2]

Meanings flow from the acts of God in history, and not least from the virgin birth. Of course, not every meaning we can imagine is a true meaning. I have rejected two: protecting Christ from hereditary concupiscence and avoiding the hereditary stain of original sin. The virgin birth does not intend these meanings. These were read into the virgin birth from our own biases, rather than flowing from God's Word. Yet from the virgin birth do flow great and rich meanings, including these: it is a sign of the full divinity and full humanity of Christ; it acts to oppose the ontological naturalism of a closed materialistic universe; it served to hide information from the enemy; it was used by God to establish the kingdom in Jesus; it reveals Mary to be wiser than Eve, and, even more so, through Mary's obedience reverses the damage caused to the reputation of women by Eve's deception. The virgin birth is a rich treasure for us.

Now we turn to what is a most significant meaning of the virgin birth: it is the foundation and image of our new birth into God's new creation: first, our adoption into the royal family of Christ, and second, our parthenogenesis (being 'born again') by his Spirit. We are familiar with the first, adoption. We began to examine this idea in Chapter 4, a 'solution' afforded by the virgin birth to the challenge of the curse of Jeremiah on Jehoiakim and Jehoiachin that seemed to threaten the Davidic covenant and the coming of the royal Messiah. So we will examine how this divine work of the Trinity, which provided for Christ's adoption by Joseph into the royal line, grounds the trinitarian metaphor of our adoption into God's royal family. Then we will examine a second metaphor, also grounded in the virgin birth: our parthenogenesis, our 'virgin birth' into new life in Christ. This term 'parthenogenesis' is an unusual phrasing for a wonderful reality for Christ and for us. When Barth reflects on the teaching of Jesus in John 6 concerning who it is who follows him and why, he says: 'This is how it is in attachment to Jesus Christ, "Ye have not chosen me" – whether by accepting a tradition or exercising your own judgment – "but I have chosen you".'[3] Here he establishes a decisive direction in the relationship between himself and his disciples: we do not follow Jesus of ourselves, but he chooses us. Barth goes on to say, 'If only in analogy to the existence of Jesus Christ, yet very really in this analogy, they, too, as the children of God exist in repetition, confirmation and revelation not only of the manner but also of the will and act of God as the One from whom they derive.'[4] Though his language is dense, nevertheless Barth asserts with his usual intensity that we are born into God's family by the act of God just as Christ is the incarnate Son by the act of the Spirit. Dustin Resch explains Barth by saying, 'Just as Christ himself was conceived and born by the power of the Holy Spirit, so are Christians begotten of God the Holy Spirit to take up their new vocation.'[5] Just as Jesus Christ was born of a virgin ('parthenos', virgin) with no sufficient human agency, so we are born ('genesis', birth) of God's Spirit without sufficient human agency. We, too, are virgin born, parthenogenesis. I want to examine these two great metaphors of adoption and parthenogenesis which derive from the virgin birth and lead us into experiencing its riches.

To Ground Our Adoption into the Royal Family of Christ

> For you did not receive the spirit of slavery to fall back into fear, but you have received the Spirit of adoption as sons, by whom we cry, 'Abba! Father!' (Rom. 8:15)

> God is called Father not infrequently but usually in the sense of the Father of Christ or the creator of the world, but [too] seldom in his relation to men or Christians. (Will B. Selbie)[6]

The New Testament echoes with news of our adoption into God's family. It is anticipated by Christ's words in Mark 3:35: 'whoever does the will of God, he is my brother and sister and mother.' Adoption is explicitly taught by Paul in Romans 8:15; Galatians 4:5; and Ephesians 5:1: we are adopted as sons. We are called 'sons of God' (and so also 'daughters') by Jesus in Matthew 5:9 and Luke 20:36, and three times by Paul in Romans 8:14,19 and Galatians 3:26. The idea is not entirely unknown in the Old Testament, as we shall see, but the concrete references to 'adoption' in the New Testament and the fulfilled emphasis is new in this period. What caused this transition? Perhaps the new Roman culture, which we will explore, but I suggest that the source may be far more personal: the adoption of Jesus by Joseph.

So the virgin birth, and the adoption of Christ which followed, lays the solid groundwork for a key theological metaphor and New Testament fulfilment: our adoption as children of God. The obvious concern must be stated here, an objection which is likely in the minds of some readers: Jesus was not adopted. That is, the verb, 'adopt' is never used in the biblical accounts of Joseph's relationship to Jesus, nor do the Evangelists explicitly show Joseph as adopting by any terms related to 'adoption'. True. Further, Jewish law had no place for adoption into inheritance of family title or family wealth. Also true. We must certainly respect the silence of the Bible on this account. Yet there is something else that must not be ignored. The Evangelists represented a paternal relationship between Jesus and

Joseph; this must be acknowledged if we are to avoid the word-concept fallacy.[7] We know from the Gospel of John that some people called Joseph the father of Jesus: 'They said, "Is not this Jesus, the son of Joseph, whose father and mother we know?"' (John 6:42). Were these townfolk affirming the paternity of Joseph against the claim of the virgin birth, or were they ignorant of the claim? Of course, there is no such explicit claim in John's 'nativity' ('the Word became flesh', John 1:14). For that reason alone, such an affirmation of Joseph's fatherhood might weigh significantly here. Stronger yet is Luke's own claim. Having just said that Jesus was not the son of Joseph (Luke 1:34–35), Luke writes of Joseph and Mary, referring to Joseph as 'father': 'And *his father* and his mother marveled at what was said about him' (Luke 2:33, emphasis added). Luke had many other ways to represent the confusing relationship that existed between Mary and Joseph and Jesus other than using terms of familial relations. He could have simply written, 'And Joseph and Mary marvelled at what was said about him.' But Luke chose 'his father and his mother'. Even more clearly, when Jesus was discovered in the temple, Mary declares, 'Behold, *your father* and I have been searching for you in great distress' (Luke 2:48, emphasis added). Not only is the possessive pronoun used again ('your father', parallel to 'his father' in Luke 2:23), but of all people, certainly Mary (the speaker, as opposed to Luke as narrator) is *not* confused on this point. Luke, Mary, and Joseph have settled on fatherhood as their explicit way to express the relationship of Joseph to Jesus. This affirms the reality of adoption in this text, even if it is only an implicit or an informal adoption. Further, this at least allows for the possibility of (some kind of) formal adoption, though this is by no means a necessity. So we can now ask: Might this implicit adoption provide the type, the model, and the grounds for our own explicit adoption into God's family?

The implicit case for adoption has been established from the biblical text because Joseph is named as Jesus' father. Yet perhaps an even stronger case for the adoption of Christ might be made. Jesus is said to be descended from David and an inheritor of the right to rule. He is the branch and the root of David, and so the King. A sample of significant texts are worth reviewing here, without specific comment on each (without repeating synoptic parallels):

- Matthew 2:2: 'Where is he who has been born king of the Jews? For we saw his star when it rose and have come to worship him.'
- Matthew 21:5: 'This took place to fulfill what was spoken by the prophet, saying, "Say to the daughter of Zion, 'Behold, your king is coming to you, humble, and mounted on a donkey, on a colt, the foal of a beast of burden.'"'
- Matthew 27:11: 'Now Jesus stood before the governor, and the governor asked him, "Are you the King of the Jews?" Jesus said, "You have said so."'
- Luke 1:32: 'He will be great and will be called the Son of the Most High. And the Lord God will give to him the throne of his father David.'
- Luke 23:2: 'And they began to accuse him, saying, "We found this man misleading our nation and forbidding us to give tribute to Caesar, and saying that he himself is Christ, a king."'
- John 1:49: 'Nathanael answered him, "Rabbi, you are the Son of God! You are the King of Israel!"'
- Acts 17:7: '. . . and Jason has received them, and they are all acting against the decrees of Caesar, saying that there is another king, Jesus.'
- Romans 1:3: '. . . concerning his Son, who was descended from David according to the flesh.'
- Romans 15:12: 'And again Isaiah says, "The root of Jesse will come, even he who arises to rule the Gentiles; in him will the Gentiles hope."'
- Revelation 5:5: 'And one of the elders said to me, "Weep no more; behold, the Lion of the tribe of Judah, the Root of David, has conquered, so that he can open the scroll and its seven seals."'
- Revelation: 22:16 'I, Jesus, have sent my angel to testify to you about these things for the churches. I am the root and the descendant of David, the bright morning star.'

There are many interpretive issues here that I am ignoring; I will leave them to others. Still the force of all these texts, taken together, serves as *witness* to the inherited Kingship which came to Jesus by his virgin birth. There are two moves that might undermine this claim. First, if an interpreter is willing to ignore the testimony of the text of Matthew and Luke to the virgin birth (as perhaps idiosyncratic and so non-canonical), we might understand the force of these texts differently – simple inheritance by birth to Joseph in the royal line. Yet that is not a move I am able to make given my stated goal of understanding the meaning of the virgin birth as presented by the authors of the gospels and in the context of the whole canon. Another possible move might be to show that, text by text, these references offer a meaning other than to affirm that Christ has inherited the kingdom through David. Yet even then we are left with the historical agreement of the church that Jesus is King in the line of David, as promised by the prophets. This is the united agreement of historical theology, unanimously asserted throughout the history of God's people, and the expectation of the Old Testament. Indeed, the coming royal Messiah is the treasure of the Old Testament and the one hope. Not least among these witnesses is Jeremiah, the very one who 'caused' our problem when he 'decertified' Jehoiachin and his descendants from the kingdom (Jer. 22). Yet he also wrote, 'Behold, the days are coming, declares the LORD, when I will raise up for David a righteous Branch, and he shall reign as king and deal wisely, and shall execute justice and righteousness in the land' (Jer. 23:5). Prophecy declares that God will raise up a messianic king to rule in the line of David. The gospels reveal that Jesus claimed the right to rule in the Davidic line. Yet Jesus was born to Mary, and no gospel explicitly attests to her royal line. How then did he gain the right to rule and fulfil the many prophecies that the Messiah would be a king in the line of David? This does not come to Jesus by the bloodline of Joseph, if (as the virgin birth requires) Jesus is not related to Joseph. Yet Jesus did inherit the right to rule. It seems that the virgin birth which divided him from the kingdom also provided the possibility of (or perhaps required) adoption as a means to draw him back into the royal line.

Is this what was intended by the Evangelists? Could it be that God, who oversees not only the events but also the timing of his intrusion into history, provided Roman adoption as the law of the land just at the time of Jesus' birth? The Evangelists had intentions in their writing, a significant point for this investigation. By writing what they did about Christ's virgin birth, the Evangelists also had intentions for us, an effect intended in us by what they wrote. God also has intentions. This includes not only the writing, but also the timing of the event of the incarnation. And so, if God's intentions included the cursing of Jehoiakim and Jehoiachin, and their being cut off from the royal line, God's intentions also included the restoration of the line in the Messiah. If that solution included adoption, legally and with historical context, it may well have served God's intentions to bring Christ into the world at the time of the Romans.

Adoption does have a rich history. It was known to Egyptians and Romans, but, as I noted above, it is missing in Judaism. Yigal Levin writes, 'In a nutshell, there is nothing in Jewish law, in either the Hebrew Bible or in later Halakhah, which can be seen as the model by which Jesus, Son of God, could have been considered the legal, but not genetic, heir to the Davidic throne.'[8] He proposes that the solution must be found in the current law of the day in that culture – Roman law. This may provide a rich cultural basis for Matthew and Luke's implicit assertion of Joseph's adoption of Jesus into the Davidic line and Christ's legal right to rule. Without proving the historical case one way or the other, we can observe that some means is required that goes beyond the facts given in the gospels of Matthew and Luke. Adoption, under Roman law, may have provided a legitimate means in that day, allowing Joseph to bestow the kingdom on Jesus. This is reinforced by the acceptance of both genealogies as belonging to Joseph (with neither attributed to Mary), as is the opinion of a plurality – and perhaps a majority – of exegetes (see Chapter 4). It is no coincidence that the two Evangelists who provided virgin birth claims, intentionally separating Jesus from Joseph, were also the Evangelists who provided genealogies connecting only Joseph to the royal line! So it seems that they required something 'like' adoption in order to be coherent. If that seems counter-intuitive to the culture of the day, it should make us cautious, but not averse to the possibility. In fact, if Jewish norms and customs do not provide the help we need to anticipate adoption, Roman rule may offer a timely solution. It is not 'unfair' to invoke Roman traditions as a general rule. Indeed, the cross was not Jewish but Roman, the means chosen by God for his own execution and anticipated in the Garden (the *tree* of evil knowledge), by the serpent on the pole (Num. 21), and by the curse of God for those hanged on a tree (Deut. 21:23). God selected the time and place for the incarnation so that all was prepared as he intended in order that prophecy would be fulfilled. At just the right time, Jesus died, so that he would die on a Roman cross. It is no theological reach to believe that he would be born at just the right time to be adopted. But was he adopted? If not, from where does our own adoption arise?

Strangely, adoption as a theological metaphor has suffered as an orphan, much ignored. While it receives affirmation, it suffers from inattention. As Robert A. Webb noted over a century ago, 'the evangelical doctrine of Adoption . . . has received but slender treatment at the hands of theologians.'[9] Writing in the same era, Robert Smith Candlish noted the same inattention among the Reformers, but excused them, noting that their hands were full of weighty matters: 'In that theology, the subject of adoption, or the sonship of Christ's disciples, did not, as it seems to me, occupy the place and receive the prominency to which it is, on scriptural grounds and warrants, entitled . . . Their hands were full.'[10] He forgave them this lapse because they were concerned with such weighty and necessary things. But moving backwards in time, he noted that even the early church failed, for the most part, to explore this sufficiently: 'patristic literature shows too plainly how the controversies about the supreme divinity of the Son tended to draw men's minds away from the sonship of his disciples.'[11] Now, a century later, the situation is little better. Martin Lloyd-Jones called attention to this strange gap in our theology: 'for some inexplicable reason it [adoption] is a doctrine about which we rarely hear. How often have you heard addresses or sermons on it? Why is it that, even as evangelical people, we neglect, and indeed seem to be unaware of, some of these most comforting and encouraging doctrines which are to be found in the Scriptures?'[12] If the theological meaning of adoption is neglected, how much more do we ignore the roots of adoption in the virgin birth?

Sonship, distinct from adoption, stands in a place of priority throughout the Bible, even revealed in the text before marriage or murder. As Adam is a son of God, made by God but not born to him, he is presented to us as God's son. However, as Webb noted, Adam's sonship is disputed by many, but a sure case is not hard to make both by reason and by revelation. Yet, if such a case cannot be made, perhaps adoption is even more necessary. Since Adam was not 'born' to God and if his creation by God did not establish his sonship, then another means is required. Whatever that means may be, it could be called 'adoption'. However, I want to make the case for sonship as created. God made Adam from the dust of the ground, a living creature, by the breath of his Spirit (Gen. 2:7). Made in God's own image, Adam is like God, and this 'likeness' constitutes his sonship. As Barth noted, 'To understand what must be said even concerning this model of all divine sonship, we must bear in mind that whenever Scripture speaks of sonship, in accordance with Oriental ideas and terminology, it has in view not merely the relationship of descent, but also the fatherly characteristics, determination, commission, and practical mode of life as continued in the sons or children concerned.'[13] In other words, in that culture, sonship consists primarily in image-bearing; descent is secondary. Webb notes, 'There are two terms in every relation – a *terminus a quo* [origin] and a *terminus ad quem* [terminus], in the boundaries between which lie certain relational facts. The two terms of the filial relation are persons – the father and the son.'[14] Of key significance in regard to adoption is that Webb's 'terms' are 'persons'. The latter person derives his life, in a wholly passive way, from the former, and the former exercises continued providence over the latter.[15] Though the terms 'father' and 'son' are missing from this text in Genesis, Adam's relationship qualifies as sonship.[16] Webb writes, 'When one person originates another, we call one father and the other son. The common language of men generally expresses the truth.'[17] We are further helped to perceive the meaning of the Genesis account by Luke. Reflecting on this personal Creator–created relationship, Luke himself asserts the sonship of Adam: looking back to Genesis, he closes Christ's lineage in this way: 'Adam, the son of God' (Luke 3:38). This is sonship. It would seem that no turn to adoption is necessary for Adam if this assessment is correct. Adam was God's son by creation.

While affirming explicit sonship in the text, we should also perceive adoption in the creation texts of Genesis 1 – 2. Adam, who was not birthed in the usual way of men, attaining sonship through birth, could also be said to have been adopted by God. The 'kiss' of the breath of God (Gen. 2:7) might be seen as God's adoption of this new creature into his family. This holy 'breath', a word used of the Holy Spirit and for speaking, is also a speech-act of God. That is, this 'kiss' was an act not only of creation, but also of imaging and claiming Adam as his own.[18] Peterson observes a connection between Genesis 2 and Romans 8: '[T]he Bible is a drama of epic proportions. Act one is set in the Garden of Eden with our first parents as co-stars. With Adam's fall the whole creation was plunged into the ruin of the curse. The setting of the drama was marred. Romans 8 teaches that there will be a change of scenery for the set of the last act of the drama of redemption.'[19] Here in this last act of the drama we await our adoption as sons, even though now we already cry out, 'Abba!' Could this connection between texts, which establishes a parallel between Adam and us with all creation, suggest that Adam, God's son by creation, was also 'adopted'? We must push deeper into the Old Testament.

Moving forward to Abraham, we encounter adoption, in effect, in Genesis 15. Abram was grief-stricken at the thought of having no heirs. In resignation, he suggested that his servant might serve as his heir. Here is the text:

> After these things the word of the LORD came to Abram in a vision: 'Fear not, Abram, I am your shield; your reward shall be very great.' But Abram said, 'O Lord GOD, what will you give me, for I continue childless, and the heir of my house is Eliezer of Damascus?' And Abram said, 'Behold, you have given me no offspring, and a member of my household will be my heir.' (Gen. 15:1–3)

In response to God's promise of a 'great reward', Abram falls into despair, anticipating that Eliezer will inherit this 'great reward', diminishing his enthusiasm. Even here, adoption is not explicit but it is implied in effect: one who is not a son by birth will gain the rights of sonship. And so Abram grieves because the 'great reward' is of no value to him if he has no son on whom to bestow this gift of God. But as the story progresses, God reveals that he will provide just what Abram desires: the promise of his own son. What is interesting is Abram's response. He trusts God, and Moses records the words that echo through time: 'And he believed the LORD [וְהֶאֱמִן בַּיהוָה], and he counted it to him as righteousness.' As we witness Abram's grief at childlessness and his anxiety as he anticipates a 'default adoption', we are not surprised. All those who long for a family of their own feel a deep sympathy with him. What does shock us, and what is intended to do so, is Abraham's faith. He did not receive the promise for many years, but he could say an enthusiastic 'Amen!' to YHWH's announcement that no adoption would be necessary.

There is an interesting anti-parallel between the stories of Abram and Joseph, the husband of Mary. For Abram, adoption was the problem, yet for Joseph it was the solution and the intention of God. For Abram, his faith was in God's promise of a yet-to-be-seen son by birth, yet for Joseph his faith was in God when he brought a son into his family who was not his own by birth. Both Joseph and Abram began in grief because of their assumptions (Gen. 15:2; Matt. 1:19), yet when corrected by God, both responded in faith, hope, and obedience. Abram awaited his son's birth (for another twenty-five years!), and Joseph married the virgin and (as was shown above) seems to have 'adopted' the newborn into his family – naming him Jesus (Matt. 1:24–25). His positional fatherhood is made clear by the genealogy of Jesus: 'Jacob the father of Joseph the husband of Mary, of whom Jesus was born' (Matt. 1:16). Something changed in Joseph just as something changed in Abram. Yet, in contrast with Abram's grief at an heir who was not of his own body, we witness Joseph's eager willingness to adopt an heir when God tells him to take Mary as his wife. The very flow of the text implies no further hesitation. There are many circumstances that may contribute to these divergent responses to 'adoption'. Perhaps Joseph's willingness stemmed from poverty, which, if so, meant he had no concerns about inheritance. Second, it may be that Joseph was a widower and that he brought children in from an earlier marriage, so was unconcerned about inheritance for himself. We do not know. But whatever the reasons behind their respective responses, we observe distinctly different human perspectives toward adoption. In the first story, it is a grief from which the man of God is freed, and, in the second, it is a calling to which he is ordered. In God's design, we read first of the grief of adoption, and later of the joyful obedience to adopt. In this regard, God has more in common with Joseph. If this is a correct perspective, it draws a comparison between God and Joseph, distinct from Abram. It was God and Joseph who were eager to adopt: God bringing Adam into his family, and Joseph bringing Jesus into his family.

Distinct from Abram's response, there are Old Testament images of adoption which are positive. Moses, whose death was ordered by Pharaoh before he was born (along with all other Hebrew males), was spared by adoption. In Exodus 2, Moses is preserved through the water by an ark, and then adopted by Pharaoh's daughter. Condemned to death, Moses was saved by adoption: 'and he became her son' (Exod. 2:10; Acts 7:21). By this adoption, God saved a people for himself. We may see this reflected in the words of Exodus 4:22: 'Then you shall say to Pharaoh, "Thus says the LORD, Israel is my firstborn son."' Ezekiel also has an image of adoption in one of his oracles: 'On the day you were born . . . you were cast out on the open field . . . on the day that you were born' (Ezek. 16:4–5). But God passed by and said, 'Live!' and adopted this child who had been exposed to die (vv. 6–7), later making her his bride (vv. 8–9). Here God is shown to adopt Israel. The image is not wholly clear, but Meir Malul argues rightly that this text is about a foundling, exposed to die, but adopted by God.[20] In both cases, these are very positive references to adoption, but less than sufficient grounds for the New Testament declaration of our adopted sonship.

We also see images in which God's people are offered sonship in the Old Testament. They seem to hold out a similar kind of restoration to that which Adam first experienced. Hosea 11:1–3 reads: 'When Israel was a child, I loved him, and out of Egypt I called my son . . . It was I who taught Ephraim to walk, I took them up by their arms'; and Isaiah 43:6: 'bring my sons from afar and my daughters from the end of the earth'; and Jeremiah 31:9: 'I am a father to Israel, and Ephraim is my firstborn.' Together, these and other texts are the antecedents for Paul, who wrote in 2 Corinthians 6:16–18:

> . . . as God said,
> 'I will make my dwelling among them and walk among them,
>   and I will be their God,
>   and they shall be my people.
> Therefore go out from their midst,
>   and be separate from them, says the Lord,
> and touch no unclean thing;
>   then I will welcome you,
> and I will be a father to you,
>   and you shall be sons and daughters to me,
> says the Lord Almighty.'

These images go beyond the sonship that is shared among all people in our descent from Adam, the inherited image of God tarnished by the fall. Romans 9:4 helps us here. Paul writes, 'They are Israelites, and to them belong *the adoption*, the glory, the covenants, the giving of the law, the worship, and the promises' (emphasis added). In context, these references point to the specific adoption (in emphasis above) of Abraham and his descendants by God for special duty. They are to be the womb of the Messiah! Even so, these images of God's people as his sons and daughters are not developed. They anticipate something not yet enjoyed or fully experienced. In fact, these sonship images are not named 'adoption' until Paul develops the idea in Romans 9.[21] So, while sonship with God and even adoption are not absent from the Old Testament, still the hope is not fully realized.

While it is offered and anticipated, this sonship, our adoption by God, is not yet fully experienced.

Yet it breaks out in a place of prominence in Paul's theology. Paul's two retrospective texts (Romans 9 and 2 Corinthians 6) are more explicit and exceed their antecedents by intensifying and narrowing the meaning of adoption. What has changed? What is the source of the sudden emphasis and visibility? Romans 8 is a focal adoption text and it provides the source for Paul's use of the word 'adoption' when he expresses his anguish for his own people in Romans 9, 10, and 11. He writes of those who no longer know condemnation, those who are in Jesus Christ: 'You have received the Spirit of adoption as sons, by whom we cry, "Abba! Father!" The Spirit himself bears witness with our spirit that we are children of God, and if children, then heirs – heirs of God and fellow heirs with Christ' (Rom. 8:15–17). We, the adopted, are the passive subject of the active and creative force of God: the Spirit. And this work is fulfilled: 'received' tells of the effect in us of God's completed action.[22] This adoption seems to be the basis for what follows: we are adopted into God's family in order that we may share in all the rights of our older brother: 'For those whom he foreknew he also predestined to be conformed to the image of his Son, in order that he might be the firstborn among many brothers . . . He who did not spare his own Son but gave him up for us all, how will he not also with him graciously give us all things?' (vv. 29,32). Here adoption is a metaphor for salvation in which we are made Jesus' brothers. But not merely a metaphor – if 'merely' and 'metaphor' can ever be used together! Adoption is the declaration of a new relationship that is not only familial, but also makes us legal heirs. Here is adoption in all its fullness breaking into the Word in the New Testament.

This celebration continues. Consider also Paul's letter to the Galatians, where he writes, 'Know then that it is those of faith who are the sons of Abraham' (Gal. 3:7). How is it that they become sons of Abraham? 'For in Christ Jesus you are all sons of God, through faith. For as many of you as were baptized into Christ have put on

Christ' (vv. 26,27). Peterson sees adoption in this text: 'And Paul infers that union with Christ is the cause of adoption. "You are all sons of God through faith in Christ Jesus, for all of you . . . have clothed yourselves with Christ"'.[23] This adoptionist understanding is vindicated when we read in Galatians 4, 'God sent forth his Son, born of woman, born under the law, to redeem those who were under the law, so that we might receive *adoption as sons*. And because you are sons, God has sent the Spirit of his Son into our hearts, crying, "Abba! Father!" So you are no longer a slave, but a son, and if a son, then an heir through God' (vv. 4–7, emphasis added).[24] We are God's sons (and daughters) by this personal and trinitarian adoption involving Father, Son, and Spirit. It is by adoption that we have legal standing in God's family.

In Ephesians, adoption is also emphasized. Paul begins by noting that we are children, but neither natural nor adopted; rather, we are children of wrath (Eph. 2:3). Yet by grace this is overturned! The remedy is declared already in the first chapter: '[God] predestined us for *adoption as sons* through Jesus Christ, according to the purpose of his will, to the praise of his glorious grace, with which he has blessed us in the Beloved' (1:5–6, emphasis added). So, by adoption, we are 'members of the household of God' (2:19). We are adopted into God's family and are seated with him on the throne – gaining the right to rule.[25]

For the reasons established by the above texts, we should also understand adoption to be the means by which those who are in Christ become members of Christ's family and inherit all that is Christ's, including the right to rule. We are now in Christ's family. Christ himself speaks of this new family in Mark 3: 'And his mother and his brothers came, and standing outside they sent to him and called him . . . And looking about at those who sat around him, he said, "Here are my mother and my brothers! For whoever does the will of God, he is my brother and sister and mother"' (Mark 3:31–35). Jesus defines the real family as the adoptive family of God in Christ. In Acts and in the epistles we also find abundant references to us as 'brothers' or 'sisters' in this new family which Christ has created. This is not merely a familial way to address each other, but a reality by God's Spirit: adoption. God has adopted many people into his family, brothers and sisters together. Adoption is taught and celebrated throughout the New Testament. But what is the antecedent?

If the Old Testament references to adoption were unfulfilled, what occurs to make adoption central to the theology of the New Testament as the image for union with Christ and the reception of God's Spirit? I propose that there may be no better candidate for an antecedent to our adoption into God's family than the virgin birth, which allows, even requires, Joseph to adopt Jesus into the right to rule. Perhaps this could even be asserted more strongly. Rather than adoption being metaphor alone, it may also be a forensic reality for our justification. As Christ stemmed from the bare 'root' of Jesse and sprouted as a new shoot, so do we. That is, like Jehoiachin and his descendants, we who are the progeny of Adam have been cut off from God with no hope. We are children of wrath. And God, as mirrored by the Medo-Persian kings, cannot revoke his word once given. The curse is spoken and we are cut off. We who are children of Adam are irreversibly condemned – at least in regard to our relationship to our head, Adam. But God has announced a plan to restore Adam through the Seed. He offers a new relationship where none could have been anticipated. How will he do this? It seems we can be adopted into God's family, even into the royal line, through one who gained the right to rule and who conquered! Christ inherited the right to rule from his adoptive father, Joseph, and then conquered by his life and death, and in his resurrection established his rule. Now by the Spirit we inherit all that Christ gained when we are adopted in Christ. So our adoption is fulfilled in Christ, and we are now also conquerors with him. But why is adoption the metaphor for our shared status with Christ as sons of God? Perhaps it is because of Jesus' antecedent adoption.

Many have noted that the virgin birth is missing from Paul, at least explicitly. And adoption is also missing, at least explicitly, from the gospels. This offers an interesting symmetry: the virgin birth is present in the gospels but missing in Paul's letters, while adoption is missing in the gospels but present in Paul's letters. Is adoption in this sense Paul's affirmation of the virgin birth? If so, adoption is more than metaphor; it is God's mystery displayed to us from its hiddenness in the Old Testament and its revelation in Christ. Adoption grounds our entry into his family, established by Christ's own human adoption into the royal line. Christ's adoption provides the antecedent theological metaphor by which we can understand our place in God's family. And through our adoption God has also again displayed his covenantal faithfulness. This is God's victory; it is his glory and it is our joy.

To Image Our Parthenogenesis by the Spirit

> The virgin birth of Christ is an unmistakable reminder that salvation can never come through human effort, but must be the work of God himself. Our salvation only comes about through the supernatural work of God. (Wayne Grudem)[26]

Having explored our adoption in Christ and like that of Christ, we now turn to our virgin birth, our parthenogenesis, like Christ's. While the word 'parthenogenesis' may be unfamiliar, the power and truth of it should never be far from us. It is this: we do not hold in ourselves the power of salvation – our birth into the family of God. In Genesis 1, the Spirit of God hovers over the deep. God speaks. The heavens and earth are created out of nothing. All that was made, God birthed, neither out of the tension between good and evil, nor between warring gods, but by the unopposed speech-act of God, anticipated by the brooding of the Spirit over the deep. Creation came as a kind of 'virgin birth' through God alone. One-sided. God-initiated. God-completed. Similarly, when the Spirit hovered over Mary, God announced by his angel what would be. Mary declared, 'Let it be to me according to your word.' Then the Son of God became a man by virginal conception: parthenogenesis, virginal genesis, virgin birth. And when the Spirit comes upon the elect, we, too, are given life. Parthenogenesis. We receive life from God alone, beyond human willing. John wrote in his gospel, 'But to all who did receive him, who believed in his name, he gave the right to become children of God, who were born, not of blood nor of the will of the flesh nor of the will of man, but of God' (John 1:12,13). This is our 'parthenogenesis', our spiritual virgin birth, in which we are born not of the will of any man or woman, certainly not of ourselves, but of God alone. Interestingly, certainly not without intention, John continues immediately with his nativity of Christ: 'And the Word became flesh' (v. 14). By association, is this John's 'virgin birth'?

This text in John 1:13 has an interesting textual variant that offers us some helpful confusion, further revealing the connection between the virgin birth of Christ and our spiritual birth. The text in the English Standard Version reads:

> He came to his own, and his own people did not receive him. But to all who did receive him, who believed in his name, he gave the right to become children of God, *who were born*, not of blood nor of the will of the flesh nor of the will of man, but of God. And the Word became flesh and dwelt among us, and we have seen his glory, glory as of the only Son from the Father, full of grace and truth (emphasis added).

This translation follows the best reading, in agreement with the NA-28 and USB critical Greek texts. Yet, while poorly attested, there is a variant that reads in verse 13, 'he was born' (singular) rather than 'who were born' (plural).[27] In other words, this variant offers the possibility that this phrase applies to Christ and his birth. If this variant were original, then John would be testifying to Christ's virgin birth: 'not of blood nor of the will of the flesh nor of the will of man, but of God'. John provides a three-fold denial of human agency either of our spiritual birth or, if the variant were original, for *that (singular) birth* – Christ's virgin birth. This peculiar and singular reading has support among only a very limited number of texts, none of them Greek (one Latin text and some in other early languages). However, John Pryor observes something quite interesting: there are significant early witnesses to the singular, including Irenaeus ('Against Heresies' 3.16.2; 3.19.2), Tertullian ('The Body of Christ', 19) and perhaps

Justin and Ignatius; and even later, in Latin (rather than Greek), Origen and Augustine. Such witnesses to the singular, in opposition to the weighty textual authority, is intriguing.[28] Pryor rightly concludes that 'there are insufficient grounds to overthrow the plural reading . . . [but] puzzles remain, particularly over the certainty of Irenaeus and Tertullian'.[29] It is precisely the puzzle that is interesting for this study: the fact that a barely attested variant seems to garner support among some significant Fathers and even some later scholars. Intentionally or unintentionally, Irenaeus and Tertullian and others adopt a reading that seems to reveal a bias to 'confuse' the relationship between our spiritual birth and Christ's virginal conception and birth as they read this gospel account. Are they discerning just such a congruence in the mind of the author, John? If so, John may have selected and used language which was intentionally descriptive of virgin birth in order to speak of our spiritual birth. Notice that he did so as his introduction to Christ's birth in verse 14, highlighting parthenogenesis for both.

In these few short introductory verses of John 1, three models of 'virgin birth' seem to come together: creation, our spiritual birth, and the incarnation. Each of these is a kind of parthenogenesis because the means of the birth (or genesis) comes not from within the material universe, but from God. That the virgin birth of Christ refutes ontological naturalism (a closed materialistic universe), we have considered earlier. But it is helpful to see that our own spiritual birth may be connected by that same hovering of God's Spirit, creating what is from that which is not, just as God did in creation and in the incarnation.

Barth draws a connection between the virgin birth and another miracle: resurrection and the empty tomb.

> Now it is no accident that for us the Virgin birth is paralleled by the miracle of which the Easter witness speaks, the miracle of the empty tomb. These two miracles belong together. They constitute as it were a single sign . . . The virgin birth denotes particularly the mystery of revelation . . . The mystery at the beginning becomes active and knowable . . . The same objective content is signified in the one case by the

miracle of the Virgin birth, in the other by the miracle of the empty tomb . . . The mystery at the beginning is the basis of the mystery at the end; and by the mystery of the end the mystery of the beginning becomes active and knowable.[30]

We saw the parallel above between the virgin birth and our spiritual birth; now we see a similar parallel between Jesus' resurrection and his birth. Returning to the former connection, Barth writes:

The Easter happening now described in this way is understood as a special act of God. It is certainly understood as a special act of God in the texts. But if it is restricted to the development of the faith of the disciples, what can this mean? A kind of *parthenogenesis* of faith without any external cause; without any cause in an external event which begets it? A faith which is in the true and proper sense other-worldly? . . . Well, nothing is impossible with God. Even according to the texts it was God, and God alone, who created the faith of the disciples – or the original form of faith which is here in question. And certainly God might have created this faith in the form of a *creatio ex nihilo* . . . If only we had one example in the Bible of God creating a faith out of nothing in this way! . . . But most definitely they do not demand it. Like the rest of the Bible, they speak of a foundation of faith which comes to those who have it, of a faith which is described in terms of its object.[31]

This needs a careful explanation. Barth is more than cautious here about linking the miracle of our Easter faith with the miracles of the virgin birth or creation. This is specifically because they arose *ex nihilo* – from nothing. Barth insists properly that our faith does not come out of *nothing*, but is grounded in the real and historical resurrection of Christ. We must never take special delight in paradox (faith from nothing), as if we enjoy paradox for paradox's sake. Our delight must be a love of truth. Yet, as we will see, this is not all that Barth says in this regard. There is yet a deep connection between the three creation miracles: creation, virgin birth, and new birth in Christ.

Indeed, our faith does arise out of nothing – at least nothing in ourselves. Human fear, not faith, was the first response to the advent of Christ and his resurrection. This is seen clearly in the apostles who were filled with fear on the very morning of the new creation, a fear which continued in those first terrible days after the resurrection. So clearly are we to see this fear that fear is the closing thought in the Gospel of Mark: 'And they went out and fled from the tomb, for trembling and astonishment had seized them, and they said nothing to anyone, for they were afraid' (Mark 16:8, the last verse of Mark as attested by the best manuscript evidence). In fact, in the Greek text, as in the English, 'fear' is the last word.[32] So, in God's people, even in his closest disciples, faith was born out of nothing which could be found in them. And the connection is in Christ. Just as Jesus was conceived out of nothing found in Mary alone – nothing in Mary or in all of nature – and just as the world was created out of nothing – nothing in nature itself – so also is faith born in us out of nothing in us. And with this, Barth agreed:

> In other words, if we are clear that with the Holy Spirit, God Himself is declared to be the author of the sign of the Virgin birth, then we know that in acknowledging the reality of this sign we have *a priori* renounced all understanding of it as a natural possibility, even when we are tempted to do so by a consideration so inviting as that of natural parthenogenesis, for example. We are already committed, then, to an acknowledgement of a pure divine beginning, and of a limiting of all natural possibilities, and this forbids us at the very outset to indulge in any reflection as to whether and how this reality can be anything else but a pure divine beginning.[33]

Here Barth uses an intriguing twist of phrase to catch our attention: 'natural parthenogenesis'. The text allows no room for such speculation, no room for human explanations for the genesis of the work of regeneration. And just as we have in the virgin birth a creation from nothing, a creation through the Holy Spirit, not by 'natural possibility' – so is our faith. This is creation from nothing in the human, nothing in nature. That established, Barth then connects the virgin birth of Christ with our birth as sons (and daughters) of God: 'Through the Holy Spirit and only through the Holy Spirit can man be there for God, be free for God's work on him, believe, be a recipient of His revelation, the object of the divine reconciliation . . . The freedom which the Holy Spirit gives in this understanding . . . is the freedom of the Church, of the children of God.'[34] This is the connection made by John himself in John 1:13.[35]

Just as the virgin birth was a work of parthenogenesis, while not unrelated to Mary's willingness to conceive (anti-parallel to Eve's willingness to conceive sin), it was a work of God alone. So also is our Easter faith.[36] Robert Candlish said in his Cunningham Lectures at Edinburgh in 1866, 'This is the work of the Spirit in regeneration. Is it not a work corresponding closely to his agency in the human birth of Christ? He generated Christ's humanity that he might continue to be the Son. He regenerates our humanity that we may become sons.'[37] He continues, with reference to John 1:12–14: 'I cannot but conclude that John intends to represent the sonship of those who receive "the Word", and believe on his name, as substantially the same relation with the sonship of "the Word" himself.'[38] Also Barth wrote, 'The virginity of Mary in the birth of the Lord is the denial, not of man in the presence of God, but of any power, attribute or capacity in him for God.'[39] Here, too, Barth is using the lens of the virgin birth to clarify the reality of our position before God. We are passive, dead, and God is active, alive. That we live in him, before him, has nothing to do with our capacity for him, but rather God's readiness to be known – so doing all of the work. It is parthenogenesis into sonship by faith.

John's affirmation of our parthenogenesis is not limited to John 1, but continues in John 3. We are virgin-born miracles of God's Spirit hovering over us and granting us life. So Jesus says to Nicodemus, 'The wind blows where it wishes, and you hear its sound, but you do not know where it comes from or where it goes. So it is with everyone who is born of the Spirit' (John 3:8). We do not give spiritual birth to ourselves, nor does any person will that new birth; rather, we are uniquely born of God, a parthenogenesis. We are virgin-born.

Barth further explains it in this way, connecting adoption and parthenogenesis: 'And this human nature, the only one we know and the only one there actually is, has of itself no capacity for being adopted by God's Word into unity with Himself. Upon this human nature a mystery must be wrought in order that this may be made possible. And this mystery must consist in its receiving the capacity for God which it does not possess. This mystery is signified by the *natus ex virgine* [born of a virgin].'[40] Here he makes the connection not only with our spiritual birth, but also with our adoption. Of course. We only become God's 'fellow workers' when God has accomplished this task entirely on his own for us. This is God's glory: a people who can delight in him. But it is not of our doing; this is God's glory also because it is all his work for us by his virgin incarnation, death on the cross, and resurrection. In Christ, we are virgin-born.

Doctrine: The Spirit's Call to Action

How do these two meanings instruct us? What is our doctrinal call to action? The text tells us that, like Christ, we are given rights which are ours not by birth but by adoption. Moreover, it tells us that, like Christ, we are virgin-born, without sufficient cause in ourselves. The meaning of this is that God has reached out to us. He has rescued his helpless enemies and made us part of his family. We would not be too far off-centre if we found our response in Paul himself in Romans 8. Here we first see that glory is connected to suffering: 'we are children of God, and if children, then heirs – heirs of God and fellow heirs with Christ, provided we suffer with him in order that we may also be glorified with him' (vv. 16,17). This is the hinge verse in Paul's argument in Romans 8, connecting God's work by his Spirit to adopt us, with the suffering we see now, to the glory we will share with Christ. He investigates this theme through the next section, writing, 'And not only the creation, but we ourselves, who have the firstfruits of the Spirit, groan inwardly as we wait eagerly for adoption as sons' (v. 23). Again he unites the ideas of Spirit, adoption, and the glory of our hope. He returns to this a third time in the verse that establishes what is often called the order of salvation, the *ordo salutis*, in vv. 28–30. We, the adopted brothers of the Firstborn, are from eternity foreknown and predestined and called, and are, within time, justified, and glorified. This is what William Perkins (1558–1602) called the Golden Chain – though while based on this text, his outline was a good deal more complex! Having just confirmed our adoption, Paul asks the question we are asking in this regard: 'What then shall we say [do!] to these things?' (v. 31). The answer then and now is to delight in the God who has adopted us and made us his own with no work from us. We will certainly conquer, not as a result of anything in us and not prevented by anything that is outside of us. For nothing outside of us – not tribulation, distress, persecution, famine, nakedness or danger or sword – can cut us off from the God who loves us in Christ. This truth makes us joyfully bold!

What response does John intend in us by declaring our parthenogenesis by God? The rest of his chapter, and the rest of his gospel, is a call to follow and know God, whom Christ makes known. It is precisely because we have been made like him that we can truly know him. In fact, Christ sums up his ministry in this way in John 17: 'this is eternal life, that they know you the only true God, and Jesus Christ whom you have sent' (v. 3). We are virgin-born by God in order to know God. This is our new ability, our vocation, and our joy.

Conclusion

The Virgin Birth: Theological Treasure

For the Son of God to be born of a virgin? I mean, really. To believe that he rose from the dead and bodily ascended into heaven? How utterly ridiculous. To believe in miracles? Or that those who obey God will rise from the dead and those who do not will burn in hell? God assumed from the beginning that the wise of the world would view Christians as fools . . . and he has not been disappointed. (Antonin Scalia)[1]

Still a Shibboleth . . . With Meaning

With a sharp wit, like that of St Paul, and the rhetoric of irony, Scalia calls Christians not to fear being considered fools by the educated of the world. Even as he does so, he reminds us again that the virgin birth is still a shibboleth. Even so, it is not the only Christian shibboleth, for we could also include all miracles and, of course, the 'problem' of hell. Shibboleths are provided by God, and so they are important as shibboleths. But, as we have seen, the virgin birth is not only a dividing point. I have tried to show that the virgin birth, as intended by the Evangelists, is a rich theological treasure:

- Preserving the full humanity and the full divinity of Christ
- Standing against the bias of naturalism
- Bestowing the kingdom on Christ
- Hiding information from the enemy
- Revealing Mary to be wiser than Eve
- 'Redeeming' women

- Celebrating adoption and our adoption in Christ
- Serving as an analogy for faith

This is hardly a complete list. These meanings, drawn from many sources (and, even more, drawn from many ways of thinking about theology – exegetical, historical, biblical, and systematic), are offered to call us to delight in God more deeply as we see his work in us through the Virgin-Born. This study should also whet our appetite to discover more of the treasure for us in God's glorious work through the virgin birth of our Lord and Saviour Jesus Christ. I am eager to learn more of the rich treasures of meaning that God will show my readers.

What If I Am Wrong?

Let me turn to the question on which I urge all of my graduate students to reflect: What if I am wrong? Authors have not only intent, but also responsibility. What if my thesis is favourably received, but is incorrect? How then might my thesis mislead the church? C.S. Lewis wrote, 'A new book is still on its trial and the amateur is not in a position to judge it. It has to be tested against the great body of Christian thought down the ages, and all its hidden implications (often unsuspected by the author himself) have to be brought to light.'[2] I may not be able to discern whether what I have written has lasting value and certainly not all the possible ways it might mislead, but I can at least consider this issue reflectively. Let me begin with two foundational positions which underlie this work. First, the Evangelists (and God) have perlocutionary intent of accomplished effects in the readers by all that they write, including the affirmation of the virgin birth. Said another way: regardless of our willingness to affirm or deny the truth content of the biblical authors' affirmation of the virgin birth, they wrote with an intent to effect action(s) in us, their readers. Second, and still foundational, I affirm that this authorial intent can be discerned (either correctly or incorrectly). That authors have meaning and intents and that their meaning can be discerned (rightly or wrongly) is argued by others. Depending upon this work of others, I am applying this thesis to the virgin birth. In doing so I hope to move my readers to reflect on the richness of the meaning of the virgin birth. I believe this to be not only solid ground and safe, but for those caught up in the defence or denial of the virgin birth – or perhaps for those who are weary of the discussion – this idea may allow reflection on the virgin birth in a productive way, a way in keeping with authorial intent. My specific proposal is to offer an assessment of many possible meanings of the virgin birth, the intentions of the Evangelists (and of God!) in the lives of the readers which flow from the virgin birth. In these I could mislead to the extent that I may be incorrect. In this book I have raised two meanings which I reject and eight meanings which I affirm. However, none of these ideas are novel; this is merely a collection and presentation of the work of others into one book for evaluation. Even as you, the reader, assess the validity of each of the meanings discussed here, I have spurred you into action that honours God: the study of his Word. I hope I have also whetted your appetite for continued investigations into the meanings intended for us by the Evangelists' affirmation of the virgin birth. It is more than *mere* shibboleth. Such an intent, and such an effect, cannot mislead. The greatest danger to us all is in how we do this work. Let Athanasius's warning be our guide: 'Similarly, anyone who wishes to understand the mind of the sacred writers must first cleanse his own life, and approach the saints by copying their deeds.'[3] Let us pursue God's mind in this purity of spirit. May the church truly follow God's Spirit, who leads us to enact the drama of his Word before the world, including that of the virgin birth.

One Last Meaning for Fools

> We are fools for Christ's sake. (1 Cor. 4:10)

As I close, there is one last meaning of the virgin birth which is worth reflecting on. It was raised by Karl Barth: we must be fools for Christ's sake; we must treat Jesus as Joseph did:

Though I am very averse to the development of 'Mariology', I am very inclined to 'Josephology', because in my eyes Joseph has played a role with respect to Christ which the church should adopt. I know that the Roman Church prefers to compare its role with the glorious role of Mary. It brings the Christian message to the world in the same way in which Mary has given us Christ. But the comparison deceives. *The church cannot give birth to the Redeemer; but it can and must serve him with humble and discrete enthusiasm.* And that was exactly the role that Joseph played, who always held himself in the background and left all fame to Jesus. Exactly that should be the role of the church, if we want the world to rediscover the glory of the Word of God.[4]

We are reminded that the virgin birth is indeed part of the offence of the gospel. Those who cling to the virgin born are fools. Joseph was the very first 'fool' in this regard. For only a *foolish man* would marry a woman who claimed to be with child from God alone. So Joseph 'foolishly' embraced Mary and the Virgin-Born with 'humble and discrete enthusiasm'. Unlike us, Joseph gave Christ his identity by adoption. Our case is the reverse: we receive our identity from Christ by adoption. Yet both for Joseph and for us, to embrace the Virgin-Born is to become fools before the world. Is this not parallel to the resurrected Christ? Only fools follow the Crucified as if he is alive! Indeed, if Christ is not raised, we too are dead and have no hope. To embrace the Virgin-Born is to embrace the Crucified.

I write this 'foolishness' as I sit in a coffee shop in an Islamic country in the Middle East. All around me are men in white and women in black who reject the One who caused himself to be born of a virgin, to be murdered, and to be resurrected. To name the Virgin-Born by the One Name, to call him our Lord and our God, is foolishness – worse, blasphemy. Yet in any country and in all of history, to truly embrace the Virgin-Born as God is dangerous to our reputations, and for many, for life itself. Yet we follow Joseph, who embraced the Virgin-Born as the unique Son of God, and looked the fool. We follow Paul, who embraced the Crucified as God raised from the dead – a fool if he was not raised. We are just such 'fools'. We embrace the Virgin-Born, the Crucified, who lives for ever, as if our lives depended on him!

Bibliography

Anderson, Gary A. *The Genesis of Perfection: Adam and Eve in Jewish and Christian Imagination* (Louisville, KY: Westminster John Knox, 2001).

Anonymous. *The Apocryphal New Testament: A Collection of Apocryphal Christian Literature in an English Translation*, ed. J.K. Elliott (London, UK: Oxford University Press, 1994).

———. 'The Epistle of Barnabas', trans. J.B. Lightfoot. *Early Christian Writings* http://www.earlychristianwritings.com/text/barnabas-lightfoot.html (accessed 30 Sep. 2014).

———. 'Protevangelium of James.' *Early Church Texts* http://www.earlychurchtexts.com/main/apocgosps/protoevangelium_of_james_01.shtml (accessed 23 Jan. 2015).

Anselm. 'On the Virginal Conception and Original Sin.' Pages 357–89 in *Anselm of Canterbury: The Major Works* (ed. Brian Davies and G.R. Evans; Oxford: Oxford University Press, 1998).

———. 'Why God Became Man.' Pages 260–356 in *Anselm of Canterbury: The Major Works* (ed. Brian Davies and G.R. Evans; Oxford: Oxford University Press, 1998).

Aquinas, Thomas. 'Summa Theologica', ed. Kevin Knight. *New Advent* (2008) www.newadvent.org/summa/ (accessed 24 Oct. 2014).

Ashwin-Siejkowski, Piotr. *The Apostles' Creed and Its Early Christian Context* (London: T&T Clark, 2009).

Athanasius. *On the Incarnation* (San Bernardino, CA: Fig, 2013).

Augustine. *The City of God* (ed. Thomas Merton, trans. Marcus Dods; New York: The Modern Library, 1993).

———. 'Reply to Faustus the Manichaean.' Pages 151–345 in *Augustine: The Writings Against the Manichaeans and Against the*

Donatists. Vol. 4 of *Nicene and Post-Nicene Fathers*, Series 1 (ed. Philip Schaff; Grand Rapids, MI: Christian Classics Ethereal Library, 2001).

―――――. 'The Enchiridion, Addressed to Laurentius; Being a Treatise on Faith, Hope and Love.' Pages 237–76 in *On the Holy Trinity; Doctrinal Treatises; Moral Treatises*. Vol. 3 of *Nicene and Post-Nicene Fathers*, Series 1 (ed. Philip Schaff; Grand Rapids, MI: Christian Classics Ethereal Library, 2001).

―――――. 'Letter CXXXVII. To Volusianus.' Pages 473–81 in *The Confessions and Letters of St Augustine, with a Sketch of His Life and Work*. Vol. 1 of *Nicene and Post-Nicene Fathers*, Series 1 (ed. Philip Schaff; Grand Rapids, MI: Christian Classics Ethereal Library, 2001).

―――――. 'On Marriage and Concupiscence.' Pages 258–309 in *St Augustine: Anti-Pelagian Writings*. Vol. 5 of *Nicene and Post-Nicene Fathers*, Series 1 (ed. Philip Schaff; Grand Rapids, MI: Christian Classics Ethereal Library, 2001).

―――――. 'On Rebuke and Grace.' Pages 468–92 in *St Augustine: Anti-Pelagian Writings*. Vol. 5 of *Nicene and Post-Nicene Fathers*, Series 1 (ed. Philip Schaff; Grand Rapids, MI: Christian Classics Ethereal Library, 2001).

―――――. 'On the Soul and Its Origin.' Pages 310–73 in *St Augustine: Anti-Pelagian Writings*. Vol. 5 of *Nicene and Post-Nicene Fathers*, Series 1 (ed. Philip Schaff; Grand Rapids, MI: Christian Classics Ethereal Library, 2001).

―――――. *Trinity* (trans. Edmund Hill, Brooklyn, NY: New City, 1991).

Badham, Paul. *The Contemporary Challenge of Modernist Theology* (Cardiff: University of Wales, 1998).

Barth, Karl. *Christmas* (trans. Bernard Citron; Edinburgh: Oliver & Boyd, 1959).

―――――. *Church Dogmatics* (Peabody, MA: Hendrickson, 2nd edn, 2010).

―――――. *Credo* (New York: Scribner's Sons, 1962).

———. *Dogmatics in Outline* (New York: Philosophical Library, 1949).

Beale, G.K. 'Eden, the Temple, and the Church's Mission in the New Creation.' *Journal of the Evangelical Theological Society* 48, no. 1 (2005): pp. 5–31.

———. *The Temple and the Church's Mission: A Biblical Theology of the Dwelling Place of God* (Downers Grove, IL: InterVarsity Academic, 2004).

Bettenson, Henry. *Documents of the Christian Church* (London: Oxford University Press, 1963).

Bird, Michael. 'Andrew Lincoln and the Virgin Conception.' *Euangelion* (2014), http://www.patheos.com/blogs/euangelion/2014/09/andrew-lincoln-and-the-virgin-conception/#ixzz3Li70AI9C (accessed 12 Dec. 2014).

Brown, Raymond E. 'The Problem of the Virginal Conception of Jesus.' *Theological Studies* 33, no. 1 (1972): pp. 3–34.

Brueggemann, Walter. *To Pluck Up, To Tear Down: A Commentary on the Book of Jeremiah 1 – 25* (Grand Rapids, MI: Eerdmans, 1988).

Bullinger, E.W. *The Witness of the Stars* (Grand Rapids, MI: Kregel, rev. edn, 1967).

Calvin, John. *Commentaries on the Book of the Prophet Jeremiah and the Lamentations* (trans. John Owen; Grand Rapids, MI: Eerdmans, 1950).

———. *Commentary on Genesis* (Colorado Springs, CO: CreateSpace Independent Publishing Platform, 2011).

———. *Commentary on Matthew, Mark, and Luke*. Calvin's Commentaries (Grand Rapids, MI: n.d.), http://www.ccel.org/ccel/calvin/calcom31.html (accessed 6 Aug. 2014).

Campenhausen, Hans von. *The Virgin Birth in the Theology of the Ancient Church* (Eugene, OR: Wipf & Stock, 2011).

Candlish, Robert S. *The Fatherhood of God: Being the First Course of the Cunningham Lectures Delivered before the New College, Edinburgh, in March, 1864* (Edinburgh: Black, 1866).

Cooke, Richard J. *Did Paul Know of the Virgin Birth? An Historical Study* (New York: MacMillan, 1926).

Crisp, Oliver D., and Fred Sanders, eds. *Christology, Ancient and Modern: Explorations in Constructive Dogmatics* (Grand Rapids, MI: Zondervan, 2013).

Crowther, Kathleen M. *Adam and Eve in the Protestant Reformation* (Cambridge: Cambridge University Press, 2010).

Dixon, A.C., ed. *The Fundamentals: A Testimony to the Truth* (Chicago: Testimony, 1910).

Eusebius of Caesarea. *Commentary on Isaiah* (ed. Jonathan J. Armstrong; Downers Grove, IL: InterVarsity Academic, 2013).

————. 'Church History.' Pages 73–403 in *Eusebius Pamphilius: Church History, Life of Constantine, Oration in Praise of Constantine*. Vol. 1 of *Nicene and Post-Nicene Fathers*, Series 2 (ed. Philip Schaff; Grand Rapids, MI: Christian Classics Ethereal Library, 2001).

————. *The History of the Church from Christ to Constantine* (Minneapolis, MN: Augsburg, 1965).

Falconer, Robert. '1 Timothy 2:14,15. Interpretative Notes'. *Journal of Biblical Literature* (1941): pp. 375–9.

Feinberg, Charles Lee. *Jeremiah, A Commentary* (Grand Rapids, MI: Zondervan, 1982).

Gentry, Peter. 'No One Holy Like the Lord.' *Midwestern Journal of Theology* 12, no. 1 (2013): pp. 17–38.

————, and Stephen J. Wellum. *Kingdom Through Covenant: A Biblical–Theological Understanding of the Covenants* (Wheaton, IL: Crossway, 2012).

Goroncy, Jason. 'Barth's Interpretation of the Virgin Birth: A Sign of Mystery.' *Journal of Theological Studies* 64, no. 2 (2013): pp. 818–23.

Grudem, Wayne A. *Systematic Theology: An Introduction to Biblical Doctrine* (Grand Rapids, MI: Zondervan, 1994).

Hawthorne, Gerald F. *The Presence and the Power: The Significance of the Holy Spirit in the Life and Ministry of Jesus* (Eugene, OR: Wipf & Stock, 1991).

Hick, John. *John Hick: An Autobiography* (Oxford: Oneworld, 2002).

Hubbard, Moyer. 'Kept Safe Through Childbearing: Maternal Mortality, Justification by Faith and the Social Setting of 1 Timothy 2:15.' *Journal of the Evangelical Theological Society* 55, no. 4 (2012): pp. 743–62.

Ignatius. 'Epistle to the Ephesians.' Pages 132–63 in *The Apostolic Fathers with Justin Martyr and Irenaeus*. Vol. 1 of *Ante-Nicene Fathers* (ed. Philip Schaff; Grand Rapids, MI: Christian Classics Ethereal Library, 2001).

―――. 'Epistle to the Magnesians.' Pages 164–81 in *The Apostolic Fathers with Justin Martyr and Irenaeus*. Vol. 1 of *Ante-Nicene Fathers* (ed. Philip Schaff; Grand Rapids, MI: Christian Classics Ethereal Library, 2001).

Irenaeus. 'Against Heresies.' Pages 306–567 in *The Apostolic Fathers with Justin Martyr and Irenaeus*. Vol. 1 of *Ante-Nicene Fathers* (ed. Philip Schaff; Grand Rapids, MI: Christian Classics Ethereal Library, 2001).

Jacobs, Alan. *Original Sin: A Cultural History* (New York: Harper One, 2008).

Justin Martyr. 'Apology, the First.' Pages 159–87 in *The Apostolic Fathers with Justin Martyr and Irenaeus*. Vol. 1 of *Ante-Nicene Fathers* (ed. Philip Schaff; Grand Rapids, MI: Christian Classics Ethereal Library, 2001).

―――. 'Dialogues with Trypho.' Pages 194–270 in *The Apostolic Fathers with Justin Martyr and Irenaeus*. Vol. 1 of *Ante-Nicene Fathers* (ed. Philip Schaff; Grand Rapids, MI: Christian Classics Ethereal Library, 2001).

Kidner, Derek. *The Message of Jeremiah: Against Wind and Tide* (Downers Grove, IL: InterVarsity Press, 1987).

Kierkegaard, Søren. *Fear and Trembling* (trans. Walter Lowrie; Princeton, NJ: Princeton University Press, 1941).

Kimberley, David. '1 Tim 2:15: A Possible Understanding of a Difficult Text.' *Journal of the Evangelical Theological Society* 35, no. 4 (1992): pp. 481–6.

Köstenberger, Andreas J. 'Women's God-Ordained Roles: An Interpretation of 1 Timothy 2:15.' *Bulletin for Biblical Research* 7 (1997): pp. 107–44.

Levin, Yigal. 'Jesus, "Son of God" and "Son of David": The "Adoption" of Jesus into the Davidic Line.' *Journal for the Study of the New Testament* 28, no. 4 (2006): pp. 415–42.

Lincoln, Andrew. *Born of a Virgin? Reconceiving Jesus in the Bible, Tradition, and Theology* (Grand Rapids, MI: Eerdmans, 2013).

Lloyd-Jones, David Martyn. *God the Holy Spirit* (Wheaton, IL: Crossway, 1997).

Longman, Tremper III. *Jeremiah, Lamentations* (Peabody, MA: Hendrickson, 2008).

Luther, Martin. *Commentary on Saint Paul's Epistle to the Galatians* (New York: Robert Carter, 1844).

———. *Lectures on Genesis*, Vol. 1. *Luther's Works* (ed. Jaroslav Pelikan; St Louis, MO: Concordia, 1958).

Machen, J. Gresham. *Virgin Birth of Christ* (Grand Rapids, MI: Baker, 1965).

Macleod, Donald. *The Person of Christ* (Downers Grove, IL: InterVarsity Press, 1998).

Malul, Meir. 'Adoption of Foundlings in the Bible and Mesopotamian Documents: A Study of Some Legal Metaphors in Ezekiel 1 – 7.' *Journal for the Study of the New Testament* 46 (1990): pp. 97–126.

Marshall, I. Howard. *The Gospel of Luke: A Commentary on the Greek Text* (Grand Rapids, MI: Eerdmans, 1978).

May, Herbert G. 'The Revised Standard Version in the Classroom.' *Journal of the American Academy of Religion* 21, no. 3 (1953): pp. 174–9.

McConville, J.G. *Judgment and Promise: An Interpretation of the Book of Jeremiah* (Leicester: Apollos, 1993).

Milliner, Matthew. 'Our Lady of Wheaton.' *First Things* http://www
.firstthings.com/article/2013/10/our-lady-of-wheaton (accessed
24 Oct. 2014).

Moo, Douglas J. 'What Does It Mean Not to Teach or Have Authority
Over Men? 1 Timothy 2:11–15'. Pages 179–93 in *Recovering Biblical
Manhood and Womanhood: A Response to Evangelical Feminism* (ed.
John Piper and Wayne Grudem; Wheaton, IL: Crossway, 2006).

Murphy, Bruce Allen. *Scalia: A Court of One* (New York: Simon &
Schuster, 2014).

Nagel, Thomas. *Mind and Cosmos: Why the Materialist Neo-Darwinian
Conception of Nature Is Almost Certainly False* (New York: Oxford
University Press, 2012).

Nettelhorst, R.P. 'Genealogy of Jesus.' *Journal of the Evangelical Theological Society* 31, no. 2 (1988): pp. 169–72.

Newbigin, Lesslie. *Proper Confidence: Faith, Doubt, and Certainty in
Christian Discipleship* (Grand Rapids, MI: Eerdmans, 1995).

Origen. 'Against Celsus.' Pages 395–669 in *Fathers of the Third Century: Tertullian, Part Fourth; Minucius Felix; Commodian; Origen,
Parts First and Second*. Vol. 4 of *Ante-Nicene Fathers* (ed. Philip
Schaff; Grand Rapids, MI: Christian Classics Ethereal Library,
2001).

———. 'Commentary on Matthew.' Pages 411–512 in *The Gospel of
Peter, The Diatessaron of Tatian, The Apocalypse of Peter, The Vision
of Paul, The Apocalypse of the Virgin and Sedrach, The Testament
of Abraham, The Acts of Xanthippe and Polyxena, The Narrative of
Zosimus, The Apology of Aristides, The Epistles of Clement (Complete
Text), Origen's Commentary on John, Books 1–10, and Commentary
on Matthew, Books 1, 2, and 10–14*. Vol. 9 of *Ante-Nicene Fathers*
(ed. Philip Schaff; Grand Rapids, MI: Christian Classics Ethereal
Library, 2001).

Orr, James. *The Virgin Birth of Christ: Being Lectures Delivered under
the Auspices of the Bible Teachers' Training School, New York, April,
1907* (New York: Scribner's Sons, 1907).

Packer, J.I. *Affirming the Apostles' Creed* (Wheaton, IL: Crossway, 2008).

Pannenberg, Wolfhart. *Jesus, God and Man* (Philadelphia, PA: Westminster, 1968).

———. *Systematic Theology* (Edinburgh: Black, 2004).

Payne, Philip Barton. *Man and Woman, One in Christ: An Exegetical and Theological Study of Paul's Letters* (Grand Rapids, MI: Zondervan, 2009).

Peterson, Robert A. 'Toward a Systematic Theology of Adoption.' *Presbyterian Journal* 27, no. 2 (2001): pp. 120–31.

Phillips, John A. *Eve, the History of an Idea* (San Francisco: Harper & Row, 1984).

Phipps, William E. *Supernaturalism in Christianity: Its Growth and Cure* (Macon, GA: Mercer University, 2007).

Pius IX, Pope. 'The Immaculate Conception: Ineffabilis Deus.' *Papal Encyclicals Online* http://www.papalencyclicals.net/Pius09/p9ineff.htm (accessed 1 Sep. 2013).

Plantinga, Alvin. *Where the Conflict Really Lies: Science, Religion, and Naturalism* (New York: Oxford University Press, 2011).

Polanyi, Michael. *Personal Knowledge: Towards a Post-Critical Philosophy* (Chicago: University of Chicago Press, 1974).

Polkinghorne, John. *Belief in God in an Age of Science* (New Haven, CT: Yale University Press, 2003).

———. *The Faith of a Physicist* (ed. Kevin Sharpe; Minneapolis, MN: Augsburg Fortress, 1st edn, 1996).

Porter, Stanley E. 'What Does It Mean to Be "Saved by Childbirth" (1 Timothy 2.15)?' *Journal for the Study of the New Testament* 15, no. 49 (1993): pp. 87–102.

Pryor, John W. 'Of the Virgin Birth or the Birth of Christians? The Text of John 1:13 Once More.' *Novum Testamentum* 27, no. 4 (1985): pp. 296–318.

Resch, Dustin. *Barth's Interpretation of the Virgin Birth: A Sign of Mystery* (Farnham: Ashgate, 2012).

Roberts, Mark. 'Woman Shall Be Saved: A Closer Look at 1 Timothy 2:15.' *The Reformed Journal* 33, no. 4 (1983): pp. 18–22.

Sailhamer, John H. *Genesis Unbound: A Provocative New Look at the Creation Account* (Sisters, OR: Multnomah, 1996).

Schaff, Philip, ed. *Ante-Nicene Fathers* (10 vols; Grand Rapids, MI: Christian Classics Ethereal Library, 2001).

———, ed. *Nicene and Post-Nicene Fathers*, Series 1 (14 vols; Grand Rapids, MI: Christian Classics Ethereal Library, 2001).

———, ed. *Nicene and Post-Nicene Fathers*, Series 2 (14 vols; Grand Rapids, MI: Christian Classics Ethereal Library, 2001).

Scheumann, Jesse. '"Saved Through the Childbirth of Christ" (1 Tim. 2:15): A Complementarian View of Eve's Creation, Fall, and Redemption' (unpublished paper, 2014).

Schleiermacher, Friedrich. *The Christian Faith* (Berkeley, CA: Apocryphile, 2011).

———. *On Religion: Speeches to Its Cultured Despisers* (New York: Ungar, 1955).

Schreiner, Thomas R. 'An Interpretation of 1 Timothy 2:9–15: A Dialogue with Scholarship.' Pages 85–120 in *Women in the Church: An Analysis and Application of 1 Timothy 2:9–15* (ed. Thomas R. Schreiner and Andreas J. Köstenberger; Grand Rapids, MI: Baker, 2005).

Selbie, W.B. *The Fatherhood of God* (London: Duckworth, 1st edn, 1936).

Shead, Andrew G. *A Mouth Full of Fire: The Word of God in the Words of Jeremiah* (Downers Grove, IL: Apollos, 2012).

Shepherd of Hermas. 'The Shepherd of Hermas', trans. J.B. Lightfoot. *Early Christian Writings* http://www.earlychristianwritings.com/text/shepherd-lightfoot.html (accessed 30 Sep. 2014).

Sigal, Gerald. *The Virgin Birth Myth: The Misconception of Jesus* (Bloomington, IN: Xlibris, 2013).

De Sousa, Rodrigo. 'Is the Choice of Παρθενος In LXX Isa. 7:14 Theologically Motivated?' *Journal of Semitic Studies* 53, no. 2 (2008): pp. 211–32.

Spencer, A.D. 'Eve at Ephesus.' *Journal of the Evangelical Theological Society* 17, no. 4 (1974): pp. 215–22.

Spurgeon, Andrew. '1 Timothy 2:13–15: Paul's Retelling of Genesis 2:4 – 4:1.' *Journal of the Evangelical Theological Society* 56, no. 3 (2013): pp. 543–56.

Strauss, David Friedrich. *The Life of Jesus, Critically Examined* (trans. George Eliot; New York: Macmillan, 1892).

Tabor, James D. 'Did Paul Invent the Virgin Birth?' *Huffington Post* (2012) http://www.huffingtonpost.com/james-d-tabor/did-paul-invent-the-virgin-birth_b_2355278.html (accessed 16 Aug. 2014).

Taylor, Justin. '5 Reasons the Virgin Birth of Jesus Is Important.' *The Gospel Coalition* http://www.thegospelcoalition.org/blogs/justintaylor/2015/02/26/5-reasons-the-virgin-birth-of-jesus-is-so-important/ (accessed 3 March 2015).

Tertullian. 'Against Marcion.' Pages 269–476 in *Latin Christianity: Its Founder, Tertullian.* Vol. 3 of *Ante-Nicene Fathers* (ed. Philip Schaff; Grand Rapids, MI: Christian Classics Ethereal Library, 2001).

———. 'Against Praxeas.' Pages 597–632 in *Latin Christianity: Its Founder, Tertullian.* Vol. 3 of *Ante-Nicene Fathers* (ed. Philip Schaff; Grand Rapids, MI: Christian Classics Ethereal Library, 2001).

———. 'On the Flesh of Christ.' Pages 521–44 in *Latin Christianity: Its Founder, Tertullian.* Vol. 3 of *Ante-Nicene Fathers* (ed. Philip Schaff; Grand Rapids, MI: Christian Classics Ethereal Library, 2001).

Vanhoozer, Kevin J. *Is There a Meaning in This Text? The Bible, The Reader and the Morality of Knowledge* (Grand Rapids, MI: Zondervan, 1998).

Waetjen, Herman C. 'The Genealogy as the Key to the Gospel according to Matthew.' *Journal of Biblical Literature* 95, no. 2 (1976): pp. 205–30.

Wall, Robert. '1 Timothy 2:9–15 Reconsidered (Again)'. *Bulletin for Biblical Research* 14, no. 1 (2004): pp. 81–103.

Walton, John H. 'Isa 7:14: What's in a Name?' *Journal of the Evangelical Theological Society* 30, no. 3 (1987): pp. 289–306.

Ware, Bruce. 'The Man Christ Jesus.' *Journal of the Evangelical Theological Society* 53, no. 1 (2010): pp. 5–18.

Webb, R.A. *The Reformed Doctrine of Adoption* (Grand Rapids, MI: Eerdmans, 1947).

Wegner, Paul. 'How Many Virgin Births Are There in the Bible (Isaiah 7:14): A Prophetic Pattern Approach.' *Journal of the Evangelical Theological Society* 54, no. 3 (2011): pp. 467–84.

Wenham, Gordon John. *Genesis 1 – 15*. Word Biblical Commentary (ed. David Allen Hubbard and Glenn W. Barker; Waco, TX: Word, 1987).

Wright, Christopher J. H. *The Message of Jeremiah* (Downers Grove, IL: InterVarsity Academic, 2014).

Wright, N.T. 'God's Way of Acting.' *Christian Century* 115, no. 35 (1998): pp. 1215–17.

Youngblood, Ronald. *The Book of Genesis: An Introductory Commentary* (Grand Rapids, MI: Baker, 2nd edn, 1991).

Endnotes

Preface

[1] Augustine, *Trinity* (Brooklyn, NY: New City, 1991), 1.5–6, pp. 68–9.

Introduction

[1] N.T. Wright, 'God's Way of Acting', *Christian Century* 115, no. 35 (1998): p. 1215. He continues, 'Likewise, if you believe the Bible is "true", you will believe the birth stories; if you don't, you won't. Again, the birth stories are insignificant in themselves; they function as a test for beliefs about the Bible.'

[2] Friedrich Schleiermacher, *The Christian Faith* (Berkeley, CA: Apocryphile, 2011), sec. 97, pp. 403–4.

[3] The rest of the story can be found in Judg. 11 – 12.

[4] The Latin reads, 'Credo in Deum Patrem omnipotentem, Creatorem caeli et terrae, et in Jesum Christum, Filium Eius unicum, Dominum nostrum, *qui conceptus est de Spiritu Sancto, natus ex Maria Virgine*, passus sub Pontio Pilato, crucifixus, mortuus, et sepultus, descendit ad inferos, tertia die resurrexit a mortuis, ascendit ad caelos, sedet ad dexteram Patris omnipotentis, inde venturus est iudicare vivos et mortuos. Credo in Spiritum Sanctum, sanctam Ecclsiam catholicam, sanctorum communionem, remissionem peccatorum, carnis resurrectionem, vitam aeternam. Amen' (Karl Barth, *Credo* [New York: Scribner's Sons, 1962], p. xvii). (I have emphasized the words which affirm the virginal conception and birth.) How old, how 'apostolic', is this creed? The exact age of the creed is debated. The earliest complete text dates from the eighth century, but most scholars believe it to be much older, perhaps dating from the second century. But the exact age is less important than the acknowledgement and weight that this ancient creed has over a wide spectrum of Christian traditions. This helps us appreciate the weight it gives to the virgin birth.

5 Some have observed that the issue is better stated as 'virginal conception' rather than 'virgin birth' (e.g. Raymond E. Brown, 'The Problem of the Virginal Conception of Jesus', *Theological Studies*, 33, no. 1 (1972): pp. 3–34). This observation has some value in precision because it focuses on the miracle as declared by the gospels of Matthew (1:18–25) and Luke (1:26–37; 2:1–7). I address the terminology later in the Introduction.

6 J. Gresham Machen, *Virgin Birth of Christ* (Grand Rapids, MI: Baker, 1965), p. 1.

7 David Friedrich Strauss, *The Life of Jesus, Critically Examined* (trans. George Eliot; New York: Macmillan, 1892), p. 130.

8 Paul Badham, *The Contemporary Challenge of Modernist Theology* (Cardiff: University of Wales, 1998), p. 6. Also, Wayne Grudem wrote, 'It has been common, at least in previous generations, for those who do not accept the complete truthfulness of Scripture to deny the doctrine of the virgin birth of Christ' (*Systematic Theology: An Introduction to Biblical Doctrine* [Grand Rapids, MI: Zondervan, 1994], p. 532).

9 Of course, not everyone believes that the virgin birth should be a fault line. William E. Phipps acknowledges that it is so, but suggests, 'Both sides of the dispute have fallen into the fallacy of false disjunction, that is, thinking that a proposition must be either true or false, and little progress has been made toward a common understanding. Seldom heard is a third position, gained from an understanding of the outlook on conception that permeated ancient Mediterranean cultures. This viewpoint, which might be called "dual parenthood", avoids the either/or mode of thinking' (William E. Phipps, *Supernaturalism in Christianity: Its Growth and Cure* [Macon, GA: Mercer University, 2007], p. 18). His precise proposal is not as important as the fact that he raised such a possibility – one seldom (if ever) appreciated. In brief, his proposal suggests parents as 'procreators' who act on behalf of the Creator in childbirth, making all births 'dual parenthood' with divinity. Also, this reasoning effectively makes all births virgin births. But this thinking seems unhelpful in the controversy between naturalism and supernaturalism, for this difference is not apparent, but deep and not at all unimportant. Indeed, the virgin birth is not the issue, but a point of discussion between camps over this more significant issue. But even more significant in regard to the virgin birth is that this proposal is unhelpful because the biblical authors who wrote of the virgin birth intended to affirm something unique and meaningful – even if it could be shown that the virgin birth was unhistorical. Yet, on this proposal, all human births are dual projects between God and two human parents, and all are redefined as virgin births. For example, he writes, 'Dual parenthood

is an appropriate label for the inclusive way in which African and Asian cultures have recognized the presence of a god or goddess in any human conception' (p. 19). So this proposal seems to exclude that uniqueness, a uniqueness clearly intended by the biblical authors. It fails, then, not for cultural reasons (as he proposes), nor because it denies the traditional understanding of the virgin birth, but because it does not fit the intent of the authors, quite apart from historical facts.

10 John Hick, *John Hick: An Autobiography* (Oxford: Oneworld, 2002), p. 125. Shortly after this, he engaged in a debate with C.F.H. Henry. In the end, the presbytery affirmed his carefully worded statement.

11 Herbert G. May, 'The Revised Standard Version in the Classroom', *Journal of the American Academy of Religion* 21, no. 3 (1953): p. 174.

12 It is worth noting that in Matt. 1:23, the RSV translated Matthew's Greek citation of Isa. 7:14, *parthenos,* as 'virgin'.

13 Still, a few examples will serve here in the event that the reader wants to pursue this issue further. J.G. Machen has written the classic volume. In his *The Virgin Birth of Christ* (an exposition based on his Thomas Smyth Lectures of 1927), he argues several key points, including: that the extra-canonical affirmation of the virgin birth in the Creed can be traced to the early second century; that the gospel narratives of the virgin birth have integrity; and that the silence of much of the New Testament is not inconsistent with the fact of the virgin birth as attested by those in a position to do so. He also argues against the theory of its derivation from pagan myth on the basis that there is little agreement among those who attempt this path. Others – there are now a great company – reject the virgin birth. For example, Wolfhart Pannenberg speaks of it as 'the legend [which] stands in an irreconcilable contradiction to the Christology of the incarnation of the pre-existent Son of God found in Paul and John' (Wolfhart Pannenberg, *Jesus, God and Man* [Philadelphia, PA: Westminster, 1968], p. 143). This view brings the rejection of the virgin birth into the ranks of those who also affirm the Bible. It is worth saying here that his objection has little substance and may be based on an over-rationalistic understanding of the assertion intended by Luke (and Matthew). In fact, their assertion of the incarnation is not 'irreconcilable' with divine Sonship for it is not 'first established in time', but only exposed in time. The incarnation is not the sonship, but stands in relation to sonship. However, a full investigation of Pannenberg or the objections of others to the virgin birth is not within the scope of this project. But of course, Pannenberg, apart from his specific objections, now stands with the majority. More recently, and from outside the church, Gerald

Sigal wrote *The Virgin Birth Myth: The Misconception of Jesus*, a masterful play on words. He portrayed the virgin birth as a failed project of two gospel writers: a spin on the facts intended to make them acceptable to a Hellenistic audience and fit certain theological goals. More on Sigal later.

[14] Of course, as cited here, there exist such works as 'On Marriage and Concupiscence' by Augustine and similar treatments in which the virgin birth is used to support a theological point. This is not the same as a treatment on the virgin birth's theology and meaning for the church.

[15] The 'virginal conception' is adopted mostly among scholars for precision. It is also used to avoid any possible confusion of the doctrine of the eternal virginity of Mary with the virginity of Mary at the birth of Jesus.

1. The Virgin Birth: A Short History from the Early Church Fathers to the Modernist Movement

[1] Karl Barth, *Credo* (New York: Scribner's Sons, 1962), p. 70.

[2] Hans von Campenhausen, *The Virgin Birth in the Theology of the Ancient Church* (Eugene, OR: Wipf & Stock, 2011), p. 16. The text he is discussing here is John 1:12,13 (which we will consider later) but his point is generally applicable.

[3] Gerald Sigal, *The Virgin Birth Myth: The Misconception of Jesus* (Bloomington, IN: Xlibris, 2013), p. 15. As an interesting historical note, this is an argument which appeared earlier in the work of Anselm. He wrote, 'God can create a human being by four methods. To be specific: he can do this either from a man and a woman together, as the usual practice demonstrates, or from neither a man nor a woman, as in the case of Adam's creation, or from a man without a woman, as in the creation of Eve, or from a woman without a man – which he has not yet done . . . It has been kept in reserve for the very undertaking which we have in mind' (Anselm, 'Why God Became Man', in *Anselm of Canterbury: The Major Works* [ed. Brian Davies and G.R. Evans; Oxford: Oxford University Press, 1998], 1.8, p. 323).

[4] Andrew Lincoln, *Born of a Virgin? Reconceiving Jesus in the Bible, Tradition, and Theology* (Grand Rapids, MI: Eerdmans, 2013), p. ix. In the introduction, he affirms his exclusion from interviews with an exclamation point (!) – a bit of a sore point for him, perhaps.

[5] Lincoln, *Born of a Virgin?*, p. 95.

[6] Lincoln writes, 'The main similarity between Luke's account and ancient biographies is the subject's conception from the gods without a human

father. In only a few of the Graeco-Roman stories of the conception of heroes of sons of god is the human mother a virgin' (*Born of a Virgin?*, p. 112).

7   Michael Bird writes of Lincoln's approach: 'While I can "imagine" that, I just don't think that is what the Evangelists were doing, nor is it what they were perceived to be doing in the early church' (Michael Bird, 'Andrew Lincoln and the Virgin Conception', *Euangelion* [2014], http://www. patheos.com/blogs/euangelion/2014/09/andrew-lincoln-and-the-virgin-conception/#ixzz3Li70AI9C [accessed 12 Dec. 2014]).

8   J. Gresham Machen, *Virgin Birth of Christ* (Grand Rapids, MI: Baker, 1965), p. 322.

9   Machen, *Virgin Birth*, p. 338. It would be satisfying to explore Machen's argument further in order to validate or refute his claim, yet that is not the focus of this work. I will leave that exploration to the reader.

10   N.T. Wright, 'God's Way of Acting', *Christian Century* 115, no. 35 (1998): p. 1217.

11   Let me give a summary of his very interesting argument. His book is *The Witness of the Stars* (Grand Rapids, MI: Kregel, rev. edn, 1967). He founds his argument upon Gen. 3:15, but also upon Ps. 19, in which he understands the terms to be astronomical: 'the heavens contain a revelation from God' (p. 6). He finds a supporting text in Ps. 147:4, where God names the stars – or is it patterns of stars? He also uses Job 9:9; Isa. 13:10; Amos 5:8; and many other references (p. 8). He points out that in all the nations of the world, the signs in the stars have the same names (p. 9). While preserving the order – as all civilizations have done – he changes the starting point (p. 16). He understands Virgo as the first of the signs, referring to the first coming of the Messiah. In Libra, the second sign, he sees the crux, as showing the cross endured and Lupus slain reflecting the slaying of Christ. In Scorpio, he sees the serpent, trodden underfoot. In Sagittarius, he sees the two-natured triumph of the Redeemer. The story continues through the signs until Leo, the last sign in his ordering, who comes in conquering triumph. He understands these signs to have been written on the banners of each of the tribes of Israel – one on each banner, as they encamped around the tabernacle. He says, 'these pictures were designed to preserve, expound, and perpetuate the one first great promise and prophecy of Genesis 3:15' (p. 19). He concludes: 'such is the content of the wondrous book that is written in the heavens' (p. 27). But it was sadly distorted in Babylon: 'After the Revelation came to be written down in the Scripture, there was not the same need for the preservation of the Heavenly Volume. And after the nations had lost the original meaning

of the pictures, they invented a meaning out of the vain imagination of the thoughts of their hearts' (p. 22). While I see no way to adjudicate his argument in such a way that would declare it certain, it is nonetheless intriguing and does not conflict with the biblical message. Indeed, he certainly is able to tell God's story by the signs in the stars. But if it is true, it would argue that God's story of virgin birth is the first story, antecedent to all the others.

[12] Examples abound that show the early church was aware of this reality, including: Origen, 'Against Celsus', in *Fathers of the Third Century: Tertullian, Part Fourth; Minucius Felix; Commodian; Origen, Parts First and Second* (vol. 4 of *Ante-Nicene Fathers* (*ANF*); ed. Philip Schaff; Grand Rapids, MI: Christian Classics Ethereal Library, 2001), 6.73; Justin Martyr, 'Apology, the First', in *The Apostolic Fathers with Justin Martyr and Irenaeus* (vol. 1 of *ANF*), ch. 33; 'Dialogues with Trypho', in *The Apostolic Fathers with Justin Martyr and Irenaeus*, ch. 66; Ignatius, 'Epistle to the Magnesians', in *The Apostolic Fathers with Justin Martyr and Irenaeus*, ch. 11; and Irenaeus, 'Against Heresies', in *The Apostolic Fathers with Justin Martyr and Irenaeus*, 3.19.

[13] 'ἰδοὺ ἡ παρθένος', Isa. 7:14, LXX, Bibleworks 9.x.

[14] 'הִנֵּה הָעַלְמָה', Isa. 7:14, WTT, Bibleworks 9.x.

[15] John H. Walton, 'Isa 7:14: What's in a Name?', *JETS* 30, no. 3 (1987): p. 292.

[16] Sigal, *Virgin Birth Myth*, p. 44. Sigal also notes that the presence of the definite article, which appears with *'almah* in the Hebrew text of Isa. 7:14, indicates a reference to a specific person, rather than an emphasis of a state, unmarried or young or even of virginity because she is unmarried at the time of the prophecy. Rather, the article indicates that she is the prophet's wife or espoused. Many have rightly noticed this reality as an understanding of Isaiah's intent.

[17] Sigal, *Virgin Birth Myth*, p. 50. He writes, 'This is inconsistent not only with the Hebrew *almah*, but with the Septuagint's use of *parthenos* in Isaiah 7:14. Matthew uses *parthenos* in a manner which conforms to the pagan divine birth-myth motif.'

[18] He writes, 'These references indicate that with few exceptions *parthenos*, used in the Septuagint, means "virgin" in the exact sense of the word' (*Virgin Birth Myth*, p. 31). He also considered the specific translations of *'almah* by the Septuagint: 'Of the scriptural verses where *almah* is used, Genesis 24:43, Exodus 2:8, Isaiah 7:14, Psalm 68:26, Proverbs 30:19, Song of Songs 1:3, 6:8, only the Septuagint's Genesis 24:43 and Isaiah 7:14 translate *almah* as *parthenos*' (p. 35).

[19] The textual evidence and linguistic scholarship is univocal in this regard: the Septuagint's translation of *'almah* by *parthenos* does not indicate that they intended the concept of 'virgin' on the basis of their word choice alone. Rodrigo de Sousa references James Barr and notes that especially in Gen. and Deut., *parthenos* is used to translate 'young female' and even 'young female servant'. Also, studies of the use of *parthenos* from 150 BCE until 70 CE show a clear development from the general use: 'a young woman of marriageable age' to 'virgin' (Paul Wegner, 'How Many Virgin Births Are There in the Bible (Isaiah 7:14): A Prophetic Pattern Approach', *JETS* 54, no. 3 [2011]: p. 482). This finding is in agreement with the article on *parthenos* in the *Theological Dictionary of the New Testament*. This fact undermines any attempt to assert an intent on the part of the translators of the Septuagint to affirm a virgin birth in Isa. 7:14 by their choice of *parthenos* (Rodrigo de Sousa, 'Is the Choice of Παρθενος In LXX Isa. 7:14 Theologically Motivated?', *Journal of Semitic Studies* 53, no. 2 [2008]: p. 231). Further, a study of all the occurrences of *'almah* and *bethulah* in the OT that are translated by *parthenos* does not resolve the issue. The Greek *parthenos* could be used for the Hebrew *bethulah* or *'almah* at the time the Septuagint was translated.

[20] It is worth noting here that Matthew's intent is clear, but the translator's intent in regard to Isa. is not, even in choosing *parthenos*. The translator could simply be saying that a woman, now a virgin, will soon conceive and bear a son. On the other hand, Matthew is clear, not because of lexical considerations, but because of narrative considerations.

[21] Sigal objects to the idea of greater fulfilment in Christ. Noting that some Christians insist on a greater fulfilment in Matt., independent of what was meant and happened in Isa., he argues that they come up against context in Isa. 7:15,16: 'Who were the two kings to be forsaken before he "shall know to refuse the evil, and choose the good"? No such fulfillment took place in Jesus' day' (Sigal, *Virgin Birth Myth*, p. 57).

[22] Walton, 'Isa 7:14', p. 303.

[23] Gerald F. Hawthorne, *The Presence and the Power: The Significance of the Holy Spirit in the Life and Ministry of Jesus* (Eugene, OR: Wipf & Stock, 1991), p. 63.

[24] Donald Macleod, *The Person of Christ* (Downers Grove, IL: InterVarsity Press, 1998), p. 26.

[25] There would be value in exploring Matthew's use of 'fulfilled' ($\pi\lambda\eta\rho\delta\omega$) – a use that is notably flexible. His use here may be typological, or a didactic point from Christ's own teaching (see Luke 24:27–45 and John 5:46),

or perhaps a specific revelation of the Holy Spirit (1 Pet. 1:10–12) or another use. But such an investigation is not the focus of this study.

26 Macleod observed that, while the text of John 1:12 is not *about* Christ, it is brought to John's mind by the close context with his nativity (1:14) and the teaching of the virgin birth. Macleod writes, 'If the story of the virgin birth were legendary, John, writing thirty or forty years afterwards, would surely have denied it and set the record straight. He does not hesitate to correct other erroneous traditions (such as that Jesus had said that John himself would not die, John 21:23)' (Macleod, *Person of Christ*, p. 30). Abraham Kuyper also wrote of John 1:13, 'John undoubtedly borrowed this glorious description of our higher birth from the extraordinary act of God which scintillates in the conception and birth of Christ' (cited in Macleod, *Person of Christ*, p. 38).

27 A.C. Dixon, ed., *The Fundamentals: A Testimony to the Truth* (Chicago: Testimony, 1910), p. 18. Richard J. Cooke also explored this in depth: *Did Paul Know of the Virgin Birth? An Historical Study* (New York: MacMillan, 1926).

28 Sigal asserts that Paul did oppose the idea of the virgin birth. He writes, 'It appears that Paul was familiar with the virginal conception stories and speculations concerning Jesus' ancestry and rejected them! Paul cautions Timothy not to occupy himself "with myths and endless genealogies which promote speculations rather than the divine training that is in faith" (1 Timothy 1:4)' (*Virgin Birth Myth*, p. 59). But as intriguing as this proposal is, in the end, it is without foundation.

29 James D. Tabor, 'Did Paul Invent the Virgin Birth?', *Huffington Post* (2012) http://www.huffingtonpost.com/james-d-tabor/did-paul-invent-the-virgin-birth_b_2355278.html (accessed 16 Aug. 2014). It's worth noting that Machen observed this as well, citing Kattenbusch in 1900. Here the suggestion is made that at a former stage, Paul's teaching on the close association of Christ with the Holy Spirit resulted in the suggestion that he was conceived by the Holy Spirit, and so in Luke. Later, his teaching on Christ as the second Adam led to the idea that he was conceived, as was Adam, from only one human 'parent', and so the tradition of Matt. (Machen, *Virgin Birth*, p. 317).

30 Von Campenhausen, *The Virgin Birth in the Theology of the Ancient Church*, p. 19.

31 'The Shepherd of Hermas', trans. J.B. Lightfoot, *Early Christian Writings* http://www.earlychristianwritings.com/text/shepherd-lightfoot.html (accessed 30 Sep. 2014), 89.5 and 90.5.

32 'Shepherd of Hermas', 89.5 and 90.5.

[33] The author of 'Shepherd' also writes, confusingly, that the servant in this fifth parable is the Son of God (58:2), and also, 'He therefore took the son as advisor' (59:7). This assertion has a ring of adoptionism. Yet, against that judgement, it should be noted that earlier the author wrote, 'So he called his beloved son, who was his heir, and the friends who were his advisers, and told them what he had commanded his servant, and how much he had found done. And they rejoiced with the servant at the testimony which his master had borne to him' (55:6). Is he identifying the son as the servant here, or differentiating them? Still, nothing here requires, or even sets the expectation of, a discussion of the virgin birth.

[34] St Barnabas, 'The Epistle of Barnabas', trans. J.B. Lightfoot, *Early Christian Writings* http://www.earlychristianwritings.com/text/barnabas-lightfoot.html (accessed 30 Sep. 2014), 6.9.

[35] 'The Epistle of Barnabas', 8.5.

[36] Eusebius of Caesarea, *The History of the Church from Christ to Constantine* (Minneapolis, MN: Augsburg, 1965), 6.12, 190.

[37] Ignatius, *Ephesians* 18.2–19.1, as cited in Machen, *Virgin Birth*, p. 6 (n. 16).

[38] Machen, *Virgin Birth*, p. 7.

[39] In contrast with the OT Apocrypha, often included with the canonical collections, the NT Apocrypha and Pseudepigrapha ('false writings') are rejected by the church canon. The latter is a class of literature which is distinct because of a late date of authorship.

[40] Anonymous, *The Apocryphal New Testament: A Collection of Apocryphal Christian Literature in an English Translation*, ed. J.K. Elliott (London, UK: Oxford University Press, 1994), p. 318 (section 93).

[41] The bracketed material is original to this translation: Justin Martyr, 'Dialogues with Trypho', ch. 43. To this statement we could add his 'Apology', which he began, 'And hear again how Isaiah in express words foretold that He [Jesus] should be born of a virgin'; he continued in a similar fashion to make his case clear ('Apology, the First', ch. 33).

[42] Irenaeus, 'Against Heresies', 1.10.1.

[43] Tertullian, 'Against Praxeas', in *Latin Christianity: Its Founder, Tertullian* (vol. 3 of *ANF*), 5.9.2.

[44] Machen, *Virgin Birth*, p. 5.

[45] All of these creedal citations are from Henry Bettenson, *Documents of the Christian Church* (London: Oxford University Press, 1963), pp. 23–6.

[46] Among other texts, his exposition of Isa. 7:14, which showed nuanced care with the Hebrew and the Septuagint, affirmed his position that Mary was a virgin and gave birth to the Messiah as a virgin (Eusebius of Caesarea, *Commentary on Isaiah* [ed. Jonathan J. Armstrong; Downers Grove, IL: IVP Academic, 2013], pp. 37–8).

[47] Irenaeus, 'Against Heresies', 1.26.2.

[48] Irenaeus, 'Against Heresies', 5.1.3.

[49] Eusebius of Caesarea, 'Church History', in *Eusebius Pamphilius: Church History, Life of Constantine, Oration in Praise of Constantine* (vol. 1 of *Nicene and Post-Nicene Fathers*, Series 2; ed. Philip Schaff; Grand Rapids, MI: Christian Classics Ethereal Library, 2001), 3.27.1–4.

[50] It is worth noting that Eusebius allows that some of the Ebionites actually affirmed the virgin birth. He writes, '[They] did not deny that the Lord was born of a virgin and of the Holy Spirit. But . . . they also refused to acknowledge that he pre-existed' ('Church History', 3.27.3). Machen explains that both Origen and Eusebius wrongly attributed the name of Ebionites to the sect who accepted the virgin birth (Machen, *Virgin Birth*, p. 36).

[51] Athanasius writes rather unambiguously, 'Prophets foretold the marvel of the Virgin and of the Birth from her, saying, Behold, a virgin shall conceive and bear a son, and they shall call his name *"Emmanuel"*, which means *"God is with us"* [Isaiah 7:14]' (*On the Incarnation* [San Bernardino, CA: Fig, 2013], sec. 33).

[52] Augustine, *Trinity* (Brooklyn, NY: New City, 1991), 8.7, p. 247.

[53] David Friedrich Strauss, *The Life of Christ, Critically Examined* (trans. George Eliot; New York: MacMillan, 1892), p. 140.

[54] Strauss, *The Life of Christ*, p. 130. As cited earlier in the Introduction, Strauss wrote, 'The statement of Matthew and of Luke concerning the mode of Jesus's conception, in every age, received the following interpretation by the church that Jesus was conceived in Mary not by a human father, but by the Holy Ghost.'

[55] The volumes were mailed at the expense of Lyman to all Christian leaders: 'This book is the first of a series which will be published and sent to every pastor, evangelist, missionary, theological professor, theological student, Sunday school superintendent, Y.M.C.A. and Y.W.C.A. secretary in the English speaking world, so far as the addresses of all these can be obtained' (from the unnumbered preface page). Orr had previously published a book-length work.

[56] Such is the case only for the first edition by Testimony Publishing Company (1910), where it holds its position of priority in Chapter 1 of Volume 1 in the twelve-volume set. Later, republished by the Bible Institute of Los Angeles (1917), it appeared as a four-volume set. In this edition some articles were deleted and the order was changed. In this and successive editions (Baker, 1980) Orr's article lost its place of prominence and is found in Volume 2, Chapter 11. James Orr actually published a longer work of over three hundred pages on the virgin birth alone, just a

few years earlier: *The Virgin Birth of Christ: Being Lectures Delivered under the Auspices of the Bible Teachers' Training School, New York, April, 1907* (New York: Scribner's Sons, 1907).

[57] Orr, 'The Virgin Birth of Christ', in Dixon, *The Fundamentals*, p. 8.

[58] Schleiermacher's view was briefly displayed in the Introduction and will be looked at more closely in Chapter 3.

[59] Friedrich Schleiermacher, *On Religion: Speeches to Its Cultured Despisers* (New York: Ungar, 1955), p. 72. He continues, 'In your sense the inexplicable and strange alone is miracle, in mine it is no miracle. The more religious you are, the more miracle would you see everywhere.' By making all things a miracle, he evacuates the category of meaning.

[60] Schleiermacher, *On Religion*, pp. 9–10.

[61] Paul Badham, *The Contemporary Challenge of Modernist Theology* (Cardiff: University of Wales, 1998), p. 6.

[62] In a brief period of time, confusion arose within both Christianity and science over where the dispute really existed so that it became the norm for some Christians to be sceptical of all science, and for not a few scientists to be sceptical of all Christian (religious) claims. That is not a focus of this project, but it is well covered by Alvin Plantinga in *Where the Conflict Really Lies: Science, Religion, and Naturalism* (New York: Oxford University Press, 2011).

2. The Virgin Birth: Historic and Misguided Meanings

[1] Hans von Campenhausen, *The Virgin Birth in the Theology of the Ancient Church* (Eugene, OR: Wipf & Stock, 2011), p. 57.

[2] Anselm, 'Why God Became Man', in *Anselm of Canterbury: The Major Works* (ed. Brian Davies and G.R. Evans; Oxford: Oxford University Press, 1998), 2.16, 338.

[3] Athanasius, *On the Incarnation* (San Bernardino, CA: Fig, 2013), sec. 8, p. 17.

[4] Piotr Ashwin-Siejkowski, *The Apostles' Creed and Its Early Christian Context* (London: T&T Clark, 2009), p. 35. His own observation of this was in opposition to this reading of the Apostles' Creed: 'Hopefully the following examination will prove that the theology promoting this specific pronouncement had a different agenda' (p. 35). My hope is the same in this regard.

[5] Irenaeus, 'Against Heresies', in *The Apostolic Fathers with Justin Martyr and Irenaeus* (vol. 1 of *Ante-Nicene Fathers (ANF)*; ed. Philip Schaff;

Grand Rapids, MI: Christian Classics Ethereal Library, 2001), 1.6.4, p. 325. He notes the argument of the Gnostics: 'Whosoever being in this world does not so love a woman as to obtain possession of her, is not of the truth, nor shall attain to the truth. But whosoever being of this world has intercourse with woman, shall not attain to the truth, because he has so acted under the power of concupiscence.' This is rather contorted language, but the argument is essentially that to have sex with a woman of the world is always unspiritual concupiscence. But Irenaeus counted this as foolishness.

6   Tertullian, 'Against Marcion', in *Latin Christianity: Its Founder, Tertullian* (vol. 3 of *ANF*), 5.15, p. 462. He writes in reference to 1 Thess. 4:3,4, 'Concupiscence, however, is not ascribed to marriage even among the Gentiles, but to extravagant, unnatural, and enormous sins. The law of nature is opposed to luxury as well as to grossness and uncleanness; it does not forbid connubial intercourse, but concupiscence; and it takes care of our vessel by the honourable estate of matrimony.' For context, he wrote this in opposition to Marcion (c.85–c.160), who divided God, rejecting what he saw as the Jewish Creator God of the Old Testament in favour of the loving God and Father of Jesus Christ in the New Testament. He also rejected Christ's physical humanity.

7   'Some early theologians argued such a possibility, and even the Augustinian formulation does not simply equate lust with intercourse. The primal couple, in their blessed state, might have engaged in sexual activity free of lust, or in other words, virginally. But after the Fall, lust and intercourse can be disentangled only theoretically, and virginity means the absence of sexual intercourse' (John A. Phillips, *Eve, the History of an Idea* [San Francisco: Harper & Row, 1984], p. 143).

8   Augustine, 'On Marriage and Concupiscence', in *St Augustine: Anti-Pelagian Writings* (vol. 5 of *Nicene and Post-Nicene Fathers* (*NPNF*), Series 1; ed. Philip Schaff; Grand Rapids, MI: Christian Classics Ethereal Library, 2001), 1.17.

9   The question bothers Augustine significantly. He writes, 'There remains a question which must be discussed, and, by the help of the Lord God of truth, solved: If the motion of concupiscence in the unruly members of our first parents arose out of their sin, and only when the divine grace deserted them; and if it was on that occasion that their eyes were opened to see, or, more exactly, notice their nakedness, and that they covered their shame because the shameless motion of their members was not subject to their will, – how, then, would they have begotten children had they remained sinless as they were created?' (Augustine, *The City of*

God [ed. Thomas Merton, trans. Marcus Dods; New York: The Modern Library, 1993], 13.24, p. 440). He did not 'solve' it here.

10 Kathleen Crowther notes, 'Although Lutheran writers maintained that sexual desire had been part of human nature since the original creation of Adam and Eve, they also drew a stark contrast between pre-lapsarian and post-lapsarian human sexuality. Had Adam and Eve remained in a state of innocence, both sexual desire and sexual intercourse would have been pure and sinless. However the Fall corrupted human sexuality, tainting it with uncontrollable lust that made men and women act like animals' (Kathleen M. Crowther, *Adam and Eve in the Protestant Reformation* [Cambridge: Cambridge University Press, 2010], p. 120). She also notes Luther's own phrase: 'leprosy of lust' (Martin Luther, *Lectures on Genesis*, Vol. 1. *Luther's Works* [ed. Jaroslav Pelikan; St Louis, MO: Concordia, 1958], p. 71). For Lutherans, it is difficult and perhaps impossible to separate lust from sexual intimacy after the fall: 'Lutherans agreed that sexual desire had been corrupted by the Fall and that sexual intercourse had to be confined to marriage and directed toward procreation. [Yet even then] sexual acts could never be pure and sinless' (p. 123).

11 Augustine, 'On Marriage', p. 127. http://www.ccel.org/ccel/schaff/npnf105. xvi.v.xxvii.html accessed 12 May 2016) Elsewhere Augustine also explains this connection: 'What priest then could there be as just and holy as the only Son of God, who was not one who needed to purge his own sins by sacrifice, whether original sin or ones added in the course of human life? . . . And what could be so pure for purging the faults of mortal men as flesh born in and from a virgin's womb without any infection of earthly lust [concupiscence]?' (Augustine, *Trinity* [Brooklyn, NY: New City, 1991], 4.19, p. 166). The connection for Augustine is that concupiscence results in impurity in the parents and so impurity in the descendants. But not merely their sin: purity in the parents is necessary to avoid the transmission of original sin.

12 Augustine, 'On Marriage', 2.15. He also writes, 'The sin, however, which is derived to children from marriage does not belong to marriage, but to the evil which accrues to the human agents, from whose union marriage comes into being. The truth is, both the evil of shameful lust can exist without marriage, and marriage might have been without it. It appertains, however, to the condition of the body (not of that life, but) of this death, that marriage cannot exist without it though it may exist without marriage' (2.42). By this he asserts that it is the seed of the man, corrupted in Adam, that necessitates the passing on of original sin.

13 While I have cited only Augustine here, we could cite others in this same regard, but that is not the main point of this project. An additional

example is Origen speaking against the foolish assertions of Celsus of the corruption of God's Spirit on contact with flesh: 'He had made these remarks, because he knows not the pure and virgin birth, unaccompanied by any corruption, of that body which was to minister to the salvation of men' (Origen, 'Against Celsus', in *Fathers of the Third Century: Tertullian, Part Fourth; Minucius Felix; Commodian; Origen, Parts First and Second* [vol. 4 of *ANF*], 6.73). Here he associates virgin birth and purity in a causal relationship.

[14] Indeed it is possible that concupiscence may be a sin in the context of marriage, but this is not something that will be resolved here.

[15] Karl Barth, *Church Dogmatics* (Peabody, MA: Hendrickson, 2nd edn, 2010), I/2, p. 190.

[16] N.T. Wright, 'God's Way of Acting', *Christian Century* 115, no. 35 (1998): pp. 1215–17.

[17] Wayne Grudem, *Systematic Theology: An Introduction to Biblical Doctrine* (Grand Rapids, MI: Zondervan, 1994), p. 530.

[18] Augustine, 'On Rebuke and Grace', in *St Augustine: Anti-Pelagian Writings* (vol. 5 of *NPNF*, Series 1), p. 33. Augustine defines the first state (era of freedom) and implies the second. He writes, 'On which account we must consider with diligence and attention in what respect those pairs differ from one another – to be able not to sin, and not to be able to sin; to be able not to die, and not to be able to die; to be able not to forsake good, and not to be able to forsake good. For the first man was able not to sin, was able not to die, was able not to forsake good. Are we to say that he who had such a free will could not sin?' See also Augustine, *The City of God*, 22.30. There Augustine defines the first and the last state in regard to sin and explains conforming-freedom.

[19] Augustine, 'On the Soul and Its Origin', in *St Augustine: Anti-Pelagian Writings* (vol. 5 of *NPNF*, Series 1), 1.24, pp. 324–5.

[20] Augustine, 'On the Soul and Its Origin', 1.33, p. 329.

[21] Augustine writes, 'Was this the condition of the nature which was formed in Adam? God forbid! Inasmuch as his pure nature, however, was corrupted in him, it has run on in this condition by natural descent through all, and still is running; so that there is no deliverance for it from this ruin, except by the grace of God through our Lord Jesus Christ' (Augustine, 'On Marriage', p. 20). Here he affirms that we inherit sin through a corrupt nature, though one originally made good by God. So while not original in creation, sin is now our burden, and the sin which originated in Adam falls upon us. In regard to the key text, Luke 1:35, it does not seem (to the extent of my research) that Augustine used the virgin birth, on the basis of this text, to make a case for Christ's sinlessness.

[22] John Calvin, *Commentary on Matthew, Mark, and Luke*. Calvin's Commentaries (Grand Rapids, MI: n.d.), http://www.ccel.org/ccel/calvin/calcom31.html (accessed 6 Aug. 2014), p. 55.

[23] Grudem, *Systematic Theology*, p. 530.

[24] Alan Jacobs, *Original Sin: A Cultural History* (New York: Harper One, 2008), p. 243. I highly recommend this book. It is captivating prose written by an English professor with well-grounded theology and based on thorough historical research.

[25] The key exegetical question (for our purposes) in Luke 1:35 is whether the one born is called 'holy' because of the Holy Spirit or called the 'Son of God' because of the Holy Spirit: The angel's announcement is in three clauses: (1)'The Holy Spirit will come upon you', (2)'and the power of the Most High will overshadow you' and (3)'therefore the child to be born will be called holy --the Son of God.' The third clause (διὸ καὶ τὸ γεννώμενον ἅγιον κληθήσεται υἱὸς θεοῦ) as translated by the ESV means that he is holy because of the Holy Spirit. The NASB translates this as, 'for that reason the holy offspring shall be called the Son of God'. He is called 'Son of God' because of the Holy Spirit. The third clause, τὸ γεννώμενον ἅγιον is a substantival participle with an adjective, all in nominative case, so I would agree with the NASB which understands 'holy' as an adjective modifying the offspring. The exegetical effect is to cast doubt on whether this verse supports the idea that Jesus is holy (and so without original sin) because of the Virgin Birth. Rather, because of the Virgin Birth, the holy child is called the Son of God. That he may be holy because of the work of the Spirit should be considered an open issue, and not directly attested by this text.

[26] Barth, *Church Dogmatics*, I/2, p. 189. © Karl Barth, 2009, 2010, and T&T Clark. Used by permission of Bloomsbury Publishing Plc.

[27] Barth, *Church Dogmatics*, I/2, p. 189. He gives his reason for this in the following paragraph: the freedom of God. He notes the objection of Schleiermacher, Seeberg, Brunner, and Althaus, who all reject the idea that the virgin birth is necessary to free Christ from original sin 'because apart from Joseph He was connected with sinful humanity on his mother Mary's side'. Indeed, this is not an unimportant point: one human parent is as logically significant as two in regard to sin.

[28] Barth, *Church Dogmatics*, I/2, p. 190. But how is the virgin birth a sign? Sigal objects that a virginal conception is no sign to anyone but the woman herself (Gerald Sigal, *The Virgin Birth Myth: The Misconception of Jesus* [Bloomington, IN: Xlibris, 2013], pp. 54–5). Unlike signs in the heavens or a divided Red Sea, the virgin birth is a sign that only Mary could appre-

ciate. But with Barth we can affirm that this is a sign to us as well, attested by Mary and by God, and affirmed by Joseph and the Evangelists.

[29] Anselm, 'On the Virginal Conception and Original Sin', in *Anselm of Canterbury: The Major Works* (ed. Brian Davies and G.R. Evans [Oxford: Oxford University Press, 1998], sec. 18, p. 376. Section 18 is entitled: 'God was not conceived from a just Virgin out of necessity, as if it was impossible from a sinful woman, but rather because this was fitting.'

[30] Pope Pius IX, 'The Immaculate Conception: Ineffabilis Deus', *Papal Encyclicals Online* http://www.papalencyclicals.net/Pius09/p9ineff.htm (accessed 1 Sep. 2013). This was affirmed by Pope Pius XII in 1950 in 'Munificentissimus Deus'.

[31] Matthew Milliner, 'Our Lady of Wheaton', *First Things* http://www.firstthings.com/article/2013/10/our-lady-of-wheaton (accessed 24 Oct. 2014).

[32] Anselm, 'Why God Became Man', 2.16, p. 340 (emphasis added).

[33] There is one more point to be made here in regard to Mary. Consider again this verse: 'the Holy Spirit will come upon you, and the power of the Most High will overshadow you' (Luke 1:35). Just as the Holy Spirit comes upon God's people, sealing us and sanctifying us, could that not have been part of this transaction? What need of an immaculate conception? Also, in the sacrificial system, when the holy touches the unholy, the unholy can be made clean. This was the case for that which touched the sin offering or was splashed by its blood. How much more in the case of the Lamb of God when he took his place in the womb of the virgin?

[34] Anselm, 'Why God Became Man', sec. 2.16.

[35] Athanasius, *On the Incarnation*, sec. 17. To this we could add texts such as Exod. 29:37 and 30:29 that affirm that whatever touches the altar of God becomes holy (see also Exod. 40:9; Lev. 6:18; Num. 16:37; Isa. 6:1–6). We could also consider the burning bush in just such a light – that which God indwells becomes holy (Exod. 3). What God touches, is joined to, is made holy. It is back-to-front to think that Mary makes Jesus holy, or that the body of Jesus must be protected; rather the Son of God makes his own human body holy.

[36] Kevin J. Vanhoozer, *Is There a Meaning in This Text? The Bible, The Reader and the Morality of Knowledge* (Grand Rapids, MI: Zondervan, 1998), p. 289.

[37] To understand his affirmation, it is helpful to hear what Vanhoozer wrote earlier in his argument: 'Meaning is not . . . something that words and texts have (meaning as a noun) but rather . . . something people do (meaning as verb). Better said: a word or text only has meaning (noun) if some person means (verb) something by it' (*Is There a Meaning in This*

Text?, p. 202). Also, he is optimistic about discerning those authorial intentions: 'My point is twofold: (1) If we can interpret actions, then we can interpret texts; (2) we can only interpret actions in light of their agents' (p. 221). I wholly agree.

[38] This is a distinctive – and to some an odd – use of the word 'doctrine'. But I think it may be quite a proper use that is helpful, although different from its use as a synonym for 'theology'. 'Doctrine' is a word closely associated with 'teaching' in the NT. Eleven times in the ESV, 'doctrine' is translated from 'διδάσκω' (or some related word) that means 'to teach' or 'teaching'. This word, or its derivatives, underlies the translation 'doctrine' in Matt. 15:9; Mark 7:7; Rom. 16:17; Eph. 4:14; 1 Tim. 1:3,10; 4:6; 6:3; Titus 1:9; 2:1,10; a twelfth occurrence is Heb. 6:1, from 'λόγος'. Specifically, the Greek verb for teach is 'διδάσκω' (often translated as 'doctrine' from the participle) and the noun is 'διδασκαλία' or 'διδαχή' (which was also the name for the early church manual of instruction). It is interesting, though it proves nothing, that the only OT use of 'doctrine' by the ESV is in Job 11:4. In that case the Hebrew is 'לֶקַח', but interestingly, the Greek LXX (Septuagint, an early Greek translation of the Bible) word chosen was 'ἔργον', 'work'. At least one translator saw a deep connection between what is taught and what we do! Indeed, the goal of teaching is always changed behaviour and the goal of language is to cause action. In fact, some understand language itself to be a combination of speech and action – 'speech-act theory' (John Austin and John Searle, via Kevin Vanhoozer). This understands that language, communicative-action, includes locution (the words), illocution (the intent), and perlocution (the effect). Vanhoozer has built a trinitarian theology of meaning around the concept of God's speech-acts. It is difficult to separate the verbal ideas of 'teaching' from the intent of the speaker, which is to move the listener to action. The distinction between the demons and believers is not how much they have learned, but that faith moves to action, revealing the work of God by his Spirit. Indeed, this is the basis of considering 'doctrine', a word that translates 'teaching' and 'word', to be 'what the church does'. I will use it in this way.

3. The Virgin Birth: Historic and Biblically Grounded Meanings

[1] Donald Macleod, *The Person of Christ* (Downers Grove, IL: InterVarsity Press, 1998), p. 22.

[2] Wolfhart Pannenberg, *Systematic Theology* (Edinburgh: Black, 2004), p. 325. Here Pannenberg writes, 'The issue of the question of the deity

of Jesus Christ is the deity of the man Jesus . . . We must discover the contours of the divine sonship of Jesus in his human reality.'

[3] Bruce Ware shows an evangelical approach to a Christology from below in 'The Man Christ Jesus', *JETS* 53, no. 1 (2010): pp. 5–18.

[4] Karl Barth, *Church Dogmatics* (Peabody, MA: Hendrickson, 2nd edn, 2010), I/2, p. 177.

[5] As we saw in the first chapter, the Ebionites focus on the humanity of Christ to the exclusion of his deity, and the Docetists on Christ's deity to the exclusion of his humanity.

[6] Athanasius, *On the Incarnation* (San Bernardino, CA: Fig, 2013), sec. 18.

[7] Henry Bettenson, *Documents of the Christian Church* (London: Oxford University Press, 1963), p. 26.

[8] Bettenson, *Documents*, p. 52.

[9] Augustine, 'Letter CXXXVII. To Volusianus', in *The Confessions and Letters of St Augustine, with a Sketch of His Life and Work* (vol. 1 of *Nicene and Post-Nicene Fathers* [*NPNF*], Series 1; ed. Philip Schaff; Grand Rapids, MI: Christian Classics Ethereal Library, 2001), sec. 9, p. 476. Augustine makes a similar claim in the 'Enchiridion', referencing this same letter to Volusianus ('The Enchiridion, Addressed to Laurentius; Being a Treatise on Faith, Hope and Love', in *On the Holy Trinity; Doctrinal Treatises; Moral Treatises* [vol. 3 of *NPNF*, Series 1], 34–5, p. 249).

[10] Augustine, 'To Volusianus', sec. 2, p. 474.

[11] Anselm, 'Why God Became Man', in *Anselm of Canterbury: The Major Works* (ed. Brian Davies and G.R. Evans; Oxford: Oxford University Press, 1998), 2.8, p. 322.

[12] Anselm, 'Why God Became Man', 2.7, p. 321.

[13] Boso characteristically responds to Anselm: 'If we maintain a logical approach, as we have proposed to do, this must inevitably be the case' (2.8, p. 322). And, 'Nothing could be more solid' (2.8, p. 323). Boso is a bit too affirming – a bit too much like a bobble-headed clown, Bozo of renown.

[14] Wayne Grudem, *Systematic Theology: An Introduction to Biblical Doctrine* (Grand Rapids, MI: Zondervan, 1994), p. 530.

[15] Schleiermacher, *The Christian Faith* (Berkeley, CA: Apocryphile, 2011), 97.2, pp. 403,405.

[16] Schleiermacher, *Christian Faith*, 97.2, p. 406.

[17] Schleiermacher, *Christian Faith*, 97.2, p. 406. Even this 'miraculous' birth is severely limited in scope. He writes, 'This physiologically supernatural element does not, in itself, imply what we demand of the divine influence in the conception of the Redeemer; nor has it any influence

upon the racial character of Jesus' personality – it neither abolishes, in itself, that which carries with it a participation in the sinfulness, nor does it rob Him of what belongs to His historicity' (p. 406).

[18] Schleiermacher, *Christian Faith*, 97.3, p. 407.

[19] Schleiermacher, *Christian Faith*, 97.3, p. 408. His concern is the introduction of temporality into the Godhead, which he resolves to his own satisfaction. He also answers the affirmation of the councils that the human and divine natures cannot be said to act separately or alter each other, or be separated. While he argues that he can be shown to be in concord with the affirmations, he also argues that these ancient formulations can only serve to introduce confusion (97.4, p. 410). Further consideration of his views is left as an exercise for the reader, for it is outside my scope.

[20] Barth, *Church Dogmatics*, I/2, p. 192. Here Barth writes, 'Man is involved, but not as God's fellow-worker, not in his independence, not with control over what is to happen, but only – and even that because God has presented him with Himself – in his readiness for God. So much does God insist that He alone is Lord by espousing the cause of man. This is the mystery of grace to which the *natus ex virgine* points.'

[21] Barth, *Church Dogmatics*, I/2, p. 185.

[22] Barth, *Church Dogmatics*, I/2, p. 194.

[23] Oliver D. Crisp and Fred Sanders, eds, *Christology, Ancient and Modern: Explorations in Constructive Dogmatics* (Grand Rapids, MI: Zondervan, 2013), p. 35.

[24] Karl Barth, *Dogmatics in Outline* (New York: Philosophical Library, 1949), p. 98.

[25] Macleod, *Person of Christ*, p. 37.

[26] 'Mutation' is a modern concept. Darwin's work is 'pre-Mendelian', before George Mendel (1822–84) founded the science of genetics by studying peas. He discovered that inheritance was discrete, so that genes combined in such a way that one or the other of the inherited genes was expressed (dominant v. recessive). His work was slow to be accepted and did not affect thinking until the early twentieth century. However, Darwin thought in terms of 'blended' inheritance, combining the traits of the ancestors, as if a red-haired mother and a blond father might make an orange-haired progeny. So, for Darwin, the evolution was driven by variations (mutations) and natural selection (survival of those chance mutations which are better adapted, better fitted, to the environment). This mechanism was not directed.

[27] Born a generation after Isaac Newton, Pierre-Simon Laplace (1749–1825) built on his work. Supposedly, Laplace presented Napoleon with a copy

of his dissertation on the universe, *Celestial Mechanics*, which never mentioned God. When Napoleon challenged his work on creation which never mentioned the Creator, Laplace is said to have declared (was he anticipating Carl Sagan?), 'I have no need of that hypothesis!'

28 Barth explains his failure as a division between the sign and the thing signified: 'The thing signified needs no sign at all' (Barth, *Church Dogmatics*, I/2, pp. 179–80).

29 To call the incarnation (or birth) miraculous in any meaningful way and yet affirm naturalism is an impossibly narrow path. George Hunsinger writes of those who choose a 'middle Christology' (neither high nor low), '[Jesus] is materially decisive but not logically indispensable. He is materially decisive because the spirituality he communicates to others needed first to be achieved in his own life. But he is not logically indispensable, because there is no good reason why this same sort of spirituality might not be achieved and transmitted by another. Schleiermacher is the great exception here, because he made Jesus logically indispensable by grounding his identity as the second Adam in the virgin birth. Modern liberal theology almost never followed him in this move' (cited in Crisp and Sanders, *Christology, Ancient and Modern*, p. 58).

30 Barth, *Church Dogmatics*, I/2, p. 182.

31 Dustin Resch, *Barth's Interpretation of the Virgin Birth: A Sign of Mystery* (Farnham: Ashgate, 2012), p. 81.

32 Barth, *Church Dogmatics*, I/2, p. 180.

33 Karl Barth, *Christmas* (trans. Bernard Citron; Edinburgh: Oliver & Boyd, 1959), p. 21.

34 As an example, John Polkinghorne writes, 'It has proved impossible to distil the essence of the scientific method' (*Belief in God in an Age of Science* [New Haven, CT: Yale University Press, 2003], p. 105). I would not disagree. Yet the methodological tenets listed here have many supporters and serve to make the point.

35 Alvin Plantinga, *Where the Conflict Really Lies: Science, Religion, and Naturalism* (New York: Oxford University Press, 2011) p. ix.

36 Plantinga, *Where the Conflict Really Lies*, p. 35.

37 Plantinga, *Where the Conflict Really Lies*, p. 60.

38 Plantinga, *Where the Conflict Really Lies*, p. 307.

39 Plantinga, *Where the Conflict Really Lies*, p. 303.

40 Plantinga, *Where the Conflict Really Lies*, p. 344. Plantinga shows by careful reasoning that to accept naturalism and evolution provides a 'defeater' such that naturalism and evolution cannot be rationally held – a sufficient reason to be at least an agnostic in respect to it. Another interesting

perspective in this regard is Thomas Nagel. He also argues as a non-theist that this position is self-defeating: 'Evolutionary naturalism provides an account of our capacities that undermines their reliability, and in so doing undermines itself' (Thomas Nagel, *Mind and Cosmos: Why the Materialist Neo-Darwinian Conception of Nature Is Almost Certainly False* [New York: Oxford University Press, 2012], p. 27).

41 Citations to creation as 'God's theatre' can be found repeatedly in Calvin, including in his *Institutes*, 1.5.8, 1.6.2, 1.14.20, 2.6.1, 3.9.2, and elsewhere in his works.

42 John C. Polkinghorne, *The Faith of a Physicist* (ed. Kevin Sharpe; Minneapolis, MN: Augsburg Fortress, 1st edn, 1996), p. 51.

43 Plantinga, *Where the Conflict Really Lies*, p. 169.

44 Polkinghorne, *The Faith of a Physicist*, p. 43.

45 Plantinga, *Where the Conflict Really Lies*, p. 186.

46 Plantinga, *Where the Conflict Really Lies*, p. 311.

47 Michael Polanyi, *Personal Knowledge: Towards a Post-Critical Philosophy* (Chicago: University of Chicago Press, 1974). Anticipating his work was Augustine, for whom knowledge was personal and based, first, on belief. Lesslie Newbigin also takes this perspective (*Proper Confidence: Faith, Doubt, and Certainty in Christian Discipleship* [Grand Rapids, MI: Eerdmans, 1995]).

48 Plantinga, *Where the Conflict Really Lies*, p. 349.

49 Barth, *Church Dogmatics*, I/2, p. 198.

4. The Virgin Birth: A Mystery Revealed

1 Hans von Campenhausen, *The Virgin Birth in the Theology of the Ancient Church* (Eugene, OR: Wipf & Stock, 2011), p. 31.

2 Augustine, 'Reply to Faustus the Manichaean', in *Augustine: The Writings Against the Manichaeans and Against the Donatists* (vol. 4 of *Nicene and Post-Nicene Fathers*, Series 1; ed. Philip Schaff; Grand Rapids, MI: Christian Classics Ethereal Library, 2001), 11.5.

3 Irenaeus, 'Against Heresies', in *The Apostolic Fathers with Justin Martyr and Irenaeus* (vol. 1 of *Ante-Nicene Fathers* (*ANF*); ed. Philip Schaff; Grand Rapids, MI: Christian Classics Ethereal Library, 2001), 3.21.9.

4 Thomas Aquinas, 'Summa Theologica', ed. Kevin Knight, *New Advent* (2008) www.newadvent.org/summa/ (accessed 24 Oct. 2014), III.31.3.

5 I am indebted to Mark Carlton, then a pastor in Ogallala, NE, for first calling my attention to the key prophecy in Jer. 22 and its link to the

virgin birth in his sermon series 'The Great Christmas War'.

6 In the quote from Aquinas above, the 'crimes of the kings of Juda' refer to the judgement of God against the last living king of Israel, Jehoiachin. We will explore this in detail in this chapter.

7 It is conceivable that another royal heir of David could be installed on the throne. For example, a descendant of one of Josiah's other sons who ruled: Jehoahaz or Zedekiah. This possibility will be assessed later.

8 Irenaeus asserts that 'Jeconiah's posterity . . . [are] expressly excluded' ('Against Heresies', 3.21.9). Aquinas, standing on Ambrose, allows that this may have applied to a single generation, so that Christ's reign is not contrary to prophecy (Aquinas, 'Summa Theologica', III.31.2 [reply to objection 3]). Calvin understands this to be an eternal command specifically because it was written down: 'when a law was enacted, which was to be binding on posterity, it was written . . . [so that] it would be certain and permanent . . . It is no wonder that the Jews regarded this judgment of God with abhorrence, as though it was something monstrous' (*Commentaries on the Book of the Prophet Jeremiah and the Lamentations*, vol. 3 [trans. John Owen; Grand Rapids, MI: Eerdmans, 1950], pp. 125–6). Andrew Shead (*A Mouth Full of Fire: The Word of God in the Words of Jeremiah* [Downers Grove, IL: Apollos, 2012]) calls this verse the annunciation of 'unending exile' (p. 215) and a 'death knell rung over the institution of Judean kingship' (p. 95). J.G. McConville writes, 'It becomes plain that the dynasty is breathing its sorry last' (*Judgment and Promise: An Interpretation of the Book of Jeremiah* [Leicester: Apollos, 1993], p. 57). Walter Brueggemann writes, 'The King is rejected. With him the royal line beginning with David is ended and the royal promise nullified' (*To Pluck Up, To Tear Down: A Commentary on the Book of Jeremiah 1 – 25* [Grand Rapids, MI: Eerdmans, 1988], p. 196). Charles Lee Feinberg writes, 'In him the royal line became extinct' (*Jeremiah, A Commentary* [Grand Rapids, MI: Zondervan, 1982], p. 160). Derek Kidner writes, 'none of his direct descendants succeeded him as king, yet another branch of David's family was counted as his legal succession' (*The Message of Jeremiah: Against Wind and Tide* [Downers Grove, IL: InterVarsity Press, 1987], p. 89). Tremper Longman III noted that the dynasty was broken like the pot of v. 28 (*Jeremiah, Lamentations* [Peabody, MA: Hendrickson, 2008], p. 159). Gerald Sigal writes, 'Perhaps this genealogy is introduced to circumvent the curse of God on Jeconiah in Jeremiah 22:24–30' (*The Virgin Birth Myth: The Misconception of Jesus* [Bloomington, IN: Xlibris, 2013], p. 85), suggesting agreement with – or at least acknowledgement of – this interpretation. His point is that Jesus must be descended from

David, but not from Jehoiachin.

9   Abraham was 75 years old when he left Haran for Canaan, a trip of a few weeks or months (Gen. 12:4). When he was 86 years old, he had a son by Hagar, Ishmael. The events of Gen. 15 take place in Canaan and prior to his first child, Ishmael. His child of promise, by Sarai, was born when he was 100 years old (Gen. 17:21; 18:10; 21:5), twenty-five years after his arrival in Canaan and fifteen years after Ishmael was born, so the time of waiting since the promise was first given was between fifteen and twenty-five years.

10 Jehoiachin reigned for three months and Jeremiah's curse came during his reign (22:26 is in the present tense in regard to a reigning king, Jehoiachin/Coniah). Hananiah's curse on Jeremiah comes in Jer. 28 in the fourth year of Jehoiachin's successor, Zedekiah.

11 Jeremiah, or perhaps an editor, or redactor. But this issue is not germane to this discussion.

12 'Summa Theologica', III.31.2 (reply to objection 3).

13 Christopher J.H. Wright, *The Message of Jeremiah* (Downers Grove, IL: InterVarsity Academic, 2014), p. 242.

14 Matthew's affirmation of three groups of fourteen is confusing for readers. The resolution is not the issue here.

15 Many have noted that Matthew's genealogy (in 1:1–17) does not align into the three groups of fourteen in an obvious way. The groups of three are obvious: ancient Fathers, kings of Israel (Judah), and post-exilic Fathers. The challenges come in discerning the fourteens. Notice that each person is named twice, once as 'son' and once as 'father'. How should they be counted? A proposal which occurs to many is to count the person as 'father' but not as 'son'. But this seems to fail immediately in the first division (only thirteen) and then again in the third division (only twelve). Worse, this approach does not count Jesus in any division. Alternatively, the transition figures, those who bridge between divisions, may be counted differently for emphasis. In this approach, David is counted twice (as listed in the first and second division), and Jesus is counted twice in the third division: then all divisions have fourteen – if Jeconiah is counted only once, not twice, even though he too is a transition figure. To make this work, he would have to be left out of the kings of Israel (division 2), but counted in the division ending in Jesus (division 2) – and Christ is counted there, twice. But this is not an obvious approach. As Herman Waetjen noted, Matthew's three divisions represent four eras, not three. He observes that the history of God's people begins with Abraham, and Christ is not the end, but the begin-

ning of the fourth ('The Genealogy as the Key to the Gospel according to Matthew', *Journal of Biblical Literature* 95, no. 2 [1976]: p. 212). That might provide the hint needed. If this is correct, and if transition figures are counted as suggested above, then not only is David exalted, but also it supports counting Jesus twice and explains the corresponding impossibility of counting Jeconiah twice, highlighting Jeconiah as the problem. However, without further support, this is only an interesting conjecture.

[16] N.T. Wright, 'God's Way of Acting', *Christian Century* 115, no. 35 (1998): p. 1216. It is worth adding that in this context, a challenge to Matthew's authorship hardly affects the argument, for N.T. Wright's observation holds true for any author, editor, or redactor of Matthew.

[17] While I cannot hope to adequately cover the historical and theological options raised by the genealogies, a study of the virgin birth requires me to explore them in part. In this brief study I can show only the key possibilities. More importantly, I hope to make it clear that the resolution of the distinctions between the genealogies does not affect my proposal. Those who desire a fuller treatment may find I. Howard Marshall's commentary on Luke helpful (*The Gospel of Luke: A Commentary on the Greek Text* [Grand Rapids, MI: Eerdmans, 1978], pp. 157–65).

[18] A levirate marriage was one commanded in Mosaic law in which a childless widow was taken into the house of a surviving brother of her dead husband. He took her as his wife and raised the firstborn to bear her dead husband's name and receive his inheritance. Later children took his name (cf. Deut. 25).

[19] Tertullian, 'On the Flesh of Christ', in *Latin Christianity: Its Founder, Tertullian* (vol. 3 of *ANF*), ch. 20–22. Specifically, in ch. 20 he writes, 'It is, however, a fortunate circumstance that Matthew also, when tracing down the Lord's descent from Abraham to Mary, says, "Jacob begat Joseph the husband of Mary, of whom was born Christ."' Tertullian's first concern here is to assert the reality of the flesh of Christ against gnostic spiritualization of the flesh. Later, in ch. 22 he writes, 'He is of the seed of David in consequence of Mary's flesh' and 'Christ is "the fruit of David's loins"; none other than Mary's, since Christ came from Mary's womb', and so, perhaps, arguing for Matthew's genealogy as that of Mary.

[20] Sigal, *Virgin Birth Myth*, p. 89. Sigal notes that this reading seems to be at odds with Matt. 1:16.

[21] This observation is challenged by the fact that it is Matthew, not Luke, who includes four women as sole representatives of their generations, seeming to make Matthew's association with Mary more likely. This is quickly countered by the observation that Matthew did not attribute his

genealogy to Mary, but rather to Joseph, even though he was not averse to including women.

[22] Marshall, *Gospel of Luke*, p. 158. This reading is first attributed to Annius of Viterbo (1490).

[23] R.P. Nettelhorst, 'Genealogy of Jesus', *JETS* 31, no. 2 (1988): p. 170. Also, Marshall, *Gospel of Luke* (pp. 157–64).

[24] Sigal, *Virgin Birth Myth*, p. 113.

[25] Sigal, *Virgin Birth Myth*, p. 119. In regard to Matthew's genealogy of Joseph, Sigal writes, 'That which they did not possess they could not pass on', speaking of the right to rule. In regard to the possibility that Joseph passed it on to Jesus by adoption, he argues that this is not permitted (p. 121). He allows that there is no way to resolve the problem of Jesus' ancestry by resorting to either bloodline.

[26] Sigal, *Virgin Birth Myth*, p. 90. He continues to discuss this theory and concludes, again, that any such proposal of a matrilineal line is 'wishful thinking' (p. 101).

[27] One other possibility is that the genealogies reflect Joseph's through his mother (Matthew) and his father (Luke), with Matthew not listing Joseph's mother's name, Jacob being his maternal grandfather (Nettelhorst, 'Genealogy of Jesus', pp. 171–2). This has plausibility and would serve this proposal just as well.

[28] J. Gresham Machen, *Virgin Birth of Christ* (Grand Rapids, MI: Baker, 1965), p. 203.

[29] Machen, *Virgin Birth*, p. 204.

[30] Adoption is another option, at least logically. I will examine this later.

[31] Machen, *Virgin Birth*, p. 205.

[32] The term of relation in Luke 1:36, συγγενής, has been translated as 'cousin' by older translations, which has added to the confusion. However, the compound word is used in Luke 1:61 and 2:44 to indicate a broad family relationship, and so is better translated as 'relative'.

[33] Aquinas, 'Summa Theologica', III.31.2 (objection 2 and reply). Aquinas saw no problem in this case, because intermarriage allowed both king and priest in the same line.

[34] Gen. 14 is the grounding story in this regard. The first reference to the Messiah as Melchizedek is found in Ps. 110. The book of Hebrews makes the connection between Christ and Melchizedek in chs 5 and 6, with an extended discussion in 7.

[35] I did not establish sufficient reason to affirm this, yet it is not an unworthy proposal. For example, J.I. Packer affirms just this idea, citing F.F. Bruce (J.I. Packer, *Affirming the Apostles' Creed* [Wheaton, IL: Crossway, 2008], p. 75).

[36] That is, except for Schleiermacher, whose commitments lie not in virginal conception, but rather in an idea of the miraculous.

[37] Not everyone is convinced of this. Exceptionally, Michael Bird proposes, 'I'm also not convinced that because Jesus was known as coming from the "seed of David" that he must have been Joseph's biological son. For a start, Jesus could have been from the "seed of David" by virtue of his maternal origins in Mary. Also sonship language can be metaphorical. Paul argues that Gentiles are from the "seed" of Abraham without having a biological connection to Abraham, nor was Augustus a biological son of Julius Caesar in order to be a "son of the divine Julius". So Jesus' Davidic status does not have to be biological (in fact, some think that Mark 12:35–37 is a debate over this very point!).' I believe that is not the case when we consider texts like Rom. 1:3 and 2 Tim. 2:8 ('descended from David') (Michael Bird, 'Andrew Lincoln and the Virgin Conception', *Euangelion* [2014], http://www.patheos.com/blogs/euangelion/2014/09/andrew-lincoln-and-the-virgin-conception/#ixzz3Li70AI9C [accessed 12 Dec. 2014]).

[38] Many texts use this metaphor of a stump – as if the family tree had been cut down: Isa. 6:13; 11:1. The metaphor is reflected in Job 14:7. The metaphor of the 'sprouting stump' (life from a hidden source) is similar to the 'sprouting horn' (strength from hidden power) which anticipates Christ in Ps. 132:17. To this, possibly, could be added the references to the 'root', a word included by synthetic parallelism in Isa. 11:1; Rev. 5:5; 22:16. However, rather than the 'bare root, left after cutting down', root can mean the source of life. Both seem to be in play in the metaphor, though proving this would entail a different paper than this.

[39] Ignatius, 'Epistle to the Ephesians', in *The Apostolic Fathers with Justin Martyr and Irenaeus* (vol. 1 of *ANF*), 19.2.

[40] John H. Sailhamer, *Genesis Unbound: A Provocative New Look at the Creation Account* (Sisters, OR: Multnomah, 1996). See ch. 16, 'The Seventh Day'. Also, G.K. Beale, *The Temple and the Church's Mission: A Biblical Theology of the Dwelling Place of God* (Downers Grove, IL: InterVarsity Academic, 2004).

[41] G.K. Beale, 'Eden, the Temple, and the Church's Mission in the New Creation', *JETS* 48, no. 1 (2005): p. 7.

[42] Peter J. Gentry and Stephen J. Wellum, *Kingdom Through Covenant: A Biblical–Theological Understanding of the Covenants* (Wheaton, IL: Crossway, 2012), p. 628.

[43] It seems likely that Seth, the line of promise, married the daughters of Cain who were outside the line of promise. This fits with the OT concern

for the people of God that they marry only within the line of promise.

44 There is no need to prove this conjecture here. However, if it is correct, it may be the root for future injunctions which prohibit the people of God from intermarrying with those who are not of the people of God. Representatively, I note Calvin (John Calvin, *Commentary on Genesis* [Colorado Springs, CO: CreateSpace Independent Publishing Platform, 2011]), chap. 6.1); Ron Youngblood, who makes a good textual case from the OT and NT (*The Book of Genesis: An Introductory Commentary* [Grand Rapids, MI: Baker, 2nd edn, 1991], p. 82); and Gordon Wenham, who gives a helpful and succinct case for each of the three classic positions: angelic, royal, and Sethite, settling on the angelic (*Genesis 1 – 15*. Word Biblical Commentary [ed. David Allen Hubbard and Glenn W. Barker; Waco, TX: Word, 1987], pp. 139–40). What is interesting about Wenham is that he supports his angelic position by affirming that the Christian worldview insists that we are not materialists, so angelic paternity should not seem more incredible to us than the virgin birth!

45 Our confusion over this event is nowhere more poignantly depicted than by Kierkegaard in *Fear and Trembling*! In this work Søren Kierkegaard (1813–55), writing as Johannes de Silentio, wrestles with the meaning of the sacrifice of Isaac. After considering many possibilities, Johannes pronounces, 'Abraham I cannot understand, in a certain sense there is nothing I can learn from him but astonishment. If people fancy that by considering the outcome of this story they might let themselves be moved to believe, they deceive themselves and want to swindle God out of the first movement of faith, the infinite resignation' (Søren Kierkegaard, *Fear and Trembling* [trans. Walter Lowrie; Princeton, NJ: Princeton University Press, 1941], p. 50).

46 Islam continues to identify Ishmael as the son of promise and the one who was almost killed on Mt Moriah.

47 Ignatius, 'Epistle to the Ephesians', 19.2.

5. The Virgin Birth: A Chiastic Reversal

1 Anselm, 'Why God Became Man', in *Anselm of Canterbury: The Major Works* (ed. Brian Davies and G.R. Evans; Oxford: Oxford University Press, 1998), 1.8, p. 323.

2 I discovered this quote in Aquinas, 'Summa Theologica', ed. Kevin Knight, *New Advent* (2008) www.newadvent.org/summa/ (accessed 24 Oct. 2014), III.31.4, where he cites Augustine (QQ. lxxxiii, qu. 11).

3   My chapter title, the connection I draw between Eve and Mary, and my use of 1 Tim. 2:12–15 (later in the chapter) may cause some to think that I am an egalitarian (understanding men and women to share parity and equality of roles in the community of believers and/or in the family). While I am a complementarian (understanding men and women to be equals but with distinct roles in God's economy), I am not considering the issue of the roles of men and women in this study. I will not take up the discussion here, nor will I advance my position here. Instead, I want to understand the meaning of the virgin birth. All other concerns are secondary to this study. If my arguments are considered in that light, they may be of more value to the reader.

4   My translation from the Greek text, Anonymous, 'Protevangelium of James', *Early Church Texts* http://www.earlychurchtexts.com/main/apocgosps/proto-evangelium_of_james_01.shtml (accessed 23 Jan. 2015), sec. 11.

5   Irenaeus, 'Against Heresies', in *The Apostolic Fathers with Justin Martyr and Irenaeus* (vol. 1 of *Ante-Nicene Fathers*; ed. Philip Schaff; Grand Rapids, MI: Christian Classics Ethereal Library, 2001), 3.21.10.

6   Irenaeus, 'Against Heresies', 3.22.4. He also wrote, 'And if the former did disobey God, yet the latter was persuaded to be obedient to God, in order that the virgin Mary might become the patroness (*advocata*) of the virgin Eve. And thus, as the human race fell into bondage to death by means of a virgin, so it is rescued by a virgin; virginal disobedience having been balanced in the opposite scale by virginal obedience' (5.19.1).

7   This late work is also known as the 'Gospel of James' or the 'Infancy Gospel of James', and later translations and expansions are called 'The Armenian Gospel of the Infancy'. Do not be confused by alternative spellings for the Protevangelium, including 'Protoevangelium' (with an 'o'). Also, don't confuse this with what is also called the 'protoevangelium' (sometimes 'protoevangelion'), which refers to God's first declaration of redemption in Gen. 3:15: 'I will put enmity between you and the woman, and between your offspring and her offspring; he shall bruise your head, and you shall bruise his heel.'

8   This work was rejected well before the era of higher criticism. Origen knew of this work, which speaks of its relatively early date. He writes, 'But some say, basing it on a tradition in the Gospel according to Peter, as it is entitled, or "The Book of James", that the brethren of Jesus were sons of Joseph by a former wife, whom he married before Mary' (Origen, 'Commentary on Matthew', in *The Gospel of Peter, The Diatessaron of Tatian, The Apocalypse of Peter, The Vision of Paul, The Apocalypse of the Virgin and Sedrach, The Testament of Abraham, The Acts of Xanthippe and Polyxena, The Narrative*

of Zosimus, The Apology of Aristides, The Epistles of Clement [Complete Text], Origen's Commentary on John, Books 1–10, and Commentary on Matthew, Books 1, 2, and 10–14 [vol. 9 of *Ante-Nicene Fathers*; ed. Philip Schaff; Grand Rapids, MI: Christian Classics Ethereal Library, 2001], 10.17). Eusebius also acknowledged the Gos. Pet. as universally rejected (in contrast to 1 Pet.): 'The so-called Acts of Pet., however, and the Gospel which bears his name, and the Preaching and the Apocalypse, as they are called, we know have not been universally accepted, because no ecclesiastical writer, ancient or modern, has made use of testimonies drawn from them' (Eusebius of Caesarea, 'Church History', in *Eusebius Pamphilius: Church History, Life of Constantine, Oration in Praise of Constantine* [vol. 1 of *Nicene and Post-Nicene Fathers*, Series 2; ed. Philip Schaff; Grand Rapids, MI: Christian Classics Ethereal Library, 2001], 3.3.2).

9 It is worth observing that this text has its own agenda distinct from the Bible – at odds with the Bible at times. This includes not merely extra details not in the Bible, but details at odds with the Bible, including the annunciation happening in Jerusalem in the temple, rather than in Galilee.

10 Similar usages of the Hebrew 'with her' (עִמָּהּ) can be found in Judg. 13:5 and Ruth 1:22, carrying the sense of physical proximity. But the same consonants with different vowel pointing reads 'her people' in Num. 15:30. This form was used by Moses. But given that the vowel pointing was added later, by others and not by Moses, the use is ambiguous, requiring context. Was Moses indicating the unfulfilled covenant duty of Adam to protect Eve, rather than his proximity: 'to Adam, [who was of] her people'? Ezra 7:25 reflects a similar construction: 'to all her people', which could parallel 'to Adam her people'. This is perhaps awkward because she had only 'one people' (other than herself) at that time, not a whole clan. Such a reading is in no way certain, though it does raise a distinct possibility. In the end, as noted above, it does not make a critical difference to the argument.

11 Gary A. Anderson, *The Genesis of Perfection: Adam and Eve in Jewish and Christian Imagination* (Louisville, KY: Westminster John Knox, 2001), p. 92. He notes this is the tradition of *conceptio per aurem*, conception by ear.

12 The Garden snake was not clearly angelic in nature in Gen. 3. Indeed, the text delays this clarification until Rev. 12, though there are indications and hints through the canon. Peter Gentry notes that the biblical term 'seraph' refers to an angelic being which is depicted as a winged snake on Hebrew seals and that this is congruent with Isa. 6, and perhaps 2 Kgs 18 and Num. 21 ('No One Holy Like the Lord', *Midwestern Journal of Theology* 12, no. 1 [2013]: p. 31). I would observe that, while Gen. 3 uses

not the word 'seraph' but rather 'nahash' for 'snake', yet the connection of concepts is intriguing. Could the 'talking snake' have been an angel/demon, a winged seraph, who spoke to Eve? Such conjecture is not necessary to observe that the one who confronted Eve was indeed the fallen angelic being Satan.

13 Karl Barth, *Dogmatics in Outline* (New York: Philosophical Library, 1949), p. 99.

14 I could cite numerous authorities here, but the observation is quite plain. The woman said, 'We may eat of the fruit of the trees in the garden, but God said, "You shall not eat of the fruit of the tree that is in the midst of the garden, neither shall you touch it, lest you die."' First, God did not say the tree was in the 'middle'. Second, he said nothing of 'touching'. And third, she diminishes the threat of death by a change in the verbal force from 'dying you will die' to 'lest you die'. Luther (I cannot resist citing one authority) clearly observed, 'Eve should have maintained, "If I eat, I shall surely die"' (Martin Luther, *Lectures on Genesis*, Vol. 1. *Luther's Works* [ed. Jaroslav Pelikan; St Louis, MO: Concordia, 1958], p. 155).

15 In Luke 1:18, Zechariah challenges the promise of the angel and is reprimanded for his lack of faith in God's power.

16 Anderson, *The Genesis of Perfection*, p. 16.

17 Mark Roberts, 'Woman Shall Be Saved: A Closer Look at 1 Timothy 2:15', *The Reformed Journal* 33, no. 4 (1983): p. 21.

18 Even so, my notes and citations will be far less than exhaustive on this text which has produced no end of scholarly opinion. I intend this section to be sufficient to help the reader understand the issues, and to provide enough leads for further study.

19 The exegetical path I will follow through this text is informed by the excellent unpublished paper of one of my students, Jesse Scheumann: '"Saved Through the Childbirth of Christ" (1 Tim. 2:15): A Complementarian View of Eve's Creation, Fall, and Redemption' (2014).

20 This text forms the framework of Christian marriage today. The father presents the bride (Gen. 2:22b). Then the groom declares his vows (Gen. 2:23a), saying, 'This at last is bone of my bones and flesh of my flesh.' Adam's words seem to commit him to caring for his wife as his own body, which may be paraphrased in Eph. 5:28: 'husbands should love their wives as their own bodies.' Then the woman takes the name of her husband (Gen. 2:23b), for as in English 'man' is related to 'woman', so in Hebrew. Then the disembodied officiant, God or Moses, gives the sermon, which begins with the first 'therefore' in the Bible. Of v. 25, a review of the wedding party's 'apparel', little needs to be said here.

21 Andrew Spurgeon, '1 Timothy 2:13–15: Paul's Retelling of Genesis 2:4 – 4:1', *JETS* 56, no. 3 (2013): p. 544.

22 David Kimberley, '1 Tim 2:15: A Possible Understanding of a Difficult Text', *JETS* 35, no. 4 (1992): p. 486.

23 Thomas Schreiner disagrees with this conclusion, being concerned about the slide of Eve into Mary as subject. See 'An Interpretation of 1 Timothy 2:9–15: A Dialogue with Scholarship', in *Women in the Church: An Analysis and Application of 1 Timothy 2:9–15* (ed. Thomas R. Schreiner and Andreas J. Köstenberger; Grand Rapids, MI: Baker, 2005), pp. 116–17.

24 Stanley E. Porter, 'What Does It Mean to Be "Saved by Childbirth" (1 Timothy 2.15)?', *Journal for the Study of the New Testament* 15, no. 49 (1993): pp. 93–4. As noted elsewhere in this exegetical discussion, I cannot support Porter's final conclusion, but thus far, he speaks correctly of Paul's use of this word 'save'.

25 Moyer Hubbard argues that this text refers to the hope for safe delivery of babies for the Ephesian women who live in grinding poverty. He argues for an exceptional use of 'save' by Paul in a non-salvific sense. His support rests on two usages of 'saved' in Paul. In 2 Tim. 4:18 he seems to use 'save' to mean 'safe conduct', but in context, salvation is intended by Paul. The other is 1 Cor. 3:15, in which 'saved' may mean 'escape' the fire. But again, the context is clearly salvation through the 'fire'. His proposal does not stand. His full argument can be found in Moyer Hubbard, 'Kept Safe Through Childbearing: Maternal Mortality, Justification by Faith and the Social Setting of 1 Timothy 2:15', *JETS* 55, no. 4 (2012): pp. 743–62.

26 Stanley Porter argues well for instrumentality, but with the rather odd argument that it is by means of their personal childbearing through which individual women are saved. See Porter, 'What Does It Mean to Be "Saved by Childbirth"?', pp. 87–102.

27 Douglas J. Moo, 'What Does It Mean Not to Teach or Have Authority Over Men? 1 Timothy 2:11–15', in *Recovering Biblical Manhood and Womanhood: A Response to Evangelical Feminism* (ed. John Piper and Wayne Grudem; Wheaton, IL: Crossway, 2006), p. 192.

28 Philip Barton Payne, *Man and Woman, One in Christ: An Exegetical and Theological Study of Paul's Letters* (Grand Rapids, MI: Zondervan, 2009), p. 431. Specifically, Payne notes that of the sixty-one uses of the article by Paul in 1 Timothy, fifty-five usages are individualizing, specific rather than generic; one is generic (1 Tim. 4:8, but this distinguishes a class, which is still specific rather than generic); and six are ambiguous (possibly generic), but even these are individualizing. Moreover, all uses of the article in a prepositional phrase (like '*dia*') are

individualizing. A.D. Spencer agrees ('Eve at Ephesus', *JETS* 17, no. 4 [1974]: p. 222). Mark Roberts also agrees, writing, 'Rather, through this special instance of childbearing, woman fulfills God's prophetic curse upon the serpent, thus exacting revenge upon Satan and being "saved" from the import of her deception and transgression' ('Woman Shall Be Saved', p. 21). There are a few who would object to this understanding, including Hubbard (as noted above), Porter (as noted above), and Andreas Köstenberger, who takes this term as synecdoche (one specific standing for a larger and more complex idea) for the entire role of wife–mother, writing: 'it seems perfectly permissible to understand [childbirth] . . . as in 1 Tim 2:15 as referring, not merely to the giving of birth to children, but to the having of a family, with all that this entails' ('Women's God-Ordained Roles: An Interpretation of 1 Timothy 2:15', *Bulletin for Biblical Research* 7 [1997], p. 141). This is in agreement with Robert Falconer, '1 Timothy 2:14,15. Interpretative Notes', *Journal of Biblical Literature* (1941): pp. 375–9.

29 Falconer, '1 Timothy 2:14,15. Interpretative Notes', p. 376. Falconer notes that the early Latin Fathers did understand this text to refer to the 'great childbearing', so the Messiah. As he writes, 'Mary . . . thus redressed the balance of Eve.' However, the later Greek Fathers generally rejected this, because it does not harmonize with the last clause of v. 15. To the contrary, I will argue that only this understanding provides a consistent reading.

30 Paul makes another reference to this Genesis promise of the seed who crushes in Rom. 16:20: 'The God of peace will soon crush Satan under *your* feet' (emphasis added). It could be objected that the one who crushes the serpent here is not 'the seed' but the church, because by the promise of the protoevangelium of Gen. 3:15 the victory is due to 'the seed'. Indeed, the singular versus plural matters to Paul, as he notes in Gal. 3:16. Yet, while Christ, the singular Seed of the protoevangelium, strikes first and fatally, the victory is shared by his offspring, the seed of the Seed. It is this that Paul celebrates in Rom. 16:20.

31 Payne, *Man and Woman, One in Christ*, p. 440.

32 Scheumann, '"Saved Through the Childbirth of Christ"', p. 27.

33 Barth, *Dogmatics in Outline*, p. 99.

34 Robert Wall, '1 Timothy 2:9–15 Reconsidered (Again)', *Bulletin for Biblical Research* 14, no. 1 (2004), p. 98. To this, Payne adds, 'The shift from "Eve" to "women" to "she" adds to the natural association of Eve as a representative of women in general' (Payne, *Man and Woman, One in Christ*, p. 420).

35 Payne, *Man and Woman, One in Christ*, p. 437.

6. The Virgin Birth: A New Birth for a New Creation

1   Dustin Resch, *Barth's Interpretation of the Virgin Birth: A Sign of Mystery* (Farnham: Ashgate, 2012), p. 86.

2   Justin Taylor, '5 Reasons the Virgin Birth of Jesus Is Important', *The GospelCoalition*http://www.thegospelcoalition.org/blogs/justintaylor/2015/02/26/5-reasons-the-virgin-birth-of-jesus-is-so-important/ (accessed 3 March 2015).

3   Karl Barth, *Church Dogmatics* (Peabody, MA: Hendrickson, 2nd edn, 2010), IV/3.2, p. 528.

4   Barth, *Church Dogmatics*, IV/3.2, p. 533.

5   Resch, *Barth's Interpretation of the Virgin Birth*, p. 154.

6   W.B. Selbie, *The Fatherhood of God* (London: Duckworth, 1st edn, 1936), p. 65.

7   As D.A. Carson and others have pointed out, we must not ignore the concept intended by the author because of the lack of a specific word.

8   Yigal Levin, 'Jesus, "Son of God" and "Son of David": The "Adoption" of Jesus into the Davidic Line', *Journal for the Study of the New Testament* 28, no. 4 (2006), p. 425.

9   R.A. Webb, *The Reformed Doctrine of Adoption* (Grand Rapids, MI: Eerdmans, 1947), p. 17. This is noted also by Robert A. Peterson, who cites John Calvin and Sinclair Ferguson as exceptions, noting the lack in Charles Hodge, Louis Berkhof, and Anthony Hoekema and most other Protestant systematic theologians (Robert A. Peterson, 'Toward a Systematic Theology of Adoption', *Presbyterian Journal* 27, no. 2 [2001]: p. 120).

10   Robert S. Candlish, *The Fatherhood of God: Being the First Course of the Cunningham Lectures Delivered before the New College, Edinburgh, in March, 1864* (Edinburgh: Black, 1866), p. 266.

11   Candlish, *The Fatherhood of God*, p. 267.

12   David Martyn Lloyd-Jones, *God the Holy Spirit* (Wheaton, IL: Crossway, 1997), p. 179.

13   Barth, *Church Dogmatics*, IV/3.2, p. 534.

14   Webb, *The Reformed Doctrine of Adoption*, p. 43.

15   Webb, *The Reformed Doctrine of Adoption*, p. 44.

16   Significant to this argument is 'like nature'. This draws the middle ground between the same nature (e.g. Christ only) and a wholly distinct nature (e.g. a squirrel). '[O]f like nature' draws on the concept of 'image' in which man was made. If this is sonship, some might object that this makes angels also 'sons', for so they are called. Nothing would prevent us from so supposing but, if so, other distinctions would still separate

us. A paucity of information makes significant clarity problematic. That said, the lack of any indication of 'image' being a part of angelic being is sufficient for doubt.

[17] Webb, *The Reformed Doctrine of Adoption*, p. 45.

[18] Ezek. 37 could be considered here, with his image of the dry bones brought to life by the Spirit of God. Also John 3, where the Spirit blows into God's people, bringing life.

[19] Peterson, 'Toward a Systematic Theology of Adoption', p. 130.

[20] Meir Malul, 'Adoption of Foundlings in the Bible and Mesopotamian Documents: A Study of Some Legal Metaphors in Ezekiel 1 – 7', *Journal for the Study of the New Testament* 46 (1990): p. 99. He wrote, 'More specifically, it will be argued that the declaration בְּדָמַיִךְ בְּחֲיִי (v. 6) may well have been a formal adoption declaration.'

[21] It is worth making mention here of the earlier text in Gal. 4:6. Paul wrote, 'And because you are sons, God has sent the Spirit of his Son into our hearts, crying, "Abba! Father!"' The texts are parallel.

[22] The Greek is 'ἐλάβετε', aorist tense. In context, this represents God's proleptically completed action in us. It is an eschatological pronouncement.

[23] Peterson, 'Toward a Systematic Theology of Adoption', p. 122.

[24] It is worth adding that while 'born of woman' is not an explicit reference to the virgin birth, it may yet be a reference by Paul to just this event. As many proponents of the virgin birth point out, including F.F. Bruce and J.G. Machen, Paul could have said 'born of a virgin'. Yet some understand this as Paul's affirmation of the virgin birth, including Luther, who wrote of this in his commentary on Gal. 4:7. Recognizing that many of the 'ancient doctors' took exception to Paul's failure to use the word 'virgin' in regard to 'born of a woman', Luther affirmed that Paul had other primary goals. Even so, he writes, 'when he nameth but only the woman-kind, saying, "made of a woman", it is as if he should have said made of a virgin' (*Commentary on Saint Paul's Epistle to the Galatians* [New York: Robert Carter, 1844], p. 361). For Luther, even Paul is calling our attention, in a subtle way, to Mary's virginity.

[25] Peterson, 'Toward a Systematic Theology of Adoption', p. 127.

[26] Wayne Grudem, *Systematic Theology: An Introduction to Biblical Doctrine* (Grand Rapids, MI: Zondervan, 1994), p. 530.

[27] John W. Pryor, 'Of the Virgin Birth or the Birth of Christians? The Text of John 1:13 Once More', *Novum Testamentum* 27, no. 4 (1985): p. 296. The options are the plural, οἳ . . . ἐγεννήθησαν and the singular, ὃς . . . ἐγεννήθη. Pryor's paper is a thorough investigation of

this textual variant, including supporters of the singular reading, such as Adolf von Harnack.

28 It is worth observing that Tertullian's and Irenaeus's citations are at odds even with texts which were extant in their day. That other texts in agreement with them might have existed, we cannot say.

29 Pryor, 'Of the Virgin Birth or the Birth of Christians?', p. 318.

30 Barth, *Church Dogmatics*, I/2, p. 182.

31 Barth, *Church Dogmatics*, IV/1, p. 339–40. © Karl Barth, 2009, 2010, and T&T Clark. Used by permission of Bloomsbury Publishing Plc.'

32 Actually, the text ends with the phrase 'ἐφοβοῦντο γάρ, and so the final words are, literally, 'fear for'. The final conjunction ('for', '*gar*') is a post-positive, meaning that it appears in the second position in a relative clause, so, 'for fear'.

33 Barth, *Church Dogmatics*, I/2, p. 198.

34 Barth, *Church Dogmatics*, I/2, p. 198.

35 To say more in regard to Barth, he acknowledges our creation as believers as a kind of parthenogenesis, a creation from nothing, but not only: 'We do not, therefore, only believe that we are called and are the children – on the basis of a parthenogenesis or *creatio ex nihilo* of our faith regarded as an act of God. We are the children of God because we who could not say this of ourselves, however strong our faith, are addressed as such by the Son of God who was made flesh and raised again in the flesh' (Barth, *Church Dogmatics*, IV/1, p. 351). He wants to never minimize the decisive work of Christ; we are created in him on the grounds of the real death of Christ and our death in his death, and God's 'Yes' to us in Christ (see also IV/1, p. 664).

36 To say this is not to be in radical disagreement with Barth, but to follow him here. Dustin Resch writes, 'For Barth, Mary's virginity is an expression of God's judgment upon humanity that reveals the incapacity of humanity for God's revelation and reconciliation. By Christ being born of a powerless virgin, the sovereignty of God's grace is shown to be all the more astonishing and surprising. The incapacity for human beings to bring about the incarnation, described in the virgin birth, even indicates the incapacity of human nature as such to be adopted by the Son of God' (Resch, *Barth's Interpretation of the Virgin Birth*, p. 86).

37 Candlish, *The Fatherhood of God*, p. 229.

38 Candlish, *The Fatherhood of God*, p. 234.

39 Barth, *Church Dogmatics*, I/2, p. 188.

40 Barth, *Church Dogmatics*, I/2, p. 188–9.

Conclusion. The Virgin Birth: Theological Treasure

[1] Bruce Allen Murphy, *Scalia: A Court of One* (New York: Simon & Schuster, 2014), pp. 312–3. Address given in Baton Rouge, LA, January 2005 to Knights of Columbus. Readers should not miss that, with his sharp wit, he is affirming the virgin birth, even as he points out a pointed truth.

[2] C.S. Lewis, introduction to Athanasius, *On the Incarnation* (San Bernardino, CA: Fig, 2013), p. 2.

[3] Athanasius, *On the Incarnation*, p. 72.

[4] Jason Goroncy, 'Barth's Interpretation of the Virgin Birth: A Sign of Mystery', *Journal of Theological Studies* 64, no. 2 (2013): p. 821.

Scripture Index

Subject Index

fatherless 3
fatherly 128
Feinberg, Charles 180
Ferguson, Sinclair 191
fiancée 15
firstborn 93, 95, 131–3, 143, 182
foreknowledge 92, 143
Gabriel 14
Galilee 14, 187
Gentry, Peter 187
Gibeon 80
Goroncy Jason, 194
Gospel 182, 186, 191
Gregory of Nazianzus 89
Grudem, Wayne 39, 41–2, 56–7,
    136, 160, 172–3, 176, 189, 192

Hagar 181
Hananiah 76, 80–82, 181
Haran 181
Harnack, Adolf von 193
Hawthorne, Gerald 17, 165
heaven 23, 56, 70, 83, 97, 144
Hick, John 4, 18, 161
Hodge, Charles 191
Hoekema, Anthony 191
Holy Spirit (Ghost) 3, 6, 13, 17,
    23–5, 40–43, 47, 54, 57, 69,
    71, 98, 105, 108, 110, 119–21,
    129, 133, 140–42, 165–6, 168,
    173–4, 191
Hubbard, Moyer 189
Hunsinger, George 178
hupostasis 54, 58, 60

Ignatius 21–3, 91, 98, 138, 164,
    167, 184–5
immaculate 45–6, 174
Immanuel 14, 60
incarnation 9–10, 20, 52, 55, 57,

60, 69, 71, 102–3, 120, 126–7,
    138, 142, 161, 168–9, 174, 176,
    178, 193–4
Irenaeus 23, 25, 36, 74, 104–5,
    137–8, 164, 167–70, 179–80,
    184, 186, 193
Isaac 75, 79, 83, 95, 185
Ishmael 95, 181, 185
Islam 99, 147, 185
Israel (Israelites) 93, 132

Jacob 14, 75, 82–3, 95, 130, 182–3
Jehoahaz 180
Jehoiachin (Jeconiah, Coniah)
    73–4, 76–86, 90–92, 97–8, 121,
    125–6, 135, 180–82
Jehoiakim 73, 76–84, 91–2, 97,
    121, 126
Jephthah 1–2
Jeremiah 77, 80–82, 98, 117, 180
Jerusalem 25, 75, 77, 82–3, 106,
    187
Jesse (Father of David) 79, 81, 124,
    135
Jesus, 20, 23, 25, 46–7, 54, 90–91,
    109, 113, 124–5, 133–4, 141,
    145, 162, 172, 176, 184
Joachim 74, 106
Joash 79
Joseph 74, 85, 90, 99, 104–5, 123,
    130–31, 147
Josephology 147
Josiah 77, 85, 97, 180
Judah 74–8, 80, 82, 89, 95, 97,
    124, 180–81
Julius Caesar 184
justification 109, 135, 189

Kidner, Derek 180
Kierkegaard, Soren 185

Paternoster:
thinking faith

We trust you enjoyed reading this book
from Paternoster. If you want to be informed
of any new titles from this author and other
releases you can sign up to the Paternoster
newsletter by contacting us:

By post:
Paternoster
PO Box 6326
Bletchley
Milton Keynes
MK1 9GG

E-mail:
paternoster@authenticmedia.co.uk

Follow us:

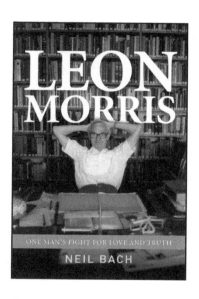

Leon Morris

One Man's Fight for Love and Truth

Neil Bach

Leon Morris's story needs to be told. In this unique and long-awaited work Neil Bach shows Leon Morris as a prodigious and original thinker from the wrong side of the world who restored the credibility of evangelical scholarship and the centrality of the cross. Many of us have been nurtured by his enormously helpful books on the cross, but few know about the obstacles that had to be overcome. The author gives us a life of Leon Morris which is true to the man, unflinching in its evaluation of his work and inspiring in its conclusions. The book claims what evangelicals have widely acknowledged: Leon Morris was, and remains, Australia's most influential international scholar and pastor.

978-1-84227-986-1

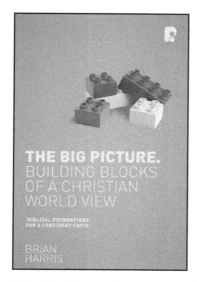

The Big Picture

*Building Blocks of a
Christian World View*

Brian Harris

The Big Picture is an accessible and stimulating exploration of the big building blocks of the Christian faith. Harris's take on the big building blocks of Christian faith is refreshing and will be appreciated by all who would like to think through different ways to follow Jesus the Christ in an ever-changing context.

'Skilfully bringing together biblically-informed theology and the everyday world, Brian Harris unpacks themes of grace, creation and Christian hope in an engaging conversational manner. The result is a book that empowers us to live out our faith wherever we are.'
Stephen Garner, Laidlaw College, Auckland, New Zealand

978-1-84227-856-7